EXPLORING TEACHER RECRUITMENT AND RETENTION

This thought-provoking collection examines the challenge of teacher shortages that is of international concern. It presents multiple perspectives, and explores the commonalities and differences in approaches from around the world to understand possible solutions for the current teacher workforce crisis.

Acknowledging that solutions to attract and retain teachers vary by country, region and in some cases locality, the contributors scrutinise a range of workforce planning interventions at local and government level, including financial incentives and early career support.

The book draws on different perspectives to understand a range of problems that negatively affect teacher recruitment and retention, unpicking key challenges, including links between the disadvantages of location and access to teachers for coastal and rural schools, rising pupil numbers, declining school budgets and the role of professional learning in raising teacher status.

Abundant in critiques, research-informed positions and context-specific discussions about the impact of teacher workforce supply and shortages, this book will be valuable reading for teacher educators, educational leaders, education policymakers and academics in the field.

Tanya Ovenden-Hope is Provost and Professor of Education at Plymouth Marjon University. She has three decades of experience as a teacher, teacher educator, senior leader and educational researcher. Her research focuses on identifying and finding solutions for inequity in education.

Rowena Passy is a Senior Research Fellow at the University of Plymouth. She has a wide range of research interests that focus on understanding and improving different aspects of our children's education.

"Ovenden-Hope and Passy draw on expertise from across the globe to provide a timely and comprehensive exploration of contextual challenges associated with isolation, teacher recruitment and retention. Part I explores a range of perspectives on recruitment and retention of teachers in England. The authors raise critical questions about shortages and workforce supply in England. Readers will enjoy the well-crafted critiques, research informed positions, and context-specific discussions about the impact of teacher workforce supply and shortages in England. Part II of the book expands the context contributions to include international perspectives on teacher recruitment and retention. The addition of international authors results in a mix of new challenges and challenges common to all the settings described in both parts of the book. Readers will benefit from learning about the similarities and differences in the language and approaches used across the globe to describe and address issues in teacher recruitment, preparation and retention. All readers will find much to stimulate their thinking on teacher supply issues. The breadth of topics and the geographic reach of contexts will provoke both connection and disruption. Ovenden-Hope and Passy have provided us with a rich mix of authors who help us think more clearly about the contextual challenges associated with global teacher recruitment and retention."

– **Professor James O'Meara**, *Dean College of Education, Texas A&M International University, President, International Council on Education for Teaching, US Focal Point, International Taskforce on Teachers for Education 2030*

EXPLORING TEACHER RECRUITMENT AND RETENTION

Contextual Challenges from International Perspectives

*Edited by Tanya Ovenden-Hope
and Rowena Passy*

Routledge
Taylor & Francis Group
LONDON AND NEW YORK

First published 2021
by Routledge
2 Park Square, Milton Park, Abingdon, Oxon OX14 4RN

and by Routledge
52 Vanderbilt Avenue, New York, NY 10017

Routledge is an imprint of the Taylor & Francis Group, an informa business

British Library Cataloguing-in-Publication Data
A catalogue record for this book is available from the British Library

Library of Congress Cataloging-in-Publication Data
A catalog record for this book has been requested

ISBN: 978-0-367-07644-3 (hbk)
ISBN: 978-0-367-07645-0 (pbk)
ISBN: 978-0-429-02182-4 (ebk)

Typeset in Bembo
by Apex CoVantage, LLC

CONTENTS

ILLUSTRATIONS

Figures

Tables

ABOUT THE EDITORS

Dr Tanya Ovenden-Hope is Provost and Professor of Education at Plymouth Marjon University and Marjon University Cornwall, UK. Tanya is a committed and enthusiastic educationalist with three decades' experience in schools, colleges and universities in England as a teacher, teacher educator, educational leader and educational researcher. She is Principal Fellow of the Higher Education Academy, Fellow of the Society of Education and Training, Founding Member of the Chartered College of Teaching and was awarded the National Enterprise Educator Award in 2014. Tanya values the importance of collaboration and has elected, invited and voluntary roles that enable her to share research and support evidence-informed practice. She is a Council Member of the Universities Council for the Education of Teachers (UCET); a Special Interest Group (SIG) Convenor and Council Member of the British Educational Research Association (BERA) and an invited member of the Paul Hamlyn Foundation Advisory Board for the Teacher Development Fund. She is also a Trustee for a number of Education Trusts. The author of over 75 papers, reports, articles and books, Tanya is dedicated to exploring social inequality and educational disparity and has spent the last ten years focusing on the challenges for coastal, rural and small schools, including issues of teacher recruitment and retention and access to funding and professional development. Tanya has used the findings of this research to inform interventions for early career teacher retention and effective mentoring in schools and colleges. Projects she has developed and led include the Education Endowment-funded RETAIN programme and the Education and Training-funded Pedagogical Mentoring Programme.

Dr Rowena Passy is a Senior Research Fellow at the Plymouth Institute of Education, University of Plymouth, where she moved in 2010 from employment as a Senior Research Officer at the National Foundation for Education Research.

Her PhD research focused on family values in education, and since then her academic interests have broadened to include issues such as school leadership, outdoor learning, widening participation and teacher training, all of which inform her research into schools in deprived coastal and educationally isolated areas. Rowena is an elected Convenor of the British Educational Research Association (BERA) Educational Research and Educational Policy-Making SIG, and a co-leader of the Peninsular Research in Outdoor Learning (PRinOL) network, a regional hub of a national network under the umbrella of the Institute for Outdoor Learning. She is Deputy Editor (Reviews) for the *Journal of Education for Teaching* and an Associate Editor for the *Journal of Experiential Education*. The author of over 50 papers, reports and chapters, Rowena was the evaluation manager of the Natural Connections Demonstration Project (2012/16), the largest outdoor learning project in the UK at the time. She is currently working on different research and evaluation projects that include a longitudinal study of an early years intervention; an evaluation of resilience training for undergraduate trainee teachers; developing and sustaining emotional health and wellbeing through physical activity in schools; an Erasmus+ project with Norway, Belgium and Italy that is focused on developing innovative curricular outdoor learning activities; and a new Erasmus+ project that is aimed at improving the quality of higher education through collaboration between different European universities and companies.

ACKNOWLEDGEMENTS

We would like to thank all the schools, trainee teachers, teachers and school leaders that have contributed to the research findings that have been used by the authors of this book.

We also want to thank our universities for giving their full support to our engagement with both this book and the underpinning research in our chapters.

We lastly want to thank Dr Philly Ricketts for her support in the final stages of the book copy-editing process.

CONTRIBUTORS

Jake Anders is Associate Professor of Educational and Social Statistics at the Institute of Education, University College London, UK.

Michele Bernini, formerly of the National Institute of Economic and Social Research, UK.

Sonia Blandford is Chief Executive Officer of Achievement for All 3 As, UK and Visiting Professor at the Institute of Education, University College London, UK and Visiting Professor at Plymouth Marjon University, UK.

Tim Cain is Professor of Education at Edge Hill University, UK.

Philippa Cordingley is Chief Executive of the Centre for the Use of Research and Evidence in Education (CUREE), UK and Visiting Professor at Plymouth Marjon University, UK.

Bart Crisp is Senior Research Manager at the Centre for the Use of Research and Evidence in Education (CUREE)

Smadar Donitsa-Schmidt is Professor of Language Education at the Kibbutzim College of Education, Israel.

Natalie Downes is a research assistant and HDR student at the University of Canberra, Australia.

Nada El-Soufi is Senior Lecturer at the University of Balamand, Lebanon.

Carol Hordatt Gentles is a Senior Lecturer at the University of the West Indies, Mona, Jamaica.

Stephen Gorard is Professor of Education and Public Policy at Durham University, UK.

Helen Gray is Principal Research Economist at the Institute for Employment Studies, UK.

John Howson is Chair of TeachVac, UK, and Visiting Professor of Education at Oxford Brookes University, UK.

Beng Huat See is Associate Professor at Durham University, UK.

Alexandra Kendall is Professor of Education at Birmingham City University, UK.

Zongqiang Li is a PhD candidate in Educational Linguistics at Griffith University, Australia.

Honggang Liu is Professor of Applied Linguistics at Northeast Normal University, China.

Ian Luke is Professor of Learning and Teaching at Plymouth Marjon University, UK.

Elizabeth Majocha is Instructor at the Gabriel Dumont Institute of Native Studies and Applied Research, Saskatoon, Saskatchewan.

Bronwen Maxwell is Head of Commissioned Research and Deputy Head of Centre for Research and Knowledge Exchange at Sheffield Hallam University, UK.

Rebecca Morris is Assistant Professor at the University of Warwick, UK.

Georgina Clare Newton is Associate Professor at the University of Warwick, UK.

Laila Niklasson is Senior Professor of Education at Mälardalen University, Sweden.

James Noble-Rogers is Executive Director of the Universities Council for the Education of Teachers (UCET), UK.

Tanya Ovenden-Hope is Professor of Education at Plymouth Marjon University, UK.

Rowena Passy is Senior Research Fellow at the University of Plymouth, UK.

Christina Preston is the retiring Chair of the Technology, Pedagogy and Education Association at De Montfort University, UK.

Philip Roberts is Associate Professor in Curriculum Inquiry and Rural Education at the University of Canberra, Australia.

Lucy Stokes is Principal Economist at the National Institute for Economic and Social Research, UK.

Shirley Van Nuland is Adjunct Professor at Ontario Tech University, Oshawa, Canada.

Linda la Velle is Professor of Education at Bath Spa University, UK and Professor Emeritus at the University of Plymouth, UK.

Catherine Whalen is Assistant Professor at the University of Northern British Columbia Prince George, Canada.

Sarah Younie is Professor of Education Innovation at De Montfort University, UK.

Ruth Zuzovsky is Professor of Science Education and a researcher at the Research Authority in the Kibbutzim College of Education, Israel.

INTRODUCTION

Rowena Passy and Tanya Ovenden-Hope

This book is a detailed investigation into the problematic question of teacher recruitment and retention. Our involvement with the teacher training and education system in England has given us a close familiarity with the situation in our home country and a recognition that different policies within the four nations of the United Kingdom have not, as yet, found ways to reduce the challenge. This localised knowledge has been given a wider perspective through working with colleagues from around the world, giving rise to discussions about similar situations in a range of different contexts and offering an opportunity to bring these ideas and experiences together. We have therefore collected the experience, research findings and observations of both national and international colleagues into a volume that presents multiple perspectives on and possible solutions for the current teacher workforce crisis.

The first section focuses on different perspectives of teacher recruitment and retention in England, and includes a range of expert insights and research that offer novel contextual thinking with which to understand the workforce supply issues. In Chapter 1, John Howson recalls his own experience from half a century ago to remind us that the current teacher supply crisis is not a new phenomenon. He argues that the responsibility to manage recruitment and training of most new teachers has not been met successfully, either by the Teacher Training Agency when it held this responsibility or by civil servants within the Department for Education (DfE); both approaches have experienced periods of oversupply and of teacher shortages. He concludes by suggesting that unless there is a period of economic turbulence – which, at the time of writing, may yet be provided by the coronavirus epidemic – the secondary sector (pupils aged 11–18) is likely to continue to experience the same challenges of teacher supply that have been a feature of the last 50 years.

James Noble-Rogers, in Chapter 2, further examines the reasons underlying the teacher supply crisis, drawing on data relating to the number of recruits to initial teacher education and on the rising number of pupils in English schools. He identifies the demographic and policy reasons why teachers are in short supply, and critiques the different incentives the government has used to attract and retain new teachers; he argues that they have been ad hoc, piecemeal and that they have not sufficiently addressed the root causes of the supply crisis. He sees the DfE (2019) recruitment and retention strategy as a positive move that, if implemented successfully, could make a difference.

Georgina Newton's Chapter 3 moves into the territory of teacher attrition. A former teacher, she reports on her research into why teachers leave teaching in England. She describes a 'hollowing-out' of the profession, in which mid-career teachers are likely to leave and the number of teachers choosing to teach until retirement is falling. She suggests that there are both 'push' factors, such as workload, data management, assessment, inspection, new initiatives and disillusionment, that propel people out of teaching, and 'pull' factors that attract individuals towards types of employment that require less emotional and physical commitment. She argues that ensuring teachers feel valued is the key to sustaining and retaining them over the long term.

The theme of valuing teachers is carried forward in Chapters 4 and 5, both of which discuss the importance of teacher continuing professional development (CPD). Linda la Velle and Alexandra Kendall suggest in Chapter 4 that much of the problem with teacher recruitment and retention stems from the low status of the teaching profession. They contend that, far from being a straightforward 'aircraft maintenance manual' exercise, learning to teach is career-long and highly complex, partly because it involves the 'problematic milieu of the classroom'. They propose an intellectual, research-informed, career-long model of teacher education, arguing that this would produce well-motivated, well-qualified and professionally satisfied teachers over the long term, and be part of the solution to problems with teacher recruitment and retention. While this would take commitment and resource from both policymakers and practitioners, they suggest that there are rich rewards to be gained from engaging with this type of long-term, research-informed CPD.

In Chapter 5 Tanya Ovenden-Hope, Sonia Blandford, Tim Cain and Bronwen Maxwell report on RETAIN, an Education Endowment Foundation-funded project, which developed and delivered a pilot programme that aimed to support early career teachers in coastal-rural schools with high levels of persistent disadvantage in Cornwall, England. The programme evaluation found that the delivery model, the how of continuing professional development (CPD), demonstrated promise of an effective CPD model. The four Cs of classroom, coaching, collaboration and child had a positive impact on early career teachers' (ECTs) self-confidence, knowledge and skills, and engaging with research helped the ECTs to have a greater understanding of the effect of persistent disadvantage on their pupils' learning. To maximise the programme's impact, however, the evaluation found that both ECTs and schools needed to engage fully with the process. At the time of writing, all ECTs who completed the programme remain in teaching.

Sarah Younie and Christina Preston in Chapter 6 focus on the supply of digital technology teachers in England. They argue that the shift in the national curriculum from information and communications technology to computing exacerbated the already-present difficulties with teacher recruitment and retention for education technology (EdTech). As leaders of two EdTech organisations that were invited by the government to advise on these matters, they recommended a focus on the three areas of reducing workload, ensuring CPD entitlement and teachers joining a community of practice (CoP). Valuing teachers and supporting them in their work, in this case viewed through professional CoPs, are seen as essential to the development of a motivated and engaged teacher workforce.

We then turn to the context of coastal schools and the locational challenges that are embedded in educationally isolated schools. Lucy Stokes, Jake Anders, Michele Bernini and Helen Gray in Chapter 7 discuss the question of pupil performance in coastal schools, drawing on a range of data to show how, on average, attainment is lower in coastal schools than in non-coastal communities. They conclude that these results reflect the greater levels of deprivation in coastal areas, and set the scene for further discussion in Tanya Ovenden-Hope and Rowena Passy's Chapter 8 on teacher workforce issues in coastal and other isolated areas. These authors present the concept of educational isolation as a place-based contextual challenge for schools that are in areas of geographic remoteness, socio-economic deprivation and cultural isolation. These locational issues restrict the schools' capacity to improve by limiting its access to key resources, which includes a high-quality workforce. The authors discuss ways in which educationally isolated schools experience teacher retention and recruitment, and conclude with recommendations to support schools who are in this position.

The final chapter in this section from an English perspective on teacher supply is by Tanya Ovenden-Hope and Ian Luke. It explores a different aspect of localised challenge: that of sense-making of education policy in relation to small schools and recruiting and sustaining teachers. They conclude that the education system in England is geared towards large urban schools and the more recently formed multi-academy trusts, in which groups of schools form an operational unit, and argue that government funding and attainment expectations should be adjusted to take account of small schools' position and make them a more attractive prospect to teachers.

We then move to the second section, which shifts the focus to international perspectives on teacher recruitment and retention. In this section, we learn about the specific contexts in which teacher supply operates and the difficulties that exist in securing a workforce that meets the classroom need. In Chapter 10, Philippa Cordingley and Bart Crisp follow the thread of previous chapters by reporting on an international research project in which they examine the impact of national or system-level continuing professional development and learning (CPDL) on teacher recruitment and retention. They argue that there is evidence which suggests that CPDL can be a potent tool in improving rates of teacher recruitment and retention, but only when the nature and purpose of the CPDL is considered in depth.

Somewhat controversially, given the tenor of other chapters in the book, in Chapter 11, Beng Huat See, Stephen Gorard, Rebecca Morris and Nada El-Soufi suggest that the most promising approach to encourage teacher recruitment and retention is the use of financial inducements, but only if they contract teachers to stay in those schools/areas for a period or continue to teach the shortage subjects. The authors present a summary of a systematic review of international research on what works in attracting and retaining teachers in challenging schools, and argue that research that examines the effect of other measures such as mentoring and induction, CPD and alternative routes to teaching is not robust enough to draw causal conclusions. They call for robust research into these areas.

The next six chapters describe and analyse the teacher supply situation in different countries. The authors of Chapter 12, Shirley Van Nuland, Catherine Whalen and Elizabeth Majocha, discuss high attrition rates in Canada and illustrate ways in which the different provinces are endeavouring to increase the support for novice teachers so they can make a successful transition to teaching. They describe a range of teacher education, induction and mentoring activities that are aimed at giving these new teachers the resilience important for teacher retention, and conclude with a series of recommendations that include preparing teachers more thoroughly for their training, developing CoPs and valuing their work, all of which are seen as fundamentally important in supporting and motivating teachers for the long term.

In Chapter 13, Honggang Liu and Zongqiang Li return to the theme of financial incentives for teachers, arguing that the combination of the Free Teacher Education/Public-funded Teacher Education (FTE/PFTE) and its sister FTE-MAEd programme are showing promise in counteracting the high attrition rates in China. Students participating in the FTE/PFTE are given free tuition, free accommodation and a stipend for the duration of their studies. After graduation, students are contracted to serve for a period of six to ten years in schools in their home provinces; in return, they have access to master's level CPD through the FTE-MAEd programme, and guaranteed income and welfare benefits during their working lifetime and in retirement. In addition, because they were trained at a top university, they have a high status during their working lives and are treated as future leaders in their schools.

This carefully planned Chinese approach contrasts with Smadar Donitsa-Schmidt and Ruth Zuzovsky's analysis of the teacher workforce in Israel in Chapter 14, where there is simultaneously a teacher shortage in the Jewish sector and a teacher surplus in the Arab one. Both phenomena have severe implications for the Israeli education system, with the Jewish sector schools employing numerous unqualified teachers, and the Arab sector schools tending to hire part-time teachers, which contributes to job insecurity, burnout and lower job satisfaction. The authors critique national policy actions, which they say have been ineffective in changing the situation over the past decade.

In Chapter 15, Carole Hordatt Gentles discusses the attrition of Jamaican teachers through migration over the past 20 years, with teachers lured by foreign recruiters who offer attractive salaries for teaching jobs overseas. She, too, is critical of government policies, arguing that they have done little to stem the tide of migration and have failed to take into account the poor working conditions, low status, lack of voice and poor professional support that teachers are likely to experience. She suggests that redressing these issues could offer viable solutions to managing the crisis of teacher migration from Jamaica.

The complex teacher supply situation in Sweden is examined by Laila Niklasson in Chapter 16 through documents from the Swedish Government, the Swedish Associations of Local Governments and the National Union of Teachers in Sweden. The author argues that the combination of private and state institutions overseeing the school workforce in Sweden creates a tension between ensuring sufficient high-quality teachers are trained and guaranteeing there are enough adults at the front of the classroom. Currently, a large number of teachers are coming up to retirement age at the same time that there is an overall increase in pupil numbers, which presents an imminent additional challenge for teacher supply.

In the final substantive chapter, Philip Roberts and Natalie Downes examine the contextual situation in 'hard-to-staff' schools in Australia. Focusing on rural, regional and remote schools, they argue that the spatial dimension of these schools is often overlooked. In a nation where over 85 per cent of the population live in urban areas within 50 kilometres of the coast, urban and cosmopolitan considerations are writ large in current approaches to teacher recruitment and retention. They suggest that hard-to-staff rural, regional and remote schools exist beyond this imagined society, as do hard-to-staff urban schools, which are often characterised by their social segregation. The last chapter in the book, the Afterword, brings the collection together under the umbrella of the United Nations Development Goal 4 of Quality Education, calling for a collaborative, coherent response to the current situation.

We could perhaps describe the book as an international application of Wright Mills' (2000) *Sociological Imagination*: the policy-induced private troubles of teachers, expressed in high levels of attrition and a reluctance to enter and/or commit to the profession for the long term, have become public issues in all our contributors' countries, at the same time that young people's education is seen as a pivotal factor in a sustainable future (UN, 2015). In some cases, the situation is complicated further by demographic changes that include a rise in the number of pupils, and/or the loss of teachers through, for example, retirement or migration. We hope that the rich understanding of these policy issues, and their potential solutions, provided by these chapters can contribute to a situation in which governments have the imagination to grasp 'the larger historical scene in terms of its meaning for the inner life and external career' (Wright Mills, 2000, p. 5) of all our teachers.

References

Department for Education [DfE]. (2019). *Teacher recruitment and retention strategy.* London: DfE. Retrieved from gov.uk website: https://assets.publishing.service.gov.uk/government/uploads/system/uploads/attachment_data/file/786856/DFE_Teacher_Retention_Strategy_Report.pdf

United Nations. (2015, September 25). *Transforming our world: The 2030 agenda for sustainable development.* Resolution adopted by the General Assembly. A/RES/70/1. Retrieved from UN website: www.un.org/ga/search/view_doc.asp?symbol=A/RES/70/1&Lang=E

Wright Mills, C. (2000). *The sociological imagination: Fortieth anniversary edition.* Oxford: Oxford University Press.

PART I

Perspectives on teacher recruitment and retention in England

1

SHORTAGES, WHAT SHORTAGES? EXPLORING SCHOOL WORKFORCE SUPPLY IN ENGLAND

John Howson

Shortages, what shortages?

In December 1970, I received a phone call from the headteacher of a local comprehensive school asking me if I wanted a temporary job until the summer teaching at the school: he had two vacancies to fill, one in science and the other in design and technology. I did not find the phone call at all unusual. Throughout the mid-1960s in England, when I was in the Sixth Form, it was quite common for some of those who remained for a third year in the Sixth Form (in order to take the Oxford and Cambridge University entrance examinations at the end of the autumn term) to take up teaching posts after Christmas when these Oxbridge examinations were over, always filling teaching vacancies in local secondary modern schools.

This was my introduction to teaching, and also to the issue of staff shortages. Schools struggled to recruit teachers for the demographic upturn experienced during the early 1970s in the secondary sector. In addition, there was a demand for extra teachers as a result of the government finally extending the school leaving age in 1972 to 16 from 15, where it had been since the late 1940s. This rise in the leaving age, long foreshadowed as an objective from the time of the passing of the 1944 Education Act, followed the delay in implementation forced upon the previous Labour government by the economic crisis of late 1967.

Teacher supply did not feature as an issue after the mid-1970s, when the school population returned to more usual levels, until the mid-1980s, except in one respect. The move to create a largely comprehensive secondary school system meant a move away from class teachers to a subject teacher staffing model in the secondary sector, even in the remaining secondary modern schools. Despite demands for the employment of more subject specialists at secondary education level, the class teacher model remained, as it still does, the dominant means of learning in the primary school sector (the term elementary school disappeared in England following the 1944 Education Act that introduced a break at the age of 11 between primary and secondary schooling).

Throughout the period under discussion, the formal starting age for schooling in England remained the term after a pupil's fifth birthday. However, in the twenty-first century, with the growing understanding of the importance of the early years in education, many children entered the schooling system at an earlier age, often through nursery provision.

Teacher training and teacher distribution: challenges and potential solutions

There had already been demands in the 1960s, especially by the teacher associations, that all teachers needed to be trained to teach. Hiring anyone, whether a graduate or not, was not for many a satisfactory way of staffing schools funded by the state. As early as 1963, John Newsom's report, entitled 'Half our Future', reflected government thinking of the time:

> In the primary and secondary modern schools teaching methods and techniques, with all the specialized knowledge that lies behind them, are as essential as mastery of subject matter. The prospect of these schools staffed to an increasing extent by untrained graduates is, in our view, intolerable.
>
> *(Ministry of Education, 1963, p. 105)*

The demand to employ more teachers with specific subject knowledge and training created many challenges for governments over the following half-century. By the late 1980s, a teacher supply problem had once again emerged. The then House of Commons Education, Science and Arts Select Committee was moved to undertake an investigation into 'the supply of teachers for the 1990s' (House of Commons, 1989). As the then Assistant Master and Mistresses Association put it in their evidence to the Select Committee, 'We consider that some geographical shortages, especially in inner cities, reflect, in addition to low general availability of teachers, the collective view of the poor reputation of schools in certain areas' (HC, 1989, Minutes of Evidence p. 126).

Thus, by the late 1980s, the twin themes of the *sufficiency of teachers and their distribution in an increasingly market-based education system* were already being acknowledged. This was to be a recurring theme addressed by House of Commons Select Committees in various reports over the next 30 years.

One solution, suggested to the House of Commons Select Committee by the Secretary of State, Sir Keith Joseph, was the idea of school-based training (HC, 1989, Q649). This introduced the third of the important themes of the decades, the question of *how teachers should be trained*. Over the next 30 years, these various themes were rarely out of the spotlight of Select Committees and the educational community.

In the early 1990s, the government created the Teacher Training Agency (TTA) as an arm's-length organisation with a remit to oversee teacher training, as well as recruitment into the profession. Operating as it did in a market-based system, the TTA had little or no involvement in where new recruits would work, and thus a system was created that rewarded high-quality training programmes, even if they were not in areas where teachers were needed. The issue of matching teachers to the vacancies was seen as a problem for the market and not for the state. This produced a potentially wasteful misuse of resources, with teachers unable to find work in some areas but schools unable to recruit teachers elsewhere.

By the time of the economic recession in the United Kingdom between the end of the 1980s and the mid-1990s, and despite the concerns of MPs in their 1989 report (HC, 1989), recruitment into teaching had improved, and vacancy rates recorded by schools reduced accordingly. There were three years in the early 1990s when the training target for mathematics teachers set by government's internal Teacher Supply Model (TSM) that determined the number of teacher training places required each year was not only met, but exceeded. Table 1.1 shows vacancy rates in secondary schools over a ten-year period from 1986 to 1996 as a percentage of the teaching workforce in England.

In the period after the changes contained in the Education Reform Act of 1988 came into force, which included the introduction of local management of schools, and with budgets transferred from local authority control to headteachers and governing bodies, teacher vacancy rates in the secondary sector declined. The growth in the early 1990s of public sector higher education, following the conversion of the polytechnics and later the colleges of higher education into

TABLE 1.1 Vacancy rates in secondary schools 1986/96 as a percentage of the teaching force in work

Year	Vacancy Percentage
1986	1.1
1987	1.2
1988	1.0
1989	1.3
1990	1.5
1991	1.1
1992	0.5
1993	0.3
1994	0.4
1995	0.3
1996	0.3

Source: Department for Education and Science, 1986, 1987, 1988, 1989, 1990, 1991; Department of Education, 1992, 1993, 1994, 1995; Department for Education and Employment [DfEE], 1996.

degree-awarding universities in their own right, may have helped provide a supply of new graduates for whom teaching looked like an attractive career option. This appears particularly true for the increasing number of the new female graduates at that time (Graduate Teacher Training Registry [GTTR], 1991, 1992, 1993, 1994, 1995, 1996).

The Labour government won the general election in May 1997, just as the tide was turning away from a positive flow in the supply of teachers. In the summer of 1996, I provided evidence to another House of Commons Select Committee inquiry into teacher recruitment, and as a mark of concern I advised the Select Committee that:

> The history of teacher training in England and Wales during the past thirty years has been one of alternating periods of 'feast' and 'famine'. Periods of shortage have been followed by times of teacher unemployment. The current position is one where a period of relative over-supply may be being replaced by a period of significant shortage towards the end of the century unless prompt action is taken by those responsible for the overall control of the teaching profession.
>
> *(HC, 1996, p. 8)*

And so teacher supply was to continue lurching from periods of surplus numbers to shortages during the next two decades as the remainder of this chapter helps to demonstrate.

Falling postgraduate numbers and supply shortages

Although teaching remained the career of choice for many graduates, as it always had been and remains so to this day, applications to postgraduate teacher training fell in key subjects between the 1996/97 entry round and those applying to start courses in 1998/99, illustrated in Table 1.2.

The number of teacher training places at this time was controlled by the government department at Westminster responsible for schools (Department for

TABLE 1.2 Applications to secondary postgraduate teacher training courses in England 1996/97 to 1998/99 (selected subjects)

Subject	1996/97	1997/98	1998/99
Mathematics	1,873	1,579	1,288
English & Drama	3,197	3,104	3,141
Sciences (all)	3,698	3,625	2,878
Languages (all)	2,680	2,561	2,442
Technology (all)	1,549	1,605	1,595
All Secondary applications	20,654	20,074	18,904

Source: GTTR, 1996, 1997, 1998, 1999 (England only).

Education and Employment, Department of Education, Department for Children, Schools and Families, or Department for Education, depending upon the title in use at the time), and distributed through the Teacher Training Agency to most course providers. The overall level of allocations provided the benchmark by which the success or otherwise of recruitment onto teacher preparation courses could be measured. This measurement of success is still used in England to the present day.

Four subjects were responsible for the majority of the unfilled places in both years shown in Table 1.3. Across the two years, these subjects accounted for 7,930 of the 8,770 unfilled places, or some 90 per cent of unfilled places.

In the 1980s, it had been the custom in some years for governments to add back in to the following years' targets any shortfall in recruitment to training courses from a previous year, presumably in the hope that recruitment might have improved. This practice was abandoned in the late 1990s, possibly because it was creating some unachievable targets. There is, after all, no point in recruiting too many trainees on to teacher preparation courses, since each year every school has to be fully staffed, even if, as noted at the beginning of this chapter, the mix of staff is not what would ideally be required. Children cannot be sent home because there is no teacher of a particular subject available.

The era of 'Education, Education, Education', as espoused by Labour in their campaign for the general election of 1997, did not start well in terms of creating enough teachers to staff the nation's schools. Interestingly, teacher supply was not one of the key areas for the Labour education manifesto of 1997 and didn't even rate a mention at its launch (Huntly Film Archives, 1997). The introduction of tuition fees for degrees was a negative factor for recruitment. The lack of financial support for many would-be teachers, together with the uncertainty generated by the market-based model of recruitment that failed to guarantee a teaching post after qualification, may have put some graduates off teaching just at a time at the end of the 1990s when the job market for graduates was finally growing, as the United Kingdom economy emerged from recession.

By early 2000, applications to train as a teacher through the key higher education-based postgraduate routes were registering new six-year lows, at

TABLE 1.3 Unfilled places on ITT higher education courses 1997/98 to 1998/99 (selected subjects)

Subject	1997/98	1998/99	Total unfilled places
Mathematics	830	1,080	1,910
Sciences (all)	520	820	1,340
Languages (all)	920	720	1,640
Technology (all)	1,200	1,840	3,040
Total from above four subjects	3,470	4,460	7,930
All Secondary applications	3,740	5,030	8,770

Source: GTTR, 1997, 1998, 1999 (England only).

a time when vacancies for teachers, as measured by the annual January census, were reaching new highs. Vacancies levels peaked at 2,477 in the 2001 census (DfEE, 2001). As a comparison, in the School Workforce Census of 2018 (the latest available when the chapter was being written), vacancy rates in November 2018 for classroom teachers amounted to just 846 posts, but there were an additional 2,493 temporarily filled posts (Department for Education [DfE], 2019a, Table 14). After taking into account both vacancies and temporarily filled posts at all grades, there were some 3,339 recorded vacancies and temporarily filled posts in November 2018 in England, occurring at a time in the year when schools would be expected to be fully staffed.

New solutions to an old problem

The government's solution to the teacher supply crisis in 2000 was sudden and unexpected. In March 2000, the government announced the introduction of a Training Grant of £6,000 for all postgraduate trainees. This injection of cash had the effect of ensuring that the total number of applications to train as teachers by graduates went from the lowest number since 1994, before the announcement in March 2000, to the highest end-of-round number since 1994, by September 2000 (GTTR, 2000).

Although the increase in applications made a difference to the flow of new entrants into the profession, the fact that the government had also started to channel additional funds into schools increased the demand for teachers, a combination of factors that the Teacher Supply Model had not predicted. As the Department for Education and Employment's model used for predicating teacher trainee numbers was not published at that time, it is, however, difficult to be certain about this point. Teacher 'churn' increased as teachers moved between schools, creating additional costs in advertising and interviewing for schools as departing teachers needed to be replaced. To deal with this problem of increased turnover at a time of overall shortage that adversely affected those schools in high-cost areas and in schools where recruitment was always challenging, especially in some parts of London, an additional source of supply was found by schools through hiring teachers from Commonwealth countries.

For instance, in the three years between 2001 and 2004, more than 10,000 work permits for jobs including the word 'teacher' were issued to nationals of just three countries: South Africa, Australia and New Zealand (McNamara, Lewis, & Howson, 2014). Their distribution was not uniform across the country. The National Labour Market Survey in 2003 found just two per cent of overseas teachers without Qualified Teacher Status were employed across the whole of the northeast region of England, the same percentage as found just in the London Borough of Tower Hamlets (DfEE, 2003).

Alongside the postgraduate teacher Training Grant awarded to all graduates training to become a teacher and the overseas recruitment, various other initiatives were put in place to solve the shortage of teachers at the start of the new century. New schemes were often based mostly in schools rather than universities; the short-lived fast-track scheme, for instance, that was administered by the government and mirrored the scheme for accelerated promotion in the civil service, interfered with the working of the market by managing the careers of those on the scheme, and the longer-lived Teach First programme was originally designed as a short-service programme where those on the scheme would devote a few years to teaching before leaving for the world of business and commerce. These schemes emerged alongside *employment-based routes* such as the Graduate and Registered Teacher Schemes that were managed by schools rather than by the university sector. All these schemes operated outside the scope of the government's allocation methodology at that time, and it is not known whether or not their effect was factored into the output of the Teacher Supply Model that still remained largely confidential during this period.

It is somewhat ironic that just as the period of recruitment difficulties was finally coming to an end, a fourth House of Commons Select Committee inquiry into teacher recruitment and retention in the secondary sector reported in 2003/04, although it had started while schools were still facing challenges in recruiting teachers. As the government happily noted in their response to the Committee's report, the number of new recruits to teacher training rose by 51 per cent between 1999/2000 and 2003/04 (HC, 2004).

Both the higher education and school-centred training numbers were also boosted during these early years of the twenty-first century by around an additional 20 per cent as a result of recruitment through the employment-based routes, Overseas Trained Teacher Programme (OTTP) and the developing Teach First Scheme (Howson, 2008).

After the success of the Training Grant in increasing applications to postgraduate training programmes in 2000, applications continued to increase in most subjects until the they reached a peak in the 2006/07 round for recruitment onto postgraduate training courses. By that time, targets for many secondary subjects were being reduced, as it was clear that the secondary school population was in decline and fewer teachers would need to be recruited. Thus, it was not until the 2007/08 recruitment round that the target for recruitment of trainee mathematics teachers was again missed: the first time since the 2001/02 recruitment round. Even as the economy collapsed into recession, in the autumn of 2008, most secondary subjects were still meeting their targets for recruitment into training (Howson, 2008).

The banking crisis of 2008 created a period of stability in the teacher labour market. Rising applications to postgraduate courses, that reached a peak of 67,000 in the 2009/10 cycle, approaching double the number of graduates needed to train as a teacher, and applications remaining above 60,000 for the following two years (GTTR, 2013), occurred at a time when secondary school rolls were falling. In the first year after the financial crisis, perhaps as many as 4,000 teachers reactivated their registration with the then General Teaching Council for England (GTCE, 2010), adding to the stock of teachers available for work.

Uncertainty about employment opportunities also meant that fewer teachers changed their jobs during this period (Howson & McNamara, 2012).

New government, new policies

After the 2010 general election, and the appointment of Michael Gove as Secretary of State for Education, both schools and teacher preparation underwent a period of significant upheaval. The desire to move teacher preparation into schools by the Conservative part of the coalition government, seemingly not opposed by the Liberal Democrat coalition partners, saw the creation of new routes into teaching, such as the School Direct Salaried and School Direct Fee routes – successors to the former employment-based Graduate and Registered Teacher routes created in the 1990s. The Salaried Scheme paid those on it a salary much like the Teach First Scheme – such as the Graduate and Register Teacher Programmes – and there was further expansion of Teach First. Additionally, under new regulations, academies and free schools and the new 14–18 sector of University Technical Colleges and Studio Schools were no longer required to employ teachers with Qualified Teacher Status and could employ anyone as a 'teacher'. The previous Labour government had abolished the term 'instructor' and replaced it with unqualified teacher for those teaching without Qualified Teacher Status. 'Teacher', however, has never been a reserved occupational term.

This chapter is not about the struggle to retain the presence of higher education as a force in preparing teachers, although there is a story to be told about how close England came to losing the involvement of its universities in preparing teachers for a career in the classroom, with all the associated loss in research and professional development that would also have ensued. At one point, in 2013, the Department for Education even seemingly toyed with the idea of completely abolishing any centralised planning for teacher supply. This would have meant abandoning the use of the Teacher Supply Model. In 2013, head of the newly merged Teacher Training Agency and National College said in a conference speech:

> In the future I would like to see local areas deciding on the numbers of teachers they will need each year rather than a fairly arbitrary figure passed down from the Department for Education. I have asked my officials at the Teaching Agency to work with schools, academy chains and local authorities to help them to devise their own local teacher supply model. I don't think Whitehall should be deciding that nationally we need 843 geography teachers, when a more accurate figure can be worked out locally.
>
> (DfE, 2013a)

In one sense, this statement recognised the need to train teachers where they would be employed and links to the theme of how teacher training places are distributed, one of the key issues identified at the start of this chapter. After all, until the early 1970s most teacher training had taken place locally. Teacher preparation was delivered in colleges managed by the employers, whether local authorities or the main Christian denominations, mostly to school leavers, with universities largely responsible for offering teacher preparation courses only for the relatively small number of graduates willing to take such courses before entering teaching.

In recent years, while the focus of education was directed elsewhere, the government was dismantling agencies involved with the recruitment and training of teachers, eventually taking the role back fully into the Department for Education in 2017, and a new teacher supply crisis has emerged that is still with us today.

In March 2013, I wrote the following:

> How much of a mess is teacher supply in at the moment? And are we heading for another teacher shortage? Might such a shortage pit Michael Gove against the Home Secretary in demanding more immigration to allow those teachers from America and the Commonwealth that he granted QTS last year the ability to take up vacancies not filled by UK trained teachers?
>
> There are certainly straws in the wind pointing to challenges that might be looming. A head contacting Canada to source teachers; concern from the media in Kent that the county is having difficulty recruiting enough teachers; a rise of around 16 per cent in vacancies for secondary school teachers advertised during the first two months of 2013 when compared to 2012. These all point to, at the very least, a tightening of the labour market. Add to this the fact that I haven't heard as many stories about last year's crop of NQTs being reduced to stacking shelves in supermarkets because they couldn't find work as teachers, and we have the situation were the pointer is certainly swinging away from 'over supply' and towards 'in balance', even if it has yet to cross into the 'shortage' zone.
>
> *(Howson, 2013a)*

The issue of whether there was an emerging teacher supply crisis in England for secondary schools came to the fore during the summer of 2013. In September, the first hard data emerged:

> Figures released this morning by the GTTR arm of UCAS when compared against government allocations for teacher training released in August show a likely undershoot in almost all subjects. The worst subjects, where the shortfall may well be around 50 per cent, are Computer Science and Design & Technology, both subjects largely shunned by the schools participating in the government's alternative School Direct Scheme for training teachers. Even in key subjects, such as Mathematics, the shortfall is likely to be in the order of 20 per cent. In Physics it is potentially around 30 per cent.
>
> *(Howson, 2013b)*

In 2013, the Department for Education ran a separate application process for the School Direct places outside of the UCAS system, and it was not until the Initial Teacher Training Census was published in November by the Department for Education that the full extent of the downturn became apparent. In that year, the issue was confined to a few subject areas as shown in Table 1.4, but it was a warning sign for what was to come over the next few years. Even the inclusion of Teach First numbers in the ITT Census has not prevented the numbers in the census for the secondary subjects failing to meet the estimated need in some subjects in each of the last six recruitment rounds.

The 2018/19 period recorded some of the lowest recorded percentages against the DfE's perceived need, with only 25 per cent of design and technology and 47 per cent of physics places filled. On the other hand, physical education has always recruited more trainees than identified need, as has history.

In February 2019, despite the publication of a recruitment and retention strategy by the DfE in January 2019 (DfE, 2019b), data from the current round

TABLE 1.4 Percentage recruitment to Teacher Supply Model number recorded in the DfE's ITT Census since 2013

	2013/14	2014/15	2015/16	2016/17	2017/18	2018/19
Percentage of target at census date	%	%	%	%	%	%
Mathematics	86	92	95	82	79	71
English	136	137	105	96	90	110
Modern Languages	85	90	88	93	93	88
Biology		95	90	113	86	153
Physics		67	70	79	68	47
Chemistry		121	94	96	83	79
Physical Education	138	113	101	109	113	116
Other					50	43
Design & Technology	45	42	40	40	33	25
History	150	121	113	110	102	101
Geography	100	81	83	115	80	85
Computing	63	85	70	67	66	73
Art & Design	136	100	64	82	74	73
Religious Education	82	72	64	80	63	58
Music	97	81	73	89	76	72
Drama					76	83
Business Studies	88	78	64	85	80	75
Classics					84	87
All Secondary	98	94	82	87	80	83
			Inc TF	Inc TF	Inc TF	Inc TF
Primary	99	89	112	98	106	103
			Inc TF	Inc TF	Inc TF	Inc TF

Source: DfE, 2013b, 2014, 2015, 2016, 2017, 2018.

TF = Teach First

of applications provided by UCAS suggests that the 2019 recruitment round is currently on course to produce a result similar to that of the past four years (Howson, 2019).

With a growing secondary school population, insufficient trainee teachers mean that unless more teachers can either be enticed back into service or recruited from overseas, schools face a choice of either cutting curriculum hours in certain subjects, increasing group sizes or asking teachers with insufficient training to teach some subjects. It is likely that all three strategies are being employed by schools across the country in some critical subject areas.

Conclusion

This article opened with a personal recollection of a teacher supply crisis half a century ago. At the present time, despite pressure on budgets, schools are experiencing yet another teacher supply crisis.

In the past 50 years, the education service has moved from a locally administered, but centrally overseen system, to one where control is devolved to individual school sites, albeit increasingly grouped together into undemocratic trusts. The control over schooling of the Department for Education in Whitehall has become more apparent during the past half-century, whether over the curriculum, assessment or funding of the school system.

However, while government has always played an important role in determining the supply of teachers for schools in England, its hand in the creation of these teachers needed to operate the school system has often been uncertain. For about half of the period since 1970, teacher supply was managed by an agency with explicit responsibility for the recruitment and training of most new teachers. At the start of the period, and again at the present time, the responsibility is that of civil servants within the education department of the government. Neither approach has coped well with external circumstances that have affected teacher supply, with both approaches having experienced periods of both over-supply and of teacher shortages.

A modern economy needs an educated workforce. It should not be beyond the powers of politicians to ensure such a workforce is available to teach every child that the state is responsible for educating by designing a system that provides sufficient, well-trained teachers, with the highest quality preparation, and where they are needed by schools. Government should also create an appropriate career development programme that helps teachers develop their skills and expertise, as well as helps them create a career within the state school system: but that's another story. This chapter has identified the failures of policy-making by the state to always ensure sufficient, appropriately prepared teachers for all pupils in all schools.

Unless there is a period of economic turbulence, it seems likely that the secondary sector, where pupil rolls are increasing across most of England, will continue to experience the same challenges in teacher supply that have been a feature of most of the past 50 years. However, there is always the possibility that action by the government might result in teaching once again becoming a career of choice for graduates: if so, stories of teacher shortages will be consigned to the history books.

References

Department for Education [DfE]. (2013a, January 18). *Charlie Taylor's keynote speech to the North of England education conference*. Retrieved from gov.uk website: www.gov.uk/government/speeches/charlie-taylors-keynote-speech-to-the-north-of-england-education-conference

Department for Education [DfE]. (2013b). *ITT census 2013–2014*. SFR 49/2013. London: Department for Education. Retrieved from gov.uk website: www.gov.uk/government/statistics/initial-teacher-training-trainee-number-census-2013-to-2014

Department for Education [DfE]. (2014). *ITT census 2014–2015*. SFR 48/2014. London: Department for Education. Retrieved from gov.uk website: www.gov.uk/government/statistics/initial-teacher-training-trainee-number-census-2014-to-2015

Department for Education [DfE]. (2015). *ITT census, 2015–2016*. SFR 46/2015. London: Department for Education. Retrieved from gov.uk website: www.gov.uk/government/statistics/initial-teacher-training-trainee-number-census-2015-to-2016

Department for Education [DfE]. (2016). *ITT census 2016–2017*. SFR 57/2016. London: Department for Education. Retrieved from gov.uk website: www.gov.uk/government/statistics/initial-teacher-training-trainee-number-census-2016-to-2017

Department for Education [DfE]. (2017). *ITT census 2017–2018*. SFR 68/2017. London: Department for Education. Retrieved from gov.uk website: www.gov.uk/government/statistics/initial-teacher-training-trainee-number-census-2017-to-2018

Department for Education [DfE]. (2018). *ITT census 2018–2019*. London: Department for Education. Retrieved from gov.uk website: www.gov.uk/government/statistics/initial-teacher-training-trainee-number-census-2018-to-2019

Department for Education [DfE]. (2019a, June). *School workforce census 2019: Guide for schools including academies within a Multi Academy Trust*. London: Department for Education. Retrieved from gov.uk website: https://assets.publishing.service.gov.uk/government/uploads/system/uploads/attachment_data/file/809753/School_Workforce_Guide_2019_v1-0_school_and_MAT_returns.pdf

Department for Education [DfE]. (2019b, January 28). *New national strategy unveiled to boost teacher numbers*. Retrieved from gov.uk website: www.gov.uk/government/news/new-national-strategy-unveiled-to-boost-teacher-numbers

Department for Education and Employment [DfEE]. (1996). *Statistics of education: Teachers*. London: HMSO.

Department for Education and Employment [DfEE]. (2001). *Statistics of education: Teachers*. London: HMSO.

Department for Education and Employment [DfEE]. (2003). *Statistics of education: School workforce in England 2003*. London: TSO.

Department of Education and Science. (1986). *Statistics of education: Teachers*. London: HMSO.

Department of Education and Science. (1987). *Statistics of education: Teachers*. London: HMSO.

Department of Education and Science. (1988). *Statistics of education: Teachers*. London: HMSO.

Department of Education and Science. (1989). *Statistics of education: Teachers*. London: HMSO.

Department of Education and Science. (1990). *Statistics of education: Teachers*. London: HMSO.

Department of Education and Science. (1991). *Statistics of education: Teachers*. London: HMSO.

Department of Education. (1992). *Statistics of education: Teachers.* London: HMSO.

Department of Education. (1993). *Statistics of education: Teachers.* London: HMSO.

Department of Education. (1994). *Statistics of education: Teachers.* London: HMSO.

Department of Education. (1995). *Statistics of education: Teachers.* London: HMSO.

General Teaching Council for England [GTCE]. (2010). *Digest of statistics.* London: GTCE

Graduate Teacher Training Registry [GTTR]. (1991). *Annual reports.* Cheltenham: UCAS.

Graduate Teacher Training Registry [GTTR]. (1992). *Annual reports.* Cheltenham: UCAS.

Graduate Teacher Training Registry [GTTR]. (1993). *Annual reports.* Cheltenham: UCAS.

Graduate Teacher Training Registry [GTTR]. (1994). *Annual reports.* Cheltenham: UCAS.

Graduate Teacher Training Registry [GTTR]. (1995). *Annual reports.* Cheltenham: UCAS.

Graduate Teacher Training Registry [GTTR]. (1996). *Annual reports.* Cheltenham: UCAS.

Graduate Teacher Training Registry [GTTR]. (1997). *Annual reports.* Cheltenham: UCAS.

Graduate Teacher Training Registry [GTTR]. (1998). *Annual reports.* Cheltenham: UCAS.

Graduate Teacher Training Registry [GTTR]. (1999). *Annual reports.* Cheltenham: UCAS.

Graduate Teacher Training Registry [GTTR]. (2000). *Annual reports.* Cheltenham: UCAS.

Graduate Teacher Training Registry [GTTR]. (2013). *Annual reports.* Cheltenham: UCAS.

House of Commons [HC]. (1989). *Education, Science and Arts Select Committee: The supply of teachers for the 1990s. (HC 208, 1989–90).* London: HMSO.

House of Commons [HC]. (1996). *Education and Employment Committee sixth report: The professional status, recruitment and training of teachers List of Memoranda included in Minutes of Evidence. Memorandum submitted by Mr John Howson Oxford Brookes University, in Volume of Evidence of Witness Sessions, HC Session 1996–97.* London: HMSO.

House of Commons [HC]. (2004). *Government response to Inquiry into recruitment and retention of teachers in secondary schools. Education and Employment Select Committee.* London: TSO.

Howson, J. (2008). *The labour market for teachers.* London: Policy Exchange.

Howson, J. (2013a, March 19). *Is school direct working?* [blog]. Retrieved from https://johnohowson.wordpress.com/?s=is+school+direct+working&submit=Search

Howson, J. (2013b, September 9). *More news on teacher supply* [blog]. Retrieved from https://johnohowson.wordpress.com/2013/09/09/more-news-on-teacher-supply/

Howson, J. (2019). *Headline news looks good, but beware headlines* [blog]. Retrieved from https://johnohowson.wordpress.com/?s=Headline+news+looks+good&submit=Search

Howson, J., & McNamara, O. (2012). Teacher workforce planning: The interplay of market forces and government polices during a period of economic uncertainty. *Educational Research, 54*(2), 173–185.

Huntly Film Archives. (1997). *Tony Blair talks about Education, Education, Education, Film 90949.* Millbank. Uploaded 13 Jan 2014. Retrieved from www.youtube.com/watch?v=kz2ENxjJxFw (also available at www.huntleyarchives.com/preview.asp?image= 1090949).

McNamara, O., Lewis, S., Howson, J., NASUWT, University of Manchester, & Education Data Surveys. (2014). *The recruitment of overseas trained teachers.* Rednal, Birmingham: NASUWT.

Ministry of Education. (1963). *Half our future: A report of the Central Advisory Committee for Education (England).* London: HMSO.

2

THE RECRUITMENT AND RETENTION OF TEACHERS IN ENGLAND

James Noble-Rogers

Teacher training in England

In November 2017 there were some 451,900 full-time equivalent teachers working in publicly funded schools in England (down by 1.2 per cent compared to the previous year), 221,100 (0.6 per cent down) in primary schools (for pupils aged 3/5-11) and 204,200 (1.9 per cent down) in secondary schools (for pupils aged 11-16/18) (Department for Education [DfE], 2018a, p. 1). These teachers are employed by a total of 16,766 state-funded primary, 3,436 secondary and 1,043 special schools with 4.72 million, 3.26 million and 0.12 million pupils respectively (DfE, 2018b, pp. 3-4). Teachers in schools maintained by local authorities are required to hold Qualified Teacher Status (QTS) and, while teachers in free schools, studio schools and academies are technically exempt from the requirement, the vast majority do hold QTS. This is awarded on the successful completion of a course of initial teacher education (ITE) delivered by an accredited ITE provider working in partnership with schools.

ITE programmes are delivered through partnerships of higher education institutions (HEIs) working with schools, which is sometimes described as 'HEI-led', and through consortia of schools, described as School Centred Initial Teacher Training providers (SCITTs) and sometimes described as 'school-led'. Most SCITTs also work in partnership with HEIs through, for example, the validation of academic qualifications that the SCITT can deliver, such as a Postgraduate Certificate in Education (PGCE), alongside the QTS they are approved to award as an ITT provider. ITE programmes are delivered at either postgraduate level for those who already have degrees or at undergraduate level for those who do not. Postgraduate programmes typically last for one academic year, and can lead to a master's-level academic award such as a Postgraduate Certificate in Education (PGCE) or a Postgraduate Diploma in Education (PGDE), as well as to QTS. Most postgraduate programmes are delivered on a fee-paying basis with student teachers liable for fees of £9,250, although there are also some salaried routes for teachers receiving training while employed by a school; examples include School Direct (salaried), open to graduates with around three years' transferable work history, and apprenticeships.

More than 95 per cent of teachers in secondary schools qualify through a postgraduate route, as do most primary school teachers, although about 30 per cent of primary teachers qualify through three- or four-year undergraduate programmes, and the government has recently expressed an interest in developing more undergraduate secondary programmes (DfE, 2019a). All programmes must adhere to the Secretary of State's requirements for ITE programmes, which include specifications relating to entry qualifications, course structure and the amount of time spent in schools, and all are subject to regular inspection by the Office for Standards in Education (Ofsted). All programmes must also equip teachers to demonstrate that they meet the national Teachers' Standards (DfE, 2011), which means that programmes must cover each of the standards and that students are continuously assessed against these standards, both during the programme and on completion.

Although there are technically a large number of different routes into teaching delivered through a variety of partnerships, something that can prove confusing to potential applicants, the routes can in effect be boiled down to just three (although all have different sub-categories): postgraduate fee paying; postgraduate salaried; and undergraduate. In 2018/19, ITE recruitment (DfE, 2019b, p. 4) through the different routes for primary and secondary combined was:

- Postgraduate fee paying: 25,452 (74 per cent)
- Postgraduate salaried 3,799 (11 per cent)
- Undergraduate 5,335 (15 per cent).

Teacher attrition

Each year, some 10 per cent of teachers leave the profession. Further details are given in Figure 2.1 (DfE, 2019a, p. 10).

Figures for those leaving during their first few years in teaching are even starker. Over 20 per cent of teachers leave within their first two years of teaching, while 33 per cent leave within in the first five years. Figure 2.2 from the DfE's teacher recruitment and retention strategy (DfE, 2019a, p. 11) provides further details.

A report by the National Foundation for Education Research (NFER) (Worth, Lynch, Hillary, Rennie, & Andrade, 2018) published in October 2018 found that the proportion leaving the teaching profession had increased, in large part because of concerns about lack of job satisfaction and workload, and for the first time in many years the number of teachers leaving the profession exceeded the numbers joining. Teachers were found to work on average 50 hours per week, more than police officers or nurses, even after account has been taken of teacher

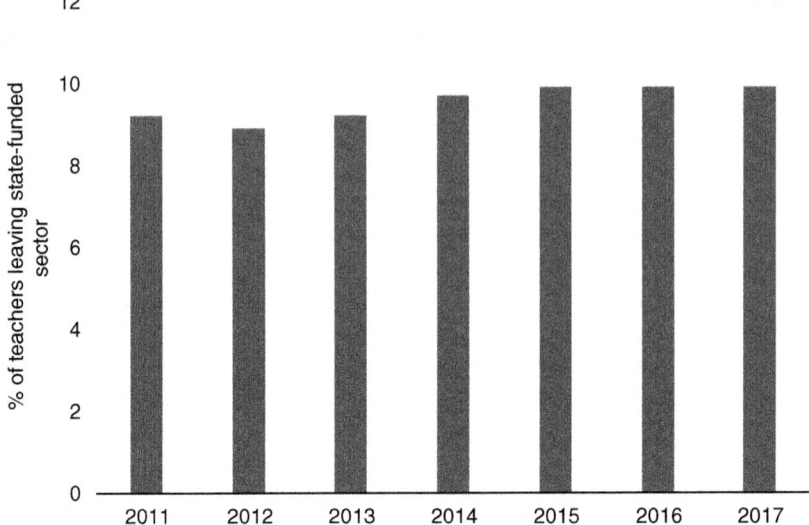

FIGURE 2.1 Percentage of teachers leaving the profession 2011/17

Source: Original source used in DfE, 2019a: see also DfE, 2018a, Table 7b.

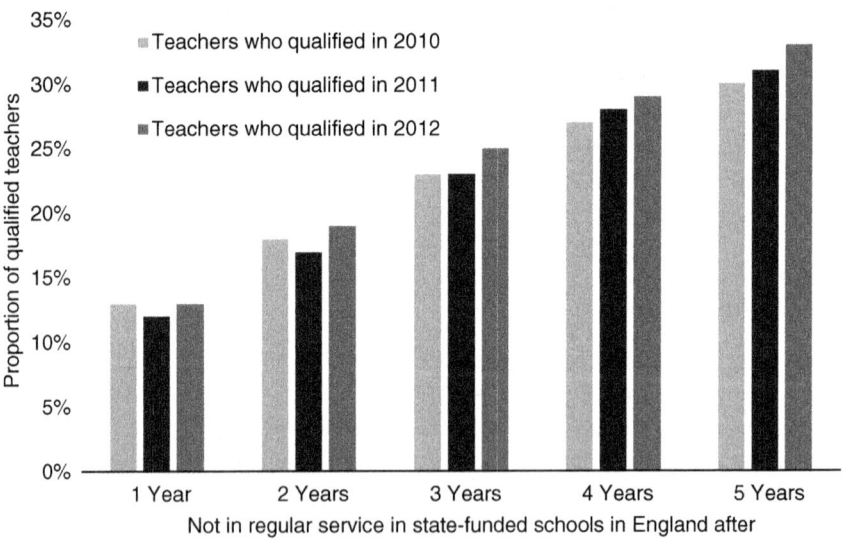

FIGURE 2.2 Proportion of teachers leaving the profession after 1, 2, 3, 4 and 5 years of service

Source: Original source used in DfE, 2019a: see also DfE, 2018a, Table 8.

holidays (Worth et al., 2018). Pay does not appear to be a determining factor, as another NFER report (Lynch, Worth, Bamford, & Wespieser, 2016) found that many people left teaching to work in less well-paid jobs, often within the education sector. Reports from other groups and organisations have produced similar results. For example, the National Audit Office (2017) reported that more teachers were leaving the profession before retirement than five years previously, and schools were finding it difficult to fill posts with the quality of teachers they required. The House of Commons Education Select Committee said that the government needed to place a greater emphasis on retaining teachers rather than on just recruiting new ones, and that rising pupil numbers and new accountability measures, such as the focus on EBacc subjects, were likely to make supply problems worse (House of Commons Education Committee, 2017). The House of Commons Public Accounts Committee suggested that the DfE needed to concentrate more on retention, and that the disparate and small-scale interventions it had taken had failed to address the underlying issues (House of Commons Committee of Public Accounts, 2018).

At the same time that an increasing proportion of teachers are leaving the profession, pupil numbers are forecast to increase, with the number in secondary schools expected to increase by 15 per cent between 2018 and 2025 (DfE, 2019a, p. 10). To meet this increasing demand, more new teachers have to be recruited into the profession, former teachers have to be attracted back and existing teachers encouraged to stay.

The student teacher recruitment crisis

The government estimates the number of new student teachers that need to be recruited to ITE programmes to meet the demand for new teachers from schools, using a Teacher Supply Model (TSM) (DfE, 2017), which takes into account factors such as forecast changes in pupil numbers, teacher wastage rates (through retirement or for other reasons), returners to the profession and policy changes that will impact on the demand for teachers in particular subject areas. For example, subjects identified as part of the English Baccalaureate – EBacc – will require a greater increase than others because of pressures on schools to focus on those subjects. The TSM produces estimates for the number of student teachers required in each phase (primary or secondary) and each secondary subject. Accredited providers of ITE then recruit students to these programmes.

The government has missed its ITE recruitment targets for the last six years (Whittaker, 2018), and Table 2.1 shows the percentage of recruitment against target in each year. In 2018/19, recruitment against the secondary TSM target was 93 per cent for secondary programmes and 103 per cent for primary. These figures do, however, mask significant variations by subject and phase, as postgraduate recruitment against target for primary and for secondary EBacc subjects in the years 2017/18–2018/19 shows (DfE, November 2018d).

Part of the reason for the current teacher recruitment crisis is demographic, with the forecast increase in pupil numbers occurring at the same time as a decline in the number of people going into higher education, the group that has traditionally supplied the bulk of entrants into ITE. In recent years the Office of Budget Responsibility (OBR) has downgraded its forecast of total student

TABLE 2.1 Percentage recruitment to ITE programmes as a percentage of target by phase and subject in 2017/18 and 2018/19

Subject/phase	% recruitment 2017/18	% recruitment 2018/19
Primary	103	103
History	100	101
Modern foreign languages	91	88
English	88	110
Biology	85	153
Chemistry	82	79
Geography	78	85
Mathematics	77	71
Physics	66	47
Computing	62	73

Source: Adapted from DfE, 2018d.

numbers, with current estimates falling from 363,000 in 2017/18 to 344,000 in 2021/22, before increasing to 350,000 in 2022/23 (Office of Budget Responsibility [OBR], 2018, p. 1) This reflects a change in the weighted population growth of 18–24-year-olds, showing declines of between 1 to 2.3 per cent in each year until 2022/23, when an increase of 1.5 per cent is expected (OBR, 2018, p. 1).

However, while the government can legitimately point to some external factors outside its control for teacher shortages, some of its own policies can be argued to have worsened the problem. For example, in the years immediately following the 2010 general election, the then Secretary of State for Education, Michael Gove, signalled a desire to increase the number and proportion of places allocated to school-led ITE programmes delivered by SCITTs and through the School Direct programme, with a corresponding decrease in the number and proportion of places allocated to HEI-led programmes (DfE, 2010). This was despite the fact that the latter partnerships were more adept at filling places. For example, in 2015 HEIs filled 88 per cent of their allocated places, compared to 65 per cent for SCITTs, 70 per cent for School Direct salaried and 54 per cent for School Direct fee paying (Noble-Rogers, 2017), which meant that places were in effect taken away from providers that could fill them in favour of providers that could not. The government's requirement that all entrants to ITE successfully complete literacy and numeracy tests before beginning their training has also damaged recruitment, not least because of a shortage of places available to take the tests at centrally funded skills test centres. However, in July 2019, as a result of pressure from UCET and following earlier relaxations that are set out later, it was announced by the Department for Education that the tests were to be abandoned (DfE, 2019c). In addition, high teacher workload resulting from government accountability measures has also had a negative effect, something the government itself seems to have recognised in its new recruitment and retention strategy (DfE, 2019a). There have also been indications that other government policies have exacerbated the teacher supply crisis. For example, the government is said to have failed to plan for the impact of policies relating to the flaws in the selection system, school funding mechanisms, the extension of the age at which people can exit education and training and an increase in the number of small schools on the demand for new teachers (See & Gorard, 2019). I would also suggest that changes to the school curriculum might have made some potential subject experts less enthused about teaching their subject in schools, as has the erosion of professional autonomy generally.

The government, prior to the publication of the 2019 recruitment and retention strategy (DfE, 2019a), had already taken a number of steps, which are discussed later, to increase recruitment to ITE programmes and to help meet its targets. To date, however, none of these have proved particularly successful and they all appear to be isolated and unconnected rather than forming part of a coherent strategy. Until the publication of the January 2019 recruitment and retention strategy, the main recruitment incentive was the payment of bursaries targeted towards those wanting to teach in key shortage areas and to those with high classification degrees. Bursaries are tax free and can be used to meet the £9,250 tuition fees and living costs. Bursary levels for 2018/19 are set out in Table 2.2.

Secondary mathematics trainees also received two additional early career payments of £5,000 each (£7,500 if teaching in specified areas of England) in their third and fifth year of teaching, if they have taught in a state-funded school in England since completing their teacher training course from the Department for Education.

While it seems reasonable to assume that bursaries do encourage and facilitate recruitment, there are concerns that the higher bursaries attract applicants interested in the money with no real commitment to teaching. Indeed, the government's own figures demonstrate poorer retention figures for teachers who received high ITE bursaries than those who did not (Vaughan, 2019). In an analysis of government data by the Labour Party, Vaughan (2019) suggested that graduates receiving the maximum bursaries were twice as likely not to enter

TABLE 2.2 ITE bursary levels for 2018/19

Eligibility 2018 to 2019	Trainee with 1st/PhD	2:1/Master's	2:2	Other
Physics, biology, chemistry, classics, computing, geography, languages	£26,000	£26,000	£26,000	£0
Secondary mathematics	£20,000	£20,000	£20,000	£0
English	£15,000	£15,000	£15,000	£0
Design and technology	£12,000	£9,000	£0	£0
History, music, religious education	£9,000	£4,000	£0	£0
Primary mathematics	£6,000	£6,000	£6,000	£0

Source: Adapted from DfE, 2018e.

teaching as those who received no bursary at all, and that 25 per cent of bursary holders overall did not enter the teaching profession. Bursaries might be more usefully set at lower levels that will make a genuine contribution to fees and living costs, and distributed more equitably across subjects and phases, without being potentially wasted on those motivated primarily by short-term financial reward and invested instead on those more likely to enter the teaching profession.

Policy changes to encourage student teacher recruitment

During 2018 the government introduced a number of additional measures aimed at maximising recruitment in response to an apparent reduction in the number of people applying through the Universities and Colleges Admission Service for ITE programmes.[1] These included relaxing the rules on literacy and numeracy skills tests by allowing applicants more than three attempts to pass the tests, and prohibiting ITE providers from requiring that applicants have prior experience in a school before being offered a place. The first of these was broadly welcomed by ITE providers, although it did increase pressure further on skills tests centres, many of which could not cope with the extra demand (Roberts, 2018), while the second was criticised because of concerns which, according to polls conducted by UCET and National Association of School Based Initial Teacher Training (NASBTT), were entirely warranted that it would lead to people being recruited who only had limited understanding of what teaching involves and would drop out of ITE as soon as they found out (Ward, 2019).

In 2018/19, the government also removed caps on the number of student teachers that accredited ITE providers were allowed to recruit in most subjects and phases other than secondary physical education, where recruitment remained strong, and expensive salaried primary programmes. Prior to then, government allocated student number places, apportioned by phase (primary/secondary) and secondary subject to individual ITE providers based on TSM estimates of national need, leading, as previously mentioned, to an increase in the number of places left unfilled. In June 2015, the government announced that from 2016/17 rather than allocating places, accredited ITE providers would be able to recruit as many teachers in each phase and subject as they like, until national targets had been reached. The government did, however, set a maximum (and rather modest) total for universities, without placing any limit (other than that implied by the national targets) on SCITTs and School Direct.

The change in government policy identified caused severe disruption to the recruitment system, with many prospective applicants refused places (even on the days of scheduled interviews) because national caps had been applied, often at midnight on the same day as targets/caps were met. UCET and other organisations had long argued for a new, open recruitment methodology, something the government had always resisted on the grounds of cost and the potential for oversupply. UCET, however, argued that sufficient constraints already existed in the system to prevent massive over-recruitment (which, as the data shows, is not really an issue anyway) through, first, the lack of capacity in schools to accommodate large numbers of additional student teachers and, second, Ofsted inspection measures relating to employment outcomes that judge ITE providers on the basis of the percentage of their student teachers that secure employment in schools. The introduction of open recruitment in most subjects and phases from 2018/19, and confirmed in the recruitment and retention strategy for the next two recruitment cycles, has probably helped to improve recruitment, while also facilitating the matching of recruitment to areas of local need; the previous system of fixed allocations took no account of regional teacher supply issues when allocating places to providers in different parts of the country.

In April 2018, in an attempt to help the government address the teacher supply crisis, the Chief Executives of UCET, NASBTT, the Chartered College of Teaching and the Teaching Schools Council wrote to the then Secretary of State for Education, Damian Hinds, with a number of constructive suggestions (UCET, 2018). These included: simplifying the way that different routes into teaching are described, focusing on the key routes of postgraduate fee paying, postgraduate salaried and undergraduate; replacing pre-entry skills tests with on-course literacy and numeracy assessments; abolishing the £9,250 tuition fees for postgraduate ITE students; shifting funding from recruitment to retention incentives; and giving all new teachers an entitlement to structured early professional development, possibly at master's degree level, that builds on and complements their ITE. A number of these suggestions are consistent with the subsequent content of the January 2019 recruitment and retention strategy (DfE, 2019a).

The Department for Education 2019 recruitment and retention strategy

Continuing problems on the recruitment and retention of teachers, which have at best only partially been addressed by measures already taken through bursaries and recruitment campaigns, led to the government in January 2019 to publish a new recruitment and retention strategy (DfE, 2019a), which in some ways represented the first cohesive and comprehensive attempt to address the crisis. The development of the strategy followed extensive consultation with key stakeholders such as UCET, NASBTT, the Chartered College of Teaching, the Teaching Schools Council, head teachers and the teacher unions. Key features include:

- An entitlement for newly qualified teachers to structured early professional development during an extended two-year induction period, with guaranteed non-contact time of 5 per cent in the second year in addition to the 10 per cent already allowed for in year one.
- Reducing teacher workload by reviewing the inspection and accountability systems.
- Working with Ofsted to address the audit culture in schools.

- Introducing a period of stability in terms of the curriculum, qualifications and assessment.
- Provision of additional support to schools for tackling poor pupil behaviour.
- Funding for heads to support key challenges (costs, capital projects, new vacancies service).
- Additional financial incentives to aid retention.
- Provision of high-quality curriculum plans and materials for NQTs.
- Development of specialist qualifications, including those for teachers who want to remain in the classroom without moving into management roles.
- Focus of support on schools in particularly challenging circumstances.
- Supporting schools introduce flexible working opportunities.
- Making the ITE application system more user-friendly.
- Review the 'vibrant' ITE market, with new providers accredited where needed and an expansion of undergraduate provision.

The new DfE recruitment and retention strategy has significant potential benefits, particularly the introduction of an Early Career Framework (ECF) that could help to attract and retain new teachers. Although the quality of ITE programmes, according to both Ofsted (Ofsted, 2018) and NQTs themselves (DfE, 2018c) is extremely high, there is a recognition that only so much ground can be covered in sufficient depth on what are, in most cases, programmes of just one academic year's duration. The ECF, which will be introduced in selected parts of the country in September 2020 prior to national roll-out in September 2021/22, has the potential to give new teachers a greater understanding in terms of subject knowledge, special educational needs (SEN)/disability and other key areas, building on and complementing what teachers will have learned during their ITE. To reach its full potential, UCET and others have argued that the ECF should be: fully funded; flexible enough to be adapted to the needs of particular NQTs working in particular school contexts; and have the potential to link to master's level credits, which several sources of evidence has shown has a positive impact on teacher effectiveness (Training and Development Agency for Schools, 2010).

UCET has argued that teaching should, over time, become an all master's-qualified profession, which it believes would boost the status of teaching, improve teacher effectiveness and attract and retain ambitious new recruits into the profession. UCET and NASBTT have also argued that the ECF should be delivered by accredited ITE providers so as to allow NQTs the option of continuing to work with their original provider, to secure synergy and consistency between ITE and the ECF and to link to the already existing quality assurance mechanisms that are in place for accredited ITE provision. The DfE decided, however, to invite an open tender for the delivery of the ECF and the development of supporting curriculum materials, with no guarantee of input from ITE providers, although it is hoped that ITE providers will have an involvement either as lead contractors or as delivery providers with bids submitted by other contractors.

The proposals to reduce workload will be crucial to the strategy's success given the findings of NFER and others about job satisfaction, and the focus on this in the recruitment and retention strategy, as well as earlier DfE advice on workload for ITE providers (DfE, 2018c), are to be welcomed. The levers the government have to address this are, however, limited. Increased autonomy (mainly at the level of chains of schools under umbrella governance arrangements rather than individual schools), budgetary constraints and continuing teacher shortages could make it difficult for government to push schools to change cultures and reduce workload pressures. The government does, however, have a number of levers it could use to address workload through the Ofsted inspection framework, something it has signalled it will do as part of the recruitment and retention strategy. It can, first of all, make it clear that Ofsted will not expect to have access to, or use if they did have access to it, detailed performance data collected by schools, the collection and storage of which might not have any direct impact on pupil learning. It can also use the inspection process to ask teachers about workload in their schools, and reflect any concerns about apparent excessive and unproductive workload in inspection reports.

Changes to the process for applying to ITE programmes could, provided the associated Information and Communications Technology (ICT) systems operate effectively, make the application process easier to navigate and make it easier for providers to recruit students. Current systems are often inflexible in that they do not make it easy for applications to be re-referred within ITE partnerships if the particular place a candidate has applied to has either been filled or is not thought to be appropriate to the candidate's particular needs. This can lead to an applicant wasting one or more of the three initial choices they are permitted during the initial stages of the applications procedure.

Conclusion

Schools in England are faced with a continuing crisis with regard to the recruitment and retention of teachers. This is to some extent because of factors outside the government's control, such as increases in pupil numbers and reductions in the age group who are traditionally more likely to want to train to become teachers, as well as economic factors such as competition from other employers for high-quality graduates. Other factors, such as the consequences of the accountability and inspection frameworks, teacher workload and school funding, are, however, the direct result of government policies because they have a negative impact on the teacher supply base provided by accredited ITE providers. The measures adopted by the government prior to 2019 were ad hoc, piecemeal and did not sufficiently address the roots of the supply crisis. It is, however, hoped that through the implementation of the DfE recruitment and retention strategy, with its emphasis on retention, professional development and workload, a positive difference in teacher recruitment and retention in England may emerge.

Note

1 However, it subsequently transpired that this reflected changes on the timing and patterns of applications rather than a year-on-year decline.

References

Department for Education [DfE]. (2010). *The importance of teaching: The Schools White Paper 2010.* London: DfE. Retrieved from gov.uk website: https://assets.publishing. service.gov.uk/government/uploads/system/uploads/attachment_data/file/175429/ CM-7980.pdf

Department for Education [DfE]. (2011). *Teacher's standards. Guidance for school leaders, school staff and governing bodies.* Retrieved from gov.uk website: https://assets. publishing.service.gov.uk/government/uploads/system/uploads/attachment_data/ file/665520/Teachers__Standards.pdf

Department for Education [DfE]. (2017, May 9). *Postgraduate Initial Teacher Training (ITT) places and the Teacher Supply Model (TSM), England 2017/18.* (SFR 42/2017). Retrieved from gov.uk website: https://assets.publishing.service.gov.uk/government/uploads/ system/uploads/attachment_data/file/655038/SFR42_2017_TSM_Main_Text.pdf

Department for Education [DfE]. (2018a, June 28). *School workforce in England: November 2017.* Retrieved from gov.uk website: https://assets.publishing.service.gov.uk/ government/uploads/system/uploads/attachment_data/file/719772/SWFC_ MainText.pdf

Department for Education [DfE]. (2018b, June 28). *Schools, pupils and their characteristics: January 2018.* Statistical publication. Retrieved from gov.uk website: https://assets. publishing.service.gov.uk/government/uploads/system/uploads/attachment_data/ file/719226/Schools_Pupils_and_their_Characteristics_2018_Main_Text.pdf

Department for Education [DfE]. (2018c, November). *Addressing teacher workload in Initial Teacher Education (ITE): Advice for ITE providers.* Retrieved from gov.uk website: https://assets.publishing.service.gov.uk/government/uploads/system/uploads/attach ment_data/file/753502/Addressing_Workload_in_ITE.pdf

Department for Education [DfE]. (2018d, November 29). *Initial Teacher Training (ITT) census for the academic year 2018 to 2019.* Retrieved from gov.uk website: www.gov.uk/ government/statistics/initial-teacher-training-trainee-number-census-2018-to-2019

Department for Education [DfE]. (2018e, April). *Initial Teacher Training bursaries funding manual, 2018 to 2019 academic year. Version 1.1.* Retrieved from gov.uk website: https:// assets.publishing.service.gov.uk/government/uploads/system/uploads/attachment_ data/file/697803/Initial_Teacher_Training_bursaries_funding_manual_18-19.pdf

Department for Education [DfE]. (2019a). *Teacher recruitment and retention strategy.* Retrieved from gov.uk website: https://assets.publishing.service.gov.uk/government/ uploads/system/uploads/attachment_data/file/786856/DFE_Teacher_Retention_ Strategy_Report.pdf

Department for Education [DfE]. (2019b). *Initial teacher training: Trainee number census 2018 to 2019, England.* Retrieved from gov.uk website: https://assets.publishing. service.gov.uk/government/uploads/system/uploads/attachment_data/file/759716/ ITT_Census_2018_to_2019_main_text.pdf

Department for Education [DfE]. (2019c, July 16). *Changes to the professional skills test for teachers.* Retrieved from gov.uk website: www.gov.uk/government/news/changes-to-the-professional-skills-test-for-teachers

House of Commons Committee of Public Accounts. (2018). *Retaining and developing the teaching workforce: Seventeenth report of session 2017–19.* (HC 460, 2017–19). Retrieved from parliaments.uk website: https://publications.parliament.uk/pa/cm201719/cmselect/cmpubacc/460/460.pdf

House of Commons Education Committee. (2017). *Recruitment and retention of teachers: Fifth report of session 2016–17.* (HC 199). Retrieved from parliaments.uk website: https://publications.parliament.uk/pa/cm201617/cmselect/cmeduc/199/199.pdf

Lynch, S., Worth, J., Bamford, S., & Wespieser, K. (2016). *Engaging teachers: NFER analysis of teacher retention.* Slough: NFER.

National Audit Office [NAO]. (2017, September 12). *Retaining and developing the teaching workforce.* Report by the Comptroller and Auditor General. (HC 307, 2017–19). Retrieved from NAO website: www.nao.org.uk/report/supporting-and-improving-the-teaching-workforce/

Noble-Rogers, J. (2017, June 14). The top to-do list priority for the DfE. *SecEd.* Retrieved from SecEd website: www.sec-ed.co.uk/editorial-comment/the-top-to-do-list-priority-for-the-dfe/

Office for Budget Responsibility [OBR]. (2018). *Forecasting student numbers for our student loans forecast.* Retrieved from OBR website: https://obr.uk/box/forecasting-student-numbers-for-our-student-loans-forecast/

Ofsted. (2018, December 4). *The annual report of Her Majesty's Chief Inspector of Education, Children's Services and Skills 2017/18.* (HC 1707). London: Ofsted. Retrieved from gov.uk website: www.gov.uk/government/publications/ofsted-annual-report-201718-education-childrens-services-and-skills

Roberts, J. (2018, August 23). Fears skills test delays will deepen recruitment crisis. *Times Educational Supplement.* Retrieved from TES website: www.tes.com/news/exclusive-fears-skills-test-delays-will-deepen-recruitment-crisis

See, B. H., & Gorard, S. (2019). Why don't we have enough teachers?: A reconsideration of the available evidence. *Research Papers in Education.* https://doi.org/10.1080/02671522.2019.1568535

Training and Development Agency for Schools. (2010). *A longitudinal review of the postgraduate professional development of teachers.* London: TDA.

UCET. (2018, April 17). *Letter from Emma Hollis, James Noble-Rogers, Dame Alison Peacock and Andrew Warren to Damian Hinds.* Retrieved from UCET website: www.ucet.ac.uk/downloads/10310-UCETNASBTTCCTTSC-Letter-to-Damian-Hinds.pdf

Vaughan, R. (2019, January 10). Millions in taxpayers cash wasted on bursaries for teachers who never set foot in a classroom. *iNews.* Retrieved from iNews website: inews.co.uk/news/education/millions-bursaries-teachers-classroom-161095

Ward, H. (2019, January 18). DfE rule sees trainees drop out over classroom 'shock'. *Times Educational Supplement.* Retrieved from TES website: www.tes.com/news/exclusive-dfe-rule-sees-trainees-drop-out-over-classroom-shock

Whittaker, F. (2018, November 29). Teacher training targets missed in most EBacc subjects. *Schools Week.* Retrieved from Schools Week website: https://schoolsweek.co.uk/teacher-training-targets-missed-in-most-ebacc-subjects/

Worth, J., Lynch, S., Hillary, J., Rennie, C., & Andrade, J. (2018). *Teacher workforce dynamics in England.* Slough: NFER.

3

WHY ARE TEACHERS LEAVING TEACHING IN ENGLAND?

Georgina Newton

Introduction

In 21 years as a classroom teacher, I said 'hello' and 'goodbye' to countless colleagues. In fact, almost every term is punctuated by formal get-togethers where all staff meet to send someone off to retirement, a school abroad, a new job or a new area of work.

I enjoyed teaching, but some colleagues clearly felt they could no longer continue, and what's more, they are not alone. Increasingly, working-age teachers are choosing to leave the profession (National Audit Office [NAO], 2017). Simultaneously, there has been a rise in pupil numbers, which means that England needs more new teachers to staff its schools for at least the next seven years. To have a robust education system, the nation needs not only enough teachers, but also enough experienced ones, so it is of critical importance that this issue is addressed (Allen & Sims, 2018).

In this chapter I present some of the findings of my master's research into why teachers leave teaching and what we could do to keep them. This mixed-methods research was conducted in 2016 and consisted of a literature review, a survey of 236 teachers and interviews with long-serving, returning, tired, career-changing and early career teachers. In presenting my findings, I suggest ways in which teachers might be encouraged to remain longer in the profession.

Leaving so soon?

Teachers are in high demand in England because of two factors: pupil numbers have swollen by approximately 10 per cent in the past eight years and working-age teachers are increasingly leaving the profession before retirement (Department for Education [DfE], 2019b). Each year around 33,000 people embark on teacher training through courses at undergraduate and postgraduate levels (NAO, 2016), but this number is insufficient to meet the demand. The government's own training targets in most secondary subjects are not achieved (Allen & Sims, 2018) and every day in England there remain over 1,000 unfilled teacher vacancies (DfE, 2019b). Some schools close early one day a week because they do not have enough staff to cover all their classes (Pidd, 2017).

Increased exit rates are evident for teachers at all stages of their careers. It is not only the more experienced who are leaving, but also the emerging leaders and the recent recruits. Attrition of early career teachers has accelerated with 32 per cent giving up teaching within the first five years (DfE, 2019a). This represents a loss of energetic and enthusiastic new teachers (CooperGibson, 2019) and later depletes the pool of available future school leaders. Primary school teachers are more likely to remain in post than their secondary colleagues.

Secondary curriculum subjects are affected by shortages of teachers in varying ways. While supply and retention rates of physical education (P.E.) and history teachers are high, only half of newly trained maths and physics teachers tend to remain in teaching beyond their fifth year (Education Policy Institute, 2018). To try to remedy this, the Department of Education (DfE) has introduced a retention element to its bursary payment (a financial incentive from the government to attract teachers into teaching) for maths teachers. A sum is paid during training, which is followed by retention payments after three and five years in the classroom. At the time of writing, similar 'golden hello' payments are also being introduced in other teacher shortage subjects, such as information technology. This bursary policy creates a lack of parity for trainee teachers across subjects, because some receive no bursary at all.

When do teachers leave?

Studies in the early 2000s found that teachers' professional lives consist of identifiable phases (Berliner, 2004; Day & Gu, 2007), which can be described as the consolidation phase (years 1–3); years of increasing effectiveness (years 4–8); followed by sustained commitment (years 9–13) (Day & Gu, 2007). These studies identified that, after around ten years of teaching, a 'career crossroads' was reached, where teachers either leave or continue in teaching until their retirement. However, more recent reports, including the annual School Workforce Census from the Department for Education, demonstrate that this cannot be relied upon as an accurate forecast of teacher numbers from 2011 onwards. Figure 3.1 shows that the number of teachers choosing to teach until retirement has fallen from 21.7 per cent in 2010, to 15.6 per cent in 2017 (DfE, 2019b, p. 5).

Figure 3.2 shows the experience levels of teachers who reported in the research underpinning this chapter that they intend to leave the profession in the next two years (Newton, 2016). It shows teachers from the second to the fifteenth year of their career are equally likely to leave. This suggests that more experienced teachers who, having weathered the early career years, might otherwise have been

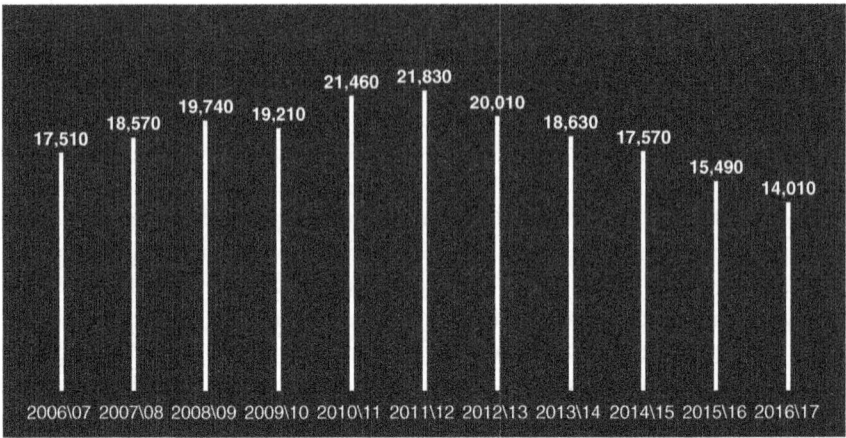

FIGURE 3.1 Number of teachers reaching retirement over the last ten years

Source: DfE, 2019b, p. 5.

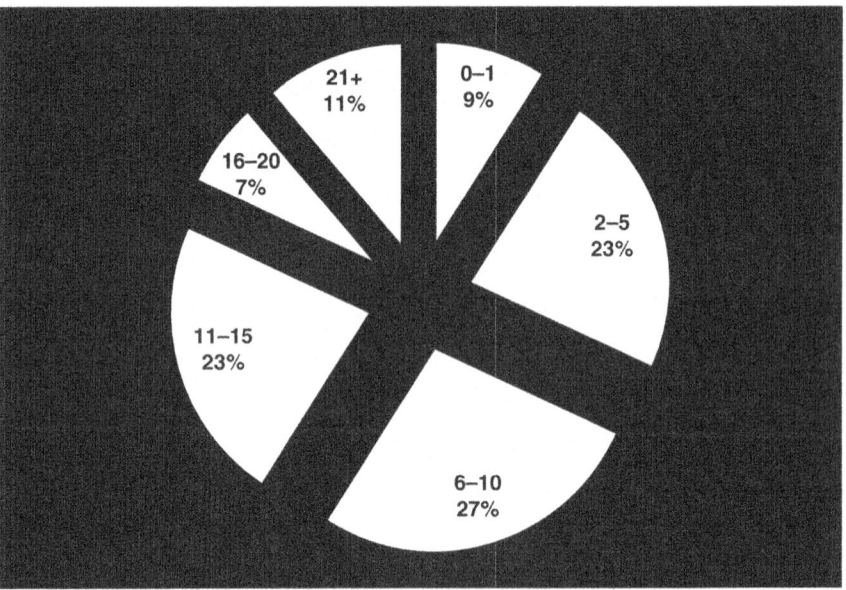

FIGURE 3.2 Experience levels (in years) of teaches intending to leave

Source: Newton, 2016, p. 36.

considering a move to senior or middle leadership, pastoral or mentoring roles are considering leaving at an equal rate to their less experienced colleagues. This represents a hollowing-out of the profession, which could be as detrimental as the early career dropout rates to levels of skill, expertise and leadership in schools.

A lower proportion of teachers reaching their most effective stage in years 5 to 8 (Berliner, 2004; Day & Gu, 2007) will affect the quality of pupil outcomes for years to come. Mid-career and experienced professionals act as mentors, role models, trainers and leaders. When pupils lose one teacher and gain another, it has been shown to affect their levels of progress and attainment (Ingersoll, 2002). When good teachers leave, pupils' education suffers even more (Allen, Mian, & Sims, 2016). Such a significant teacher shortage, coupled with the potential of more in-service leavers, demands investigation. The next section addresses some of the complex and varied factors that have led to this point.

Why do teachers leave?

To examine why teachers leave, it is helpful to understand both the small stories – those individual and personal motivations which may have the result of pushing people away – and the grand narratives of system-wide issues that result in teacher attrition. It is apparent that there are both 'push' factors out of the profession, such as workload, data, assessment, inspection, new initiatives and disillusionment that propel people out of teaching, as well as 'pull' factors that propel individuals towards other jobs requiring less emotional and physical commitment.

The majority of ex-teachers in the research underpinning this chapter cite heavy workload as one of the reasons for their decision to leave (Newton, 2016). Thousands of blogs, tweets, open letters and posts on the subject have given the issue of teacher workload much exposure. This public airing of dissatisfaction may, in itself, be detrimental to overall teacher numbers. An individual teacher, writing an opinion piece on their unreasonable workload, might feel that this is an important act as it gives vent to their frustration and creates empathy among their followers. However, publishing a profession's dissatisfactions in the public realm might actually also contribute to the problem creating negativity about the profession for those standing outside and within it. The drip-drip effect of professional intent is eroded.

Teachers who take matters into their own hands in this way may be demonstrating frustration at their lack of agency (that sense of having the power to act with intent to achieve a certain goal) in teaching. This ability to influence one's job using initiative has been recognised to be less evident in the public sector than the private or voluntary sectors (Bernecker, Klier, Stern, & Thiel, 2018). Resorting to a tweet expressing frustration at aspects of the job (as the following tweet demonstrates) might feel like a good way of venting, if it was the case that someone with the power to change things was listening.

> I left [teaching] because I felt that nobody understood.
> *(L. Hutchings, interview with a career changer, February 26, 2016)*

Teachers in this author's research cited a range of 'push' factors that resulted in their leaving the profession (Newton, 2016) and these are shown in Figure 3.3

FIGURE 3.3 Push factors causing teachers to leave the profession

Source: Newton, 2016, p. 42.

with the size of the word denoting the frequency of its use. It is clear that, for these teachers, school leaders were perceived as a pressure point pushing them away from the job.

The perceived challenges placed on staff by leaders is not just a problem in teaching. The Chartered Institute of Personnel and Development (CIPD) survey of employees in multiple sectors found that relationships with senior leaders are generally much poorer in the public sector than in the voluntary or private sectors. Employees say they do not feel their leaders treat them with respect or consult them on aspects of their work, and 25 per cent state that they do not trust their bosses to act with integrity (CIPD, 2016, p. 11). Those managers in schools who neither consult their staff nor instil confidence and respect contribute to teacher attrition.

When leaders give value and appreciation to the teacher workforce, it has been noted to reduce the negative effect of high workload. The author noted in an interview with a long-standing supply teacher that they highlighted the impact of a supportive headteacher on the staff in his school:

> There was a different ethos from the top. He inspired you to do it, and didn't force you. . . . Mr. B would lead and the teachers would follow. It was only ever supposed to be a temporary job but I was . . . gutted when I had to leave [the] school. . . . It's about being valued. We did as much work as we had to.
>
> *(Newton, 2016, p. 37)*

Is higher pay outside teaching a 'pull' factor?

In the United States, where there are also teacher retention problems, individual states take their own actions to help keep their teachers (Teacher Portal, 2020). In Wyoming, every teacher is paid a salary 50 per cent higher than the surrounding states, and there is an average of 19.6 applications for each teacher vacancy (Stoddard, 2011). In England, teachers do not generally leave teaching to achieve higher pay elsewhere, and there are signs that only a minority of leavers achieve high pay immediately (Worth & Van den Brande, 2019, p. 3). The National Foundation for Educational Research (NFER) found that it takes about three years for pay to recover to the level it was when the teacher left teaching (Worth & Van den Brande, 2019, p. 3).

Early career teachers who have highly paid career alternatives in the private sector show concern about the level of their pay as a teacher. Science, Technology, Engineering and Mathematics (STEM) teachers have been shown to stay longer in teaching when their pay is increased (Sims, 2017). Sims also finds that pay incentives early in their career may be more effective at retaining STEM teachers than rewarding them highly once they are established (Sims, 2019). However, it is a gamble for school leaders and government to assume that teacher pay is not a factor when it has declined in real terms by 10 per cent since 2010 (Organisation for Economic Cooperation and Development [OECD], 2017, p. 434). Placing a higher value on the gaining of experience than rewarding it once secured could have the unintended consequence of contributing further to the exodus of more experienced teachers.

The Department for Education would also be wise to consider that the expansion of international schools abroad presents an interesting prospect for those who want to remain in teaching but are attracted to life overseas. It is expected that over 200,000 teaching jobs in international schools will be created in the next ten years (APPG, 2019, p. 5), and 40 per cent of teachers say that they would relocate abroad if the right job offer came along (Schools Improvement, 2018).

Who leaves? And what could help them stay?

Not all teachers who leave teaching in England are lured away by exotic locations, as gender and age are seen to be contributing factors. Women in teaching outnumber men by about 4 to 1 (Dickens, 2017) and therefore proportionally more women than men intend to leave teaching, but what is noticeable is that these women are predominantly between the ages of 30 and 39 (Newton, 2016). This age-specific group could be due to increasing family commitments and the impact of this on these women's work/life balance as identified by Day and Gu (2007).

During their 30s, teachers will mostly be developing high levels of effectiveness, so it is essential to understand the concerns of this significant segment of the teacher workforce (Day & Gu, 2007). In the research underpinning this chapter, teachers in their 30s cited workload (83 per cent) as their main reason for considering leaving. Management expectations (50 per cent), family/personal commitments (35 per cent) and disillusionment (28 per cent) were additional causes (Newton, 2016). When the author asked teachers what could be done to make them want to stay, the majority (64 per cent) said they required more praise and recognition for their work; 34 per cent also said that they would welcome flexibility in their working hours (Newton, 2016).

The UK Government has taken note of the demand for teacher recognition (Department for Education, 2016) and recommendations have been made to schools to improve flexible working options (DfE, 2017). Flexibility for school teachers offers both advantages and disadvantages to schools. For teachers who are parents, a flexible approach provides opportunities to attend their children's school assemblies, sports days and parents' consultations, provided they fall on the fallow timetable day.

Solutions for overcoming timetable constraints for flexible teacher working could include:

- Two part-time teachers completing a job-share and covering for each other when one is unavailable.
- Flexible start and finish times.
- Flexible approaches to planning, preparation and assessment (PPA) time (e.g., the right to work off the school site).
- Avoidance of fortnightly timetables.
- Compressed hours.
- Time Off In Lieu (TOIL) arrangements which allow for flexible working.
- Discretionary paid or unpaid leave by prior arrangement.

(National Education Union, 2020)

Clearly, arranging part-time working to achieve a balance that is advantageous for the school, the teacher and the pupils is a complex task. For pupils in the primary years it can result in lack of consistency with one class teacher for half of a week and another teacher for the other half (DfE, 2017). In secondary schools, it can result in acknowledged timetabling difficulties and the government's published guidelines offer some solutions to these (*ibid.*). However none address the inequalities created when consistent teachers are guaranteed for older students, preparing for their high-stakes tests, and younger students' lessons are therefore assigned to multiple different part-time teachers.

An unintended consequence of secondary schools' decision to adopt a two-week timetable has been a reduction in teachers that are parents being able to afford to work part time. For example, if the teaching timetable includes Monday, Tuesday and Thursday one week and Tuesday, Wednesday and Friday the next, parents could find themselves needing to reserve childcare every day of the week, each week, which can present disproportionately high childcare costs.

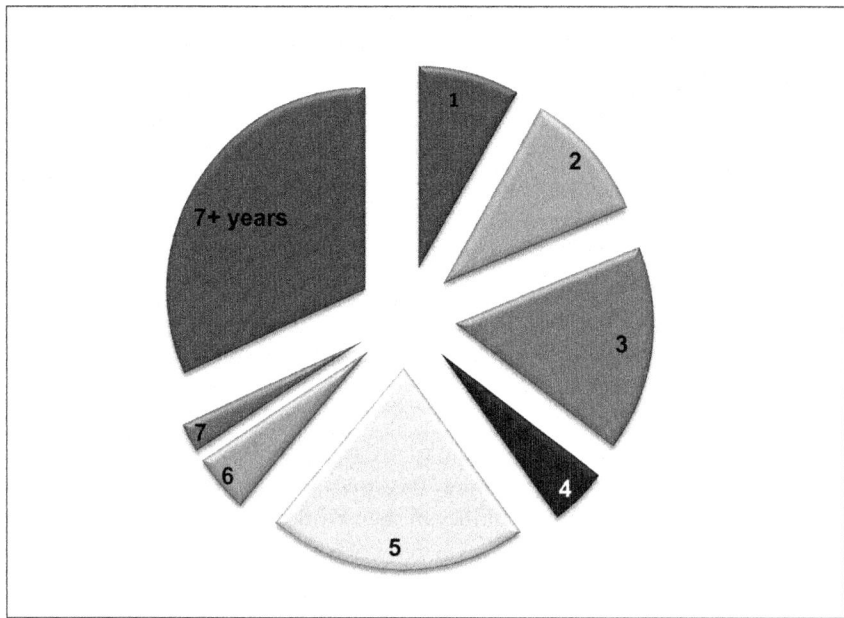

FIGURE 3.4 The number of years teachers could envisage remaining in teaching if things were better

Source: Newton, 2016, p. 44.

Listening to teachers and adjusting their working arrangements could, however, have a huge impact on the number of experienced teachers able to remain in the classroom. Annually, around 14,000 teachers make a successful return to schools following a break in their career (Worth & Van den Brande, 2019). Thanks to the high level of vocational intent shown by teachers from the outset, they often state that it is not the nature of the work itself that caused them to leave. Figure 3.4 shows that, if action was taken to address their concerns, over 81 per cent of the leavers from the profession said they would stay for at least two years and almost a third could envisage a further seven or more years in the classroom (Newton, 2016, p. 42).

Is there a light at the end of the tunnel of disillusionment?

Alongside leadership actions that might create a 'push' effect, we should consider the emotional effects of negativity around teaching. Teaching can be seen as 'emotional labour' (Nichols, Schutz, Rodgers, & Bilica, 2017, p. 406), and negative emotional impact can be of great detriment to job satisfaction (Huber, 2016). When teachers in the underpinning research were asked why they wanted to leave teaching, 60 per cent said they felt disillusioned about their job, using terms such as 'hopeless', 'useless', 'not valued', 'powerless', 'worried', 'ground down' and 'not supported' to express how this feels (Newton, 2016, p. 57).

When this disillusionment in teaching occurs in the early stages of a teaching career, it can result from a mismatch of previously held beliefs about teaching and the teachers' difficulty in coping with their early experiences of classroom events (Nichols et al., 2017). Additional pressures ensue when a new teacher's underlying professional intent does not align with the ethos of a particular school, which means that he or she is very likely to leave teaching (Lindqvist & Nordänger, 2016) without giving another school or setting the opportunity to help them succeed.

The DfE's Early Career Framework (DfE, 2019a), for delivery from 2021, will provide an opportunity for schools to embed supportive structures, including dedicated time for professional development and support from a trained mentor. This is a promising development, but the quality of implementation will be crucial to its success in retaining teachers.

The 'million dollar' question in all of this is: what can really be done to help teachers stay? As shown in Figure 3.5, my research findings suggest that teachers want praise and recognition, better relationships with their bosses, a greater sense of autonomy and more flexibility in their work (Newton, 2016, p. 40). For public-sector workers, especially, a key retention factor is that they feel good at their job (Menzies, 2015) and receive recognition for this via manager approval (Spear, Gould, & Lee, 2000).

My findings suggest that school leaders have huge potential to affect the retention figures within their own school through their approval, recognition and appreciation of teachers as reward for their emotional labour. European research states that school leadership should aim to reduce emotional stress, rather than add to it (Huber, 2016), and leaders listening to their teachers, giving praise and affirmation and making feasible adjustments to working arrangements can create a win–win scenario. The teacher gains a workable life/work balance and the school retains an experienced member of staff.

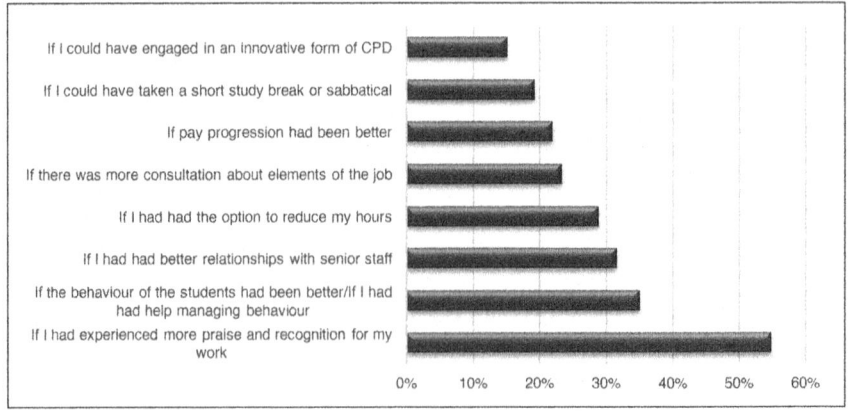

FIGURE 3.5 What could have encouraged you to stay in teaching?

Source: Newton, 2016, p. 42.

The CIPD (2016) recommends cross-function working, secondments and opportunities to work on new projects as ways of boosting skills without giving promotion. When staff do depart, leaving the door open for them to return later in a different role can add wider experience to the workplace (Hope, 2017). Around 10,000 teachers return to the classroom annually but policy initiatives aimed at increasing this number have failed to entice many (Worth & Van den Brande, 2019). Schools that take a pro-active approach to reingaging returners may find themselves able to address staffing shortages in a flexible, agile way.

Despite all this talk of teachers leaving the profession, around 14,000 in-service teachers each year reach their retirement age. These are the colleagues who give the longest and most interesting speeches at the end-of-term staff meeting before the awaited summer holiday. They attest to having had challenging times in their career, but leadership actions such as authenticity and a listening ear are cited as being among the motivational forces at work that secure long-lasting engagement (J. Offord, interview with a long-standing teacher, February 26, 2016).

> At the end of the day it's all about feeling valued.
>
> *(Newton, 2016, p. 56)*

Long-serving teachers unsurprisingly could teach us much about teaching for the long haul. It has been argued that they demonstrate personal efficacy and resilience, compensating for weakness in leadership and securing long-lasting commitment by drawing recognition from other meaningful sources (Kell, 2018). Kell (2018, p. 118) advocates 'making your own rewards' by creating a folder of great memories to provide motivation when it is needed, such as a tag from a bunch of flowers from a child, a thank-you card from grateful parents or a note from a colleague.

I conclude that what is significant is what it *feels* like to be a teacher. Feeling valued can protect teachers against both push and pull factors which might make them leave teaching. We do well when we feel confident, and we feel confident when we do well (Day & Gu, 2007). We have seen that a complex combination of individual factors can result in significant attrition. If we can create schools that value their teachers as individuals, give them confidence and manage them well, maybe it will be possible to retain them more effectively.

References

Allen, R., Mian, E. S., & Sims, S. (2016, April). *Social inequalities in access to teachers* (Social Market Foundation Commission on Inequality in Education Briefing 2). London: Social Market Foundation. Retrieved from www.smf.co.uk/wp-content/uploads/2016/04/Social-Market-Foundation-Social-inequalities-in-access-to-teachers-Embargoed-0001-280416.pdf

Allen, R., & Sims, S. (2018). *The teacher gap*. Abingdon: Routledge.

All Party Parliamentary Group for the Teaching Profession [APPG]. (2019, January 21). *Minutes of meetings*. Retrieved from APPG for the Teaching Profession: https://

appgteachingcom.files.wordpress.com/2018/02/appg_mon-21-jan-2019_minutes-final_amendedv2.pdf

Berliner, D. C. (2004). Describing the behavior and documenting the accomplishments of expert teachers. *Bulletin of Science, Technology & Society, 24*(3), 200–212.

Bernecker, A., Klier, J., Stern, S., & Thiel, L. (2018). *Sustaining high performance beyond public-sector pilot projects*. Retrieved from McKinsey & Company website: www.mckinsey.com/industries/public-sector/our-insights/sustaining-high-performance-beyond-public-sector-pilot-projects

Chartered Institute of Personnel and Development [CIPD]. (2016). *Employee outlook*. London: CIPD.

CooperGibson. (2019, June). *Schools' experiences of hosting trainees and employing newly qualified teachers*. London: Department for Education.

Day, C. G., & Gu Qing. (2007). Variations in the conditions for teachers' professional learning and development: Sustaining commitment and effectiveness over a career. *Oxford Review of Education, 33*(4), 423–443.

Department for Education [DfE]. (2016, March). *Educational excellence everywhere*. London: DfE. Retrieved from gov.uk website: https://assets.publishing.service.gov.uk/government/uploads/system/uploads/attachment_data/file/508447/Educational_Excellence_Everywhere.pdf

Department for Education [DfE]. (2017, February). *Flexible working in schools*. London: DfE. Retrieved from gov.uk website: https://assets.publishing.service.gov.uk/government/uploads/system/uploads/attachment_data/file/593990/DFE_Flex_Working_Guidance_2017_FINAL.pdf

Department for Education [DfE]. (2019a, October 11 [updated March 2, 2020]). *Supporting early career teachers*. Retrieved from gov.uk website: www.gov.uk/government/publications/supporting-early-career-teachers/supporting-early-career-teachers#the-early-career-framework

Department for Education [DfE]. (2019b, June 27). *School workforce in England: November 2018*. London: Department for Education. Retrieved from gov.uk website: www.gov.uk/government/statistics/school-workforce-in-england-november-2018

Dickens, J. (2017, June 22). *Teachers leaving faster than ever – and 10 other school workforce findings*. Schools Week. Retrieved from Schools Week website: https://schoolsweek.co.uk/teachers-leaving-faster-than-ever-and-10-other-school-workforce-findings/

Education Policy Institute. (2018, August 30). *Teaching and leadership: Supply and quality* [summary of report]. Retrieved from EPI website: https://epi.org.uk/publications-and-research/the-teacher-labour-market-in-england/

Hope, K. (2017, February 1). How long should you stay in one job? *BBC News*. Retrieved from BBC News website: www.bbc.co.uk/news/business-38828581

Huber, S. (2016). *School leadership practices and health – Selected findings from a multi-method longitudinal school leadership study*. BELMAS. London: Sage.

Ingersoll, R. (2002). The teacher shortage: A case of wrong diagnosis and wrong prescription. *NASSP Bulletin, 86*(631), 16–26.

Kell, E. (2018). *How to survive in teaching: Without imploding, exploding or walking away*. London: Bloomsbury.

Lindqvist, P., & Nordänger, U. K. (2016). Already elsewhere – A study of (skilled) teachers' choice to leave teaching. *Teaching and Teacher Education, 54*, 88–97.

Menzies, L. (2015). *Why teach?* London: Pearson.

National Audit Office [NAO]. (2016, February 10). *Training new teachers*. (HC 798, Session 2015–16). London: NAO. Retrieved from www.nao.org.uk/wp-content/uploads/2016/02/Training-new-teachers.pdf

National Audit Office [NAO]. (2017, September 12). *Retaining and developing the teaching workforce* [press release]. Retrieved from NAO website: www.nao.org.uk/press-release/retaining-and-developing-the-teaching-workforce/

National Education Union. (2020, January 16). *Special leave model policy – Checklist.* Retrieved from NEU website: https://neu.org.uk/advice/special-leave-model-policy-checklist

Newton, G. (2016, September 1). *Why do teachers quit and what could be done to make them stay?* Unpublished master's thesis, University of Staffordshire, Stoke-on-Trent.

Nichols, S. L., Schutz, P. A., Rodgers, K, & Bilica, K. (2017). Early career teachers' emotion and emerging teacher identities. *Teachers and Teaching, 23*(4), 406–421.

Organisation for Economic Cooperation and Development [OECD]. (2017). *Education at a glance.* Paris: OECD Publishing.

Pidd, H. (2017, March 10). Cuts could mean schools close early two days a week, say teachers. *The Guardian.* Retrieved from Guardian website: www.theguardian.com/education/2017/mar/10/schools-in-england-and-wales-consider-shorter-days

Schools Improvement. (2018, October 2). *Two out of five teachers would leave Britain 'next term' if they got the right job opportunity abroad.* Schools Improvement. Retrieved from Schools Improvement website: https://schoolsimprovement.net/two-out-of-five-teachers-would-leave-britain-next-term-if-they-got-the-right-job-opportunity-abroad/

Sims, S. (2017). *What happens when you pay shortage-subject teachers more money?* [report]. London: Gatsby Foundation. Retrieved from www.gatsby.org.uk/uploads/education/datalab-simulating-the-effect-of-early-career-salary-supplements-on-teacher-supply-in-england.pdf

Sims, S. (2019). *Increasing pay of early career shortage subject teachers key to averting retention crisis.* London: Gatsby Foundation.

Stoddard, C. (2011, August 19). *Monitoring cost pressures on teacher salaries in Wyoming.* [final report]. Retrieved from https://wyoleg.gov/2011/Interim%20Studies/Stoddard_indicators8_26_2011v2.pdf

Spear, M., Gould, K., & Lee, B. (2000). *Who would be a teacher? A review of factors motivating and demotivating prospective and practising teachers.* Slough: NFER.

Teacher Portal. (2020, January 10). *Teacher salary data by state.* Retrieved from Teacher Portal website: www.teacherportal.com/teacher-salaries-by-state/

Worth, J., & Van den Brande, J. (2019). *The teacher labour market in England: Annual report 2019.* Slough: NFER.

4

A HIGH-STATUS, RESEARCH-INFORMED PROFESSION

The foundation for successful teacher recruitment and retention?

Linda la Velle and Alexandra Kendall

Introduction

> As teachers are a fundamental condition for guaranteeing quality education, teachers and educators should be empowered, adequately recruited and remunerated, motivated, professionally qualified, and supported within well-resourced, efficient and effectively governed systems.
>
> (UNESCO, 2016, p. 52)

Retention in the teaching profession is a global and critical issue (Geiger & Pivovarova, 2018). In England, it is estimated that approximately one-third of newly qualified teachers will leave the profession within their first five years of teaching (Worth, 2018). Added to this is that pupil numbers in state-funded schools in England are rising and therefore increasing the pupil-to-teacher ratio in classrooms. There is also a decline in recruitment to initial teacher education and training courses: this has been below target every successive year since 2012. The final challenge is that the number of full-time teacher vacancies and temporarily filled posts have both risen since 2011. In the words of the National Foundation for Educational Research [NFER] (Worth, 2018), these issues together create the 'perfect storm' of teacher supply.

In the last two decades, a number of government initiatives and interventions have been proposed and some put into operation, including: the introduction of bursaries for shortage subjects such as physics, computing and modern foreign languages; incentive schemes for returning teachers; encouragements for overseas teachers; opportunities for flexible working; introducing early career retention payments for maths teachers; piloting a student loan reimbursement scheme for science and language teachers working in schools in certain local authorities in their third and fifth years of teaching; and, finally, a commitment of £84 million up to 2022/23 to upskill 8,000 computer science teachers (Foster, 2019). Other initiatives that were piloted, such as the proposed National Teaching Service, which aimed to place teachers in underperforming schools in areas that struggle to recruit teachers, did not get beyond the pilot stage (Hazell, 2016). Additionally, recent evidence suggests that over £22 million has been spent on bursaries for student teachers in England, many of whom do not go into teaching (Vaughn, 2019).

In spite of these various inducements, and possibly because of their comparative lack of success in improving the situation of teacher recruitment and retention, the UK Government has the stated aim to strengthen the status of the profession by the provision of structured continuing professional development and career development. It is beyond the scope of this chapter to discuss in detail the various policy initiatives that have recently been implemented. While acknowledging that raising the status of the teaching profession is a long-term aspiration, it can be argued that to date there is little sign of much difference having been made to the status quo. This chapter will argue that the provision of attractive, motivating and progressive *initial* and career-long professional development for teachers is the first step in raising the profession's status. It is also central and crucial to the ultimate aim of ensuring that all pupils have a well-qualified and motivated teacher to enable them to achieve their educational potential.

Strengthening the status of the teaching profession

To consider how the professional status of teachers might be strengthened first requires a conceptualisation of the notion of status itself. For teaching, a useful model of status has been offered by Eric Hoyle (2001). In short, Hoyle proposes that occupational status is comprised of three related aspects: prestige, esteem and status. He defines *occupational prestige* as the public perception of the relative position of an occupation in a hierarchy of occupations; *occupational status* as the category to which knowledgeable groups (for example, civil servants, politicians and social scientists, etc.) allocate a particular occupation/profession; and *occupational esteem* as the regard in which an occupation is held by the general public by virtue of the personal, rather than technical, qualities, such as care, competence, conscientiousness, that practitioners bring to their work. Hoyle goes on to argue that teachers' *occupational prestige* is comparable to 'semi-professions' such as social work, rather than the major professions such as law or medicine. In spite of having achieved official professional status in the 2001 census classification of occupations, Hoyle claims that teachers' *occupational status* is limited by the image that people hold of them, mainly because of the nature of their work with children. Teachers' *occupational esteem*, Hoyle proposes, is influenced by people's own experiences at school. However, occupational esteem is, he argues, the only aspect of their status that teachers can themselves influence, through their own practice.

In many countries, including Ireland, Finland and Australia, teaching is regarded as a high-status profession. Recruitment and retention is relatively unproblematic; teachers enjoy their work and are esteemed for it by society. In the UK, however, and particularly in England, concern about the professional status of teachers has a long-standing and far-reaching history reaching back well into the middle of the last century. A report from the United Nations Educational, Scientific and Cultural Organisation's [UNESCO] Special Intergovernmental Conference on the Status of Teachers (UNESCO, 2008) contained an extensive list of recommendations, relating to the most important professional, social, ethical and material concerns of teachers, which aimed to improve the status of the teaching profession. Among other imperatives, and with relevance to this chapter, these included:

- initial and continuing training
- recruitment
- advancement and promotion
- professional freedom
- supervision and assessment
- responsibilities and rights
- participation in educational decision-making
- conditions for effective teaching and learning.

Strengthening each of the frameworks in which these elements of teacher professionalism can grow and develop is crucial to the reinforcement of the status of the profession and, ultimately, is the responsibility of government and governance.

Taking a wider international view, the Organisation for Economic Cooperation [OECD] in their report 'Teachers Matter: Attracting, Developing and Retaining Effective Teachers' (OECD, 2005) considered the preparation, recruitment, work and careers of school teachers from 25 countries worldwide. They focused on governmental policies that contributed to attracting, developing and retaining effective teachers in schools. The report provides a comprehensive international analysis of: trends and developments in the teacher workforce; evidence of the key factors in attracting, developing and retaining effective teachers; innovative and successful teacher policies and practices; teacher policy options for countries to consider; and priorities for future work at national and international levels. That the research attracted participation by so many countries showed that issues concerning the teaching profession are a global priority for public policy. As the OECD forecast, and the recruitment and retention trends discussed have testified, this matter has acquired even more urgency in the intervening years.

Teaching as an intellectual profession

In terms of professionalism, the 1966 UNESCO report stated that

> Teaching should be regarded as a profession: it is a form of public service, which requires of teachers expert knowledge and specialized skills, acquired and maintained through rigorous and continuing study; it also

calls for a sense of personal and corporate responsibility for the education and welfare of the pupils in their charge.

(UNESCO, 2008, III.6)

As we have long argued, teaching is an intellectual, critical profession (Totterdell, Hathaway, & la Velle, 2011; Duggan & la Velle, 2019; la Velle & Flores, 2018). As such, associated with this is a vast and dynamic body of academic and professional knowledge, which is informed by research developments. Engagement with this is the career-long requirement and commitment of an effective teacher. Ken Zeichner (2014) has argued that because teachers are professionals, their initial and continuing education requires more provision than just classroom management and administrative skills. The best teachers teach from strength in knowledge, understanding and skills, incorporating, for example, reflection, emotions, beliefs, dispositions, agency, efficacy, values and so on. These elements contribute to a professional autonomy, which is increasingly necessary in the face of externally imposed educational policy because teachers today work within an environment of increasing tension and paradox in terms of accountability, work-life balance, pupil behaviour management and other reported stressors (Worth & Van den Brande, 2019).

The seminal work of Lee Shulman on teachers' knowledge bases has informed teacher education courses since the 1980s. He proposed a series of areas of knowledge for teachers (Shulman, 1986, p. 9), asking himself 'in which forms are the domains and categories of knowledge represented in the minds of teachers?' and describing the following categories of knowledge: content; general pedagogic; pedagogic content; curricular; pupil characteristics; and educational context. This led to the formulation of a 'cycle of pedagogic reasoning' (Shulman, 1987), which begins and ends with an act of comprehension on behalf of the teacher. A version of this is reproduced in Figure 4.1.

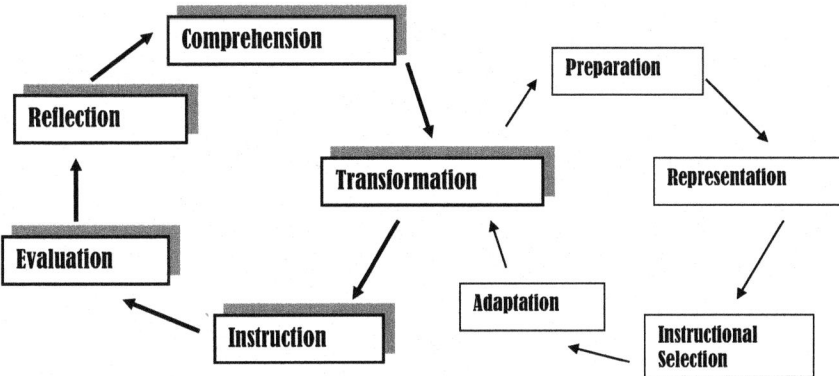

FIGURE 4.1 Shulman's Cycle of Pedagogic Reasoning

Source: Reproduced with the kind permission of Inderscience Publishers, from la Velle, Watson & Nichol, 2000.

This should be envisioned as an upwardly spiralling cycle of experience and increased understanding. Beginning and ending in something understood by the teacher (for example, a biology teacher understands about photosynthesis, a geography teacher about plate tectonics, a music teacher about key signatures), that knowledge is *transformed* into a form that can be understood by learners through an iterative process of *preparation, representation, choice of instructional techniques and adaptation (differentiation).* The lesson is then taught, the teacher evaluating the effect of her instruction to gauge its impact on the pupils' understanding (for example, by question–and–answer, observing their actions, listening to their talk), following which she reflects on her teaching and comes to a new level of comprehension in respect of what she originally understood about teaching that particular lesson.

A recently proposed model of research-based enhancement of teachers' knowledge (la Velle & Flores, 2018), based on the Shulman cycle (1987, see Figure 4.2), argues that the upward gain can be greatly enhanced by teachers' engagement, as both consumers and producers, with educational research.

In this cycle, new knowledge is generated by research, acquired by teachers to add to their levels of comprehension within the various knowledge domains, transformed into pedagogic content knowledge, used in teaching and subsequently reflected upon to enhance the original level of comprehension. Thus, teachers' professional knowledge bases as either recipients or donors of research are continuously expanded, increasing their efficacy, effectiveness and confidence. In terms of retention in the profession, this is very likely to have a positive impact not only on an individual teacher's professionalism, practice and job satisfaction, but also in terms of raising the status of the teaching profession. Both of these outcomes have a potential knock-on effect on recruitment and retention.

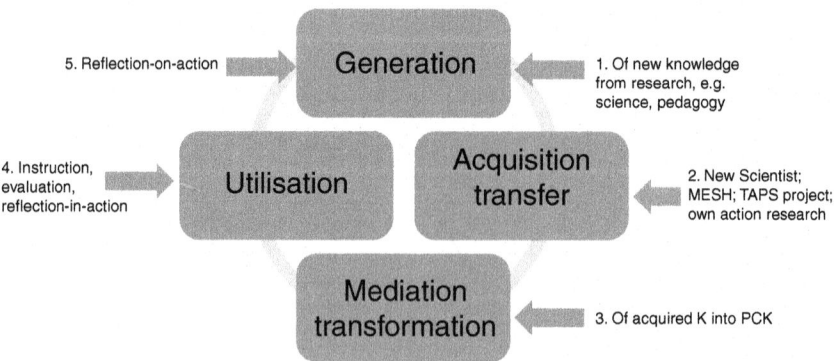

FIGURE 4.2 Research-based Knowledge Enhancement for Teaching

Source: This figure is derived in part from an article (la Velle & Flores, 2018) published in the *Journal of Education for Teaching* (copyright Routledge, Taylor & Francis Group, Informa Group Plc).

To become a fundamental element of teachers' professional practice, it is necessary to embed research-informedness into teacher education courses, both initial and continuing. The role of teacher educators themselves then becomes critical. However, as Duggan and la Velle (2019) reported, teacher educators working within higher education institutions operate under dual tensions of accountability: on one hand, to Ofsted, the UK Government's education inspection service for the quality of their initial teacher education courses, and on the other hand, as university academics, to Research England, the government authority responsible for the quality of universities' research. Nevertheless, if teaching is truly to become a research-informed profession, the roles of teacher educators, whether they are working in universities or in other educational settings, as both users and generators of research, is crucial.

In 2014, the British Educational Research Association (BERA), together with the Royal Society of Arts (RSA), produced a joint report, 'Research and The Teaching Profession, Building the Capacity for a Self-Improving System' (BERA/RSA, 2014):

> to consider what contribution research can make to the development of teachers' professional identity and practice, to the quality of teaching, to the broader project of school improvement and transformation, and, critically, to the outcomes for learners: children, young people and adults, especially those for whom the education system does not currently 'deliver'.
>
> *(p. 5)*

The report identified four ways in which research can contribute to the education of teachers. First, through the content of teacher education courses; second, through the design of teacher education courses; third, through teacher educators as consumers of research; and fourth, through teacher educators as producers of research. The enquiry drew upon evidence to build a case for 'developing and sustaining what might be termed teachers' "research literacy"' (BERA/RSA, 2014, p. 12).

Helpfully illustrated in Figure 4.3, teachers' research literacy can be viewed as a 'key dimension of teachers' broader professional identity, one that reinforces other pillars of teacher quality: notably subject knowledge and classroom practice' (p. 12).

The role of higher education in teacher education

Initial teacher education (ITE) in the UK and particularly in England is undergoing a period of sustained and unprecedented change. ITE has always occurred in a range of contexts and with varying partnership arrangements (between universities, primary and secondary schools, further education colleges and early years settings), but policy developments over the last decade have resulted in an increasingly complex and diverse range of provision (Sorensen, 2019). The

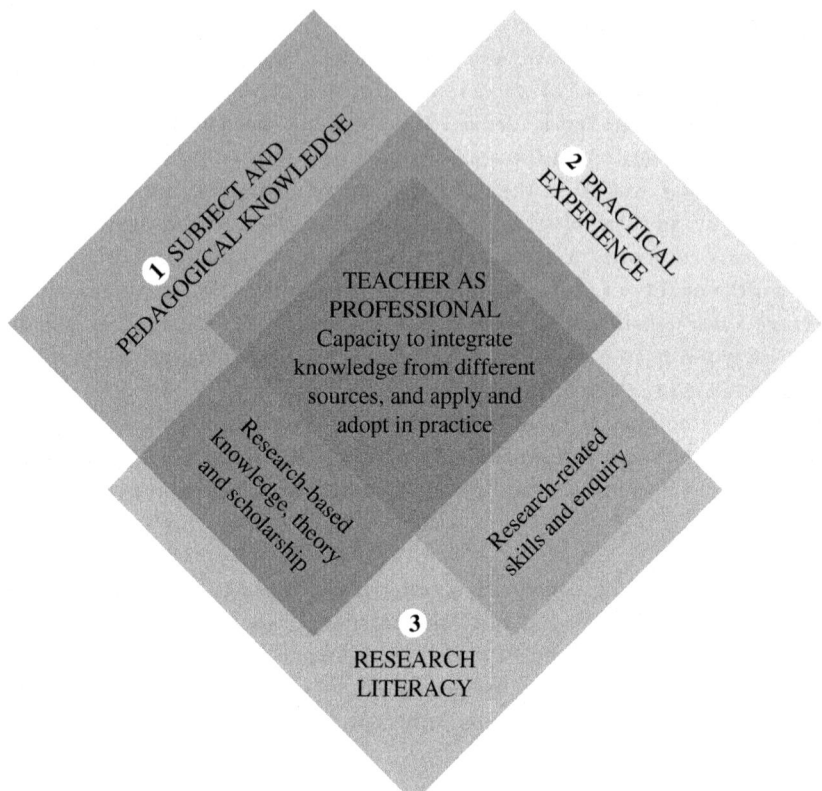

FIGURE 4.3 Dimensions of teacher effectiveness and teachers' professional identity

Source: Reproduced, with the kind permission of BERA, from: BERA/RSA, 2014, p. 10.

parts played by universities in designing, supporting and sustaining new models of ITE are many and varied. The higher education sector is distinguished by its role in the generation of new knowledge and so provides a natural environment in which initially to learn to teach and one to which to return periodically for continuing teacher education.

The current ITE infrastructure in England presents an adaptive opportunity to re-imagine the roles that universities play in teacher education partnerships. Understanding how research underpins, enhances and enriches ITE is a unique and key contribution that universities make towards securing high-quality ITE. This is also true for the provision by universities of continuing professional development for practicing teachers, particularly in the provision of master's level accreditation, as is the norm in such countries as Finland (Tirri, 2013), Australia (McLean-Davies et al., 2013) and Portugal (Flores, 2018). The relationship between master's level education and professionalism was examined and illustrated through the lenses of reflective evaluation, narrative inquiry and critique in a special issue of the *Journal of Education for Teaching* (la Velle, 2013), which included a series of articles from across the world arguing for the expectation of teaching as a master's level profession to raise its status in order to address the key issues of recruitment, career-long teacher education and retention.

The Universities' Council for the Education of Teachers (UCET) in the UK exists to promote quality in teacher education. Responding to the BERA-RSA call to 'work with its members and partners to . . . produce a sector-wide plan to strengthen research-informed practice *wherever this is required*' (2014, p. 29), UCET launched a position paper aiming to build research-informed teacher education communities (UCET, 2019) and argued for a reimagining of both initial and continuing professional development underpinned by research (Nunn, 2017). Building on the BERA-RSA (2014) review and BERA's more recent report on the close-to-practice research project (BERA, 2018), UCET supports the concept of teaching as an intellectual activity, in which research and researching enhances teachers' capacity to make a positive and enduring difference to the lives of the children and young people with whom they work.

Affirming the notion of teaching as a profession underpinned by research-informed knowledge, UCET provides an accessible 'thinking tool' to enable teacher educators to interrogate and develop aspects of their existing practice in the provision of both initial and continuing teacher education in which research has been identified as having a significant bearing. This innovative, practical and dynamic framework thus supports the development of high-quality, research-informed practice *wherever* teacher education occurs. It is organised into the four discrete but connected elements identified in the BERA/RSA (2014) report: *content* and *design* of teacher education provision and teacher educators as *consumers* and *producers* of research. Each element is exemplified by case studies.

Content of teacher education

Two important reviews of teacher education provision, that of Andrew Carter (2015) and that of the combined Royal Society and The British Academy (2018), informed UCET's position on the content of initial teacher education courses in relation to research.

UCET asserts that teaching is a scholarly, evidence-based activity and that: 'Where possible, teacher educators should introduce new teachers to pedagogies grounded in a firm evidence base' (The Royal Society of Arts & The British Academy, 2018, p. 56), thus equipping them both to undertake their own high-quality research *and* to 'understand how to interpret educational theory and research in a critical way, so they are able to deal with contested issues' (Carter, 2015, p. 8).

In relation to continuing professional development provision, UCET also welcomes the positive call for 'an agreed level of familiarity with current research in education, and evidence assisted practice in general' (Bennett, 2017, p. 2), arguing for equipping teachers to deal with 'contested issues' (Carter, 2015, p. 8) and pushing beyond the notion of research 'familiarity' to offer a bolder, more aspirational framework that sets new, more challenging expectations for the contribution of research to both ITE and CPD.

UCET thus believes that initial and continuing teacher education courses should be informed by scholarship and provide an evidenced basis of knowledge and understanding, which is derived from research that has its origin in a range of academic disciplines and epistemological traditions. Central to this is the notion of university-school partnership in teacher education. As John Furlong has argued,

> Educationalists urgently need to develop collaborative partnerships with teachers, schools and others; partnerships that are institutionalised and based on the genuine recognition that however important the university's contribution, it is always only part of the story . . . it is their commitment to the 'contestability of knowledge' that marks universities out as unique in society; and it is this commitment that goes to the very heart of what the university-based study of Education can contribute.
>
> *(Florian & Pantić, 2013, p. 8)*

Research-informed design of teacher education programmes

As we have argued, the development of pedagogical reasoning (Shulman, 1987) is a fundamental element of all good ITE provision and should become a central element of career-long professional development. Far from being a straightforward 'aircraft maintenance manual' exercise, learning to teach is not only career-long, but also highly complex and involves an appreciation of the problematic milieu of the classroom, described by Schön (1983, p. 42) as 'the swampy lowlands' of practice where important but messy issues arise that cannot simply be resolved by technical management. Loughran, Keast, HM Government, and Cooper (2016) argue that understanding the development of pedagogical reasoning and how it influences practice is a challenge for all teacher education curriculum designers and their programmes. UCET contends that this is central to all teacher education and, further, that teacher educators' own research should continue to inform this corpus of educational knowledge. This is notwithstanding the tensions described of the education academic as both teacher educator and researcher.

Teachers and teacher educators as consumers of research

UCET thus corroborates the assertion in the BERA/RSA report that

> to be at their most effective, teachers and teacher educators need to engage *with* research and enquiry – this means keeping up to date with the latest

developments in their academic subject or subjects and with developments in the discipline of education.

(BERA/RSA, 2014, p. 6)

This continuous informing and updating of the knowledge bases of teaching enables an upward spiral of increased understanding that characterises successful pedagogies (la Velle & Flores, 2018).

Teachers and teacher educators-as-researchers

UCET recognises the current tensions between research activities and regulatory regimes, such as OfSTED, and the Research and Teaching Excellence Frameworks (REF and TEF). Nevertheless, there is universal recognition that teachers researching their own practice can generate unique 'insider knowledge' that provides valuable new insights and conceptualisations of educational processes and practices (Burke & Kirton, 2006). BERA, concerned to characterise high quality in this close-to-practice (CtP) research, have defined it as 'research that focusses on aspects defined by practitioners as relevant to their practice, and often involves collaborative work between practitioners and researchers' (Wyse, Brown, Oliver, & Poblete, 2018, p. 1).

In terms of quality indicators for CtP research, they go on to state:

> High quality in CtP research requires the robust use of research design, theory and methods to address clearly defined research questions, through an iterative process of research and application that includes reflections on practice, research and context.
>
> (Wyse, et al., 2018, p. 2)

Conclusion

This chapter has argued that intellectual, research-informed, career-long teacher education is the foundation for enhancing the status of the teaching profession, which can ultimately lead to successful and sufficient recruitment to and retention in the teaching profession. It has described some initiatives aimed at raising the status of the teaching profession with the ultimate objective of recruiting and retaining well-motivated, well-qualified and professionally satisfied teachers. The opportunity now exists for providers of teacher education, both initial and continuing, to look to the design and content of their courses with a view to enhancement in terms of research-informedness. This will have a positive impact on school-university partnership and collaboration and lead to increased understanding of matters of teaching and learning in the classroom, which will lead in turn to improved outcomes for the learners. This will take commitment and resource by both policymakers and practitioners, but the payback, in terms of educational improvement, will surely be a rich reward?

References

British Educational Research Association [BERA]. (2018, November 20). *The BERA close-to-practice research report*. London: BERA. Retrieved from BERA website: www.bera.ac.uk/researchers-resources/publications/bera-statement-on-close-to-practice-research

British Educational Research Association [BERA] and the Royal Society of the Arts [RSA]. (2014). *Research and the teaching profession: Building the capacity for a self-improving education system. Final report of the BERA-RSA inquiry into the role of research in teacher education*. London: BERA. Retrieved from RSA website: www.thersa.org/discover/publications-and-articles/reports/research-and-the-teaching-profession-building-the-capacity-for-a-self-improving-education-system

Bennett, T. (2017). *Moving towards an evidence-informed teaching profession: A proposal for an initial teacher training evidence and research curriculum* [report]. London: ResearchEd. Retrieved from Dropbox website: www.dropbox.com/s/lgzx82xq3ynrzjs/ITT%20research%20proposal%20Tom%20Bennett-2.pdf?dl=0

Burke, P. J., & Kirton, A. (2006). The insider perspective: Teachers as researchers. *Reflecting Education, 2*(1), 1–4.

Carter, A. (2015, January). *Carter Review of Initial Teacher Training (ITT)*. Retrieved from gov.uk website: www.gov.uk/government/publications/carter-review-of-initial-teacher-training

Duggan, M., & la Velle, L. (2019). Embracing complexity: Understanding the experiences of university-based teacher educators in England. In N. Sorensen (Ed.), *Diversity in teacher education: Perspectives on a school-led system*. London: UCL-IOE Press.

Flores, M. A. (2018). Linking teaching and research in initial teacher education: Knowledge mobilisation and research-informed practice. *Journal of Education for Teaching, 44*(5), 621–636. https://doi.org/10.1080/02607476.2018.1516351

Florian, L., & Pantić, N. (2013). *Learning to teach part 1: Exploring the history and role of higher education in teacher education* [report]. Retrieved from AdvanceHE website: www.heacademy.ac.uk/system/files/resources/learningtoteach_part1_final.pdf

Foster, D. (2019, December 16). *Teacher recruitment and retention in England*. House of Commons Briefing Paper, number 7222. London: House of Commons. Retrieved from the House of Commons Library on the parliament.uk website: https://researchbriefings.parliament.uk/ResearchBriefing/Summary/CBP-7222

Geiger, T., & Pivovarova, M. (2018). The effects of working conditions on teacher retention. *Teachers and Teaching, 24*(6), 604–625. https://doi.org/10.1080/13540602.2018.1457524

Hazell, W. (2016, December 1). *DfE abandons National Teaching Service*. Retrieved from TES website: www.tes.com/news/exclusive-dfe-abandons-national-teaching-service

Hoyle, E. (2001). Teaching: Prestige, status and esteem. *Educational Management & Administration, 29*(2), 139–152. https://doi.org/10.1177/0263211X010292001

la Velle, L. (2013). Masterliness in the teaching profession: Global issues and local developments. *Journal of Education for Teaching, 39*(1), 2–8. https://doi.org/10.1080/026074 76.2012.733186

la Velle, L., & Flores, M. A. (2018). Perspectives on evidence-based knowledge for teachers: Acquisition, mobilisation and utilisation. *Journal of Education for Teaching, 44*(5), 524–538. https://doi.org/10.1080/02607476.2018.1516345

la Velle, L., Watson, K., & Nichol, J. (2000). Otherscope – The virtual reality microscope – Can the real learning experiences in practical science be simulated? *International Journal of Healthcare Technology and Management, 2*(5/6), 539–556. https://doi.org/10.1504/IJHTM.2000.001098

Loughran, J., Keast, S., & Cooper, R. (2016). Pedagogical reasoning in teacher education. In J. Loughran & M. L. Hamilton (Eds.), *International handbook of teacher education*. (Vol. 1, pp. 387–421). New York: Springer.

McLean-Davies, L., Anderson, M., Deans, J., Dinham, S., Griffin, P., Kameniar, B., & Tyler, D. (2013). Masterly preparation: Embedding clinical practice in a graduate pre-service teacher education programme. *Journal of Education for Teaching, 39*(1), 93–106. https://doi.org/10.1080/02607476.2012.733193

Nunn, J. (2017). *Strengthening the quality and content of initial teacher training*. Planning in Partnership. Retrieved from www.ucet.ac.uk/downloads/10385-Strengthening-the-quality-and-content-of-initial-teacher-training'-Planning-in-partnership.pdf

Organisation for Economic Cooperation and Development [OECD]. (2005). *Teachers matter: Attracting, developing and retaining effective teachers*. Paris: OECD Publications. Retrieved from OECD website: www.oecd.org/education/school/34990905.pdf

Royal Society of Arts & The British Academy. (2018, October). *Harnessing educational research*. London: RSA. Retrieved from RSA website: https://royalsociety.org/topics-policy/projects/royal-society-british-academy-educational-research/

Schön, D. (1983). *The reflective practitioner: How professionals think in action*. New York: Basic Books.

Shulman, L. (1986). Those who understand: Knowledge growth in teaching. *Educational Researcher, 15*(2), 4–14.

Shulman, L. (1987). Knowledge and teaching: Foundations of the new reform. *Harvard Educational Review, 57*(1), 1–22.

Sorensen, N. (Ed.). (2019). *Diversity in teacher education: Perspectives on a school-led system*. London: UCL-IOE Press.

Tirri, K., & Ubani, M. (2013). Education of Finnish student teachers for purposeful teaching. *Journal of Education for Teaching, 39*(1), 21–29. https://doi.org/10.1080/0260 7476.2012.733188

Totterdell, M., Hathaway, T., & la Velle, L. (2011). Mastering teaching and learning through pedagogic partnership: A vision and framework for developing 'collaborative resonance' in England. *Professional Development in Education, 37*(3), 411–437. https://doi.org/10.1080/1941525.2010.510003

Universities' Council for the Education of Teachers [UCET]. (2019). *UCET position paper: Building Research Informed Teacher Education Communities (July 2019)*. Retrieved from UCET website: www.ucet.ac.uk/10988/ucet-position-paper-building-research-informed-teacher-education communities-july-2019

United Nations Educational, Scientific and Cultural Organisation [UNESCO]. (2008). *The ILO/UNESCO recommendation concerning the status of teachers (1966) and The UNESCO recommendation concerning the status of higher-education teaching personnel*. Paris: UNESCO. Retrieved from the Right to Education website: www.right-to-education.org/sites/right-to-education.org/files/resource-attachments/ILO_UNESCO_Recommendation_Concerning_the_Status_of_Teachers_1966_En.pdf

United Nations Educational, Scientific and Cultural Organisation [UNESCO]. (2016). *Education 2030: Incheon Declaration and Framework for Action for the implementation of Sustainable Development Goal 4: Ensure inclusive and equitable quality education and promote lifelong learning opportunities for all*. Retrieved from the UNESCO digital library website: https://unesdoc.unesco.org/ark:/48223/pf0000245656

Vaughn, R. (2019, January 10). Millions in taxpayers' cash wasted on bursaries for teachers who never set foot in a classroom. *iNews*. Retrieved from iNews website: https://inews.co.uk/news/education/millions-bursaries-teachers-classroom/?fbclid=IwAR1_g8XbOttrcS8B2aDUWDX__ZdJWH75NYqVhUMntXJ4zuFv1Csjq9OHjoA

Worth, J. (2018, June 28). *Latest teacher retention statistics paint a bleak picture for teacher supply in England* [blog]. Retrieved from NFER website: www.nfer.ac.uk/news-events/nfer-blogs/latest-teacher-retention-statistics-paint-a-bleak-picture-for-teacher-supply-in-england/

Worth, J., & Van den Brande, J. (2019, February 25). *Teacher Labour Market in England – Annual Report 2019.* Slough: National Foundation for Educational Research. Retrieved from NFER website: www.nfer.ac.uk/key-topics-expertise/school-workforce/

Wyse, D., Brown, C., Oliver, S., & Poblete, X. (2018). *The BERA close-to-practice research project: Research report.* London: British Educational Research Association [BERA]. Retrieved from BERA website: www.bera.ac.uk/researchers-resources/publications/bera-statement-on-close-topractice-research

Zeichner, K. (2014). The struggle for the soul of teaching and teacher education in the USA. *Journal of Education for Teaching, 40*(5), 551–568.

5

RETAIN

A research-informed model of continuing professional development for early career teacher retention

*Tanya Ovenden-Hope, Sonia Blandford,
Tim Cain and Bronwen Maxwell*

Introduction

In 2018, after the RETAIN pilot programme had been completed, independently evaluated and the findings reported by the Education Endowment Foundation (EEF), a blog was written by Jones (2018), a lead of a Research School[1] in England, asking 'Has a solution to [teacher] retention been found?'

> So did RETAIN work? Well it looks promising. The CPD aspect appears to have increased self-efficacy, confidence and research-use. . . . Are we actually just seeing a model of good practice? . . . do we actually need to consider the how of our CPD as much as the what?
>
> *(Jones, 2018)*

How continuing professional development (CPD) is developed was central to the creation of RETAIN. The RETAIN pilot programme was a research-informed and evidence-based CPD programme for early career teachers (ECTs) in primary phase education that sought to improve teacher retention in schools with high levels of persistently disadvantaged pupils. The independent evaluation of the programme demonstrated that is was the carefully considered *how* for the CPD that supported the positive outcomes achieved.

In this chapter, we offer an overview of the rationale for developing RETAIN, the evidence for both the content and the delivery, the methodology for evaluation and an insight into the significance and reach of the findings as a potential solution for early career teacher retention challenges. Has a solution to early career teacher retention been found in RETAIN, as Jones (2018) asks? The evidence from the pilot suggests that RETAIN provides a model of high-quality, research-informed CPD that changes how teachers perceive their own self-efficacy and that this model can be applied in any context and in any country. At the time of writing, all ECTs who participated in the RETAIN pilot programme remain in the profession.

Why was RETAIN needed?

In England, as in other countries, there are concerns about the shortage of teachers in schools (Foster, 2019). These concerns are justified: the most recently published data from the British Government (Foster, 2019) show that the overall number of teachers in England has not kept pace with increasing pupil numbers, with around 42,000 full-time equivalent qualified teachers leaving the state-funded sector in the 12 months to November 2018, an attrition of 9.8 per cent; 32.3 per cent of newly qualified teachers in 2016 were recorded as not working as teachers in the state sector five years later. This is the highest five-year attrition rate for early career teachers (ECTs) since 1997 (Foster, 2019).

Teacher shortage has been described as 'a policy problem' (Cochran-Smith, 2004) with two causes: insufficient people entering teaching as a career (a problem of recruitment), and too many teachers choosing to leave teaching (a problem of retention). The problem is acute, particularly as pupil numbers are rising, and the number is forecast to continue rising until at least 2024 (Worth, Lynch, Hillary, Rennie, & Andrade, 2018), and elicited a government response in 2019 with the teacher recruitment and retention strategy (Department for Education [DfE], 2019a). When RETAIN was being developed in 2015, the 'challenge' of teacher retention was evident and looked set to increase, particularly among teachers in their first to third years of employment in England, for the reasons as noted.

There are several consequences of teacher shortages. From a policy perspective, an important one is the waste of money: it is not financially viable to train large cohorts of teachers, many of whom quit the profession within a few years. But it is in schools where the problem is most acutely felt. Despite spending time, money and effort to recruit teachers, school leaders are unable to fill vacancies with properly qualified teachers, increasingly turning to unqualified teachers or temporary replacements in academies, free schools and studio schools (allowed through an amendment in 2012 by the Secretary of State to regulations within the Education Act, 2002) (NASUWT, 2017). Furthermore, a high turnover of staff can affect the school community and make long-term planning more difficult (Brill & McCartney, 2008). In consequence, at the time of writing, the first priority of the Schools Minister is to 'ensure there are sufficient high-quality teachers in our schools . . . by delivering our teacher recruitment and retention strategy' (DfE, 2018, Section 2).

The teacher recruitment and retention strategy (DfE, 2019a) recognises that in England teacher supply is in crisis and intends to address this through four key areas where the department believes focus, investment and reform can have the biggest impact on improving teacher recruitment and retention. The four key areas are:

1   To reform the accountability system – this process has started and the schools' regulatory body in England, Ofsted, introduced a new Education Inspection Framework in May 2019 (Ofsted, 2019) that is intended to 'have an active focus on reducing teacher workload' (DfE, 2019a, p. 7).

2   To transform support for early career teachers by developing an Early Career Framework (DfE, 2019b) and phased bursaries with staggered retention payments. The Early Career Framework becomes a statutory requirement in schools in England in September 2021 and will introduce 'a fully-funded package of structured support for early career teachers time off-timetable in the second year and support for mentors' (DfE, 2019b, p. 7).

3   To develop and enhance specialist qualification in teaching and leadership. This work has begun with the creation of national professional qualifications (NPQs) that are set to launch in September 2021 and are intended to help teachers 'pursue the right career opportunities for them', including progression in teaching as well as leadership (DfE, 2019a, p. 7).

4   To create a new application system for those wanting to train as teachers. It is hoped that the new system, which is preparing for full implementation in September 2020, will 'radically simplify the process for becoming a teacher . . . [and] make application easier and more user-friendly' (DfE, 2019a, p. 7). At the time of writing, there is a range of routes into teaching in England that involve different ways of applying, for example, postgraduate accredited and undergraduate programmes through the Universities Central Application System, while an 'assessment only' route to QTS (qualified teacher status) means that applicants apply directly to a school via an accredited provider. Under the new system all routes will be supported through one application system.

The recruitment and retention strategy (DfE, 2019a) has generally been well received by educationalists as both an acknowledgement of the problems schools face with teacher supply and for the interventions being made as noted (Menzies, 2019).

The Department for Education invited the RETAIN team to share findings of the RETAIN pilot programme in a meeting in 2017. The importance of high-quality CPD was discussed; evidence for increased self-efficacy for ECTs, through continued skills development and mentoring, was recognised and the constituent elements are embedded in the recruitment and retention strategy (Department for Education, 2019a). The RETAIN model and pilot programme contributed to thinking at government and school level in England on how to solve the challenge of teacher retention.

How was RETAIN developed?

The aim of the RETAIN pilot programme was to improve ECT retention, defined as newly qualified teachers (NQTs) in the first three years of teaching, through a new research-informed model of CPD. Understanding that there was increasing ECT attrition in England, and recognising this as a challenge in many other countries, the priority in developing RETAIN became to understand the causes of poor ECT retention and to create ways in which a CPD programme could contribute to reducing ECT attrition. A review of research literature in this area demonstrated that the reasons why ECTs leave teaching are complex, especially when this is examined at an international level (Veenman, 1984; Caspersen & Raaen, 2014; Høigaard, Giske, & Sundsli, 2012).

In England, a national survey, commissioned by the National Association of Schoolmasters and Union of Women Teachers (NASUWT), found that '[a]lmost three quarters of teachers (74%) are seriously considering leaving their current job and over two-thirds of teachers (67%) are thinking of quitting the profession altogether' (NASUWT, 2019, p. 15).

The number thinking of leaving the profession was up from 69 per cent and 61 per cent respectively in 2017 (NASUWT, 2017). The NASUWT found that the main reasons for teacher and school leader dissatisfaction were the high workload, pupil behaviour, budget cuts, pay and accountability (NASUWT, 2019). However, there is also some contradictory evidence that teachers are 'not primarily motivated to leave the profession by the prospect of increased pay' (Worth et al., 2018, p. 5). This study found that teachers who leave the profession are, on average, paid 'ten per cent less than . . . when they were a teacher' (Worth et al., 2018, p. 5). The same research found that around 80 per cent of full-time teachers reported being satisfied with their income, which suggests that one major means of addressing the problem of ECT retention lies in enabling them to cope with the demands of teaching. Menzies et al. (2015) suggest that teachers primarily go into the profession to make a difference and become overwhelmed by the parts of their work that appear meaningless in relation to improving the learning of their pupils.

There is a large literature around the demands placed on ECTs; being an ECT can be a professionally challenging role in any school (DfE, 2019b). In schools in areas facing socio-economic disadvantage, these challenges can be multiplied exponentially (Ovenden-Hope & Passy, 2019). This means that the retention of teachers is most challenging in areas of disadvantage; the very areas where the need for continuity of teaching and the support of high-quality CPD are needed the most (Cordingley et al., 2015).

Veenman (1984) referred to 'reality shock', a state experienced by ECTs, caused by the heavy personal and professional demands for new teachers, and the unpredictability and complexity of their role. The reality they experience is at dissonance with their expectations of the role and this leads to anxiety, feeling vulnerable and finding it difficult to cope (Feiman-Nemser, 2003; Sabar, 2004). Although they can, and do, seek support from colleagues, often they do not want to be seen as needing support in their schools because they want to be seen as 'proper teachers' (Haggarty, Postlethwaite, Diment, & Ellins, 2011, p. 942). Additionally, they can perceive that support is given primarily to teachers who are struggling, rather than being an entitlement to professional development.

A large-scale survey of teachers in Scotland identified what ECTs felt they needed to cope with teaching. In order of priority, these were: 'Keeping up to date with teaching strategies in order to meet specific pupils' needs'; 'Knowing more about [the] Curriculum . . . and how it will impact on my practice'; 'Subject or topic-specific CPD'; and 'Behaviour management strategies' (Kennedy et al., 2008, p. 36). 'Behaviour management' is likely to refer to the need for ECTs to manage the behaviour of students, which has been found to be a major concern of ECTs (Barmby, 2006; Kitching, Morgan, & O'Leary, 2009). These findings were used to justify the inclusion of taught workshops in the RETAIN pilot programme. Relevant evidence-based and research-informed resources were created to develop ECT knowledge, skills and understanding, and delivered through expert taught workshops. The RETAIN pilot programme classroom-based workshops were designed to enhance the ECTs' ability to cope with teaching lessons by understanding both what and how to teach the children in their school context.

However, research findings also identified that there are processes that enable ECTs to cope with the demands of teaching. It is important that ECTs have the time and space for reflection on their experience. As Dimmock (2012) states: 'A key part of improving the professionalism and performance of teachers is concerned with aiding their reflective skills on past teaching events in order to enhance their future classroom effectiveness' (p. 43). This is because it is impossible to prepare teachers for every eventuality that they might meet, so it is important for teachers to be able to reflect on their experience, be willing to learn and to take a problem-solving approach to challenges. This remains as true today as it was when argued by Korthagen, Kessels, Koster, Lagerwerf, and Wubbels in 2001.

Developing effective professional reflective practice contributes to improving professional self-efficacy (Korthagen et al., 2001). Reflection is assisted by considering multiple perspectives on teaching and can be assisted by coaching and mentoring (e.g., Swafford, 2000; Blandford & Knowles, 2013; Blandford & Knowles, 2016; Tonna, Bjerkholt, & Holland, 2017). Reflection, assisted by a coach, can move teachers from a concern with routine action, in pursuit of technicist aims, towards a type of thinking in which they question their fundamental assumptions and purpose more deeply (e.g. Ward & McCotter, 2004; Harrison, Lawson, & Wortley, 2005). Schön (1983) describes professional reflective practice as a process where professionals constantly monitor their actions and make decisions based on their accumulated and informed knowledge. Coaching was therefore used in the RETAIN pilot programme as a way of supporting ECT reflection in the application of taught workshop content to practice.

Furthermore, various studies demonstrate the necessity for ECTs to be supported emotionally. In a provocatively titled article called 'Why Do New Teachers Cry?', McCann and Johannessen (2004) described the feelings of stress and frustration reported by ECTs, while Johnson et al. (2014) summarised the emotions that ECTs experience as 'dislocation, alienation, self-doubt, and sheer exhaustion' (p. 531). Hobson (2010) found that ECTs placed greater emphasis on the need for psychological or emotional support than instructional support, although the distinctions between them are 'blurred and far from clear-cut' (Hobson, 2010, p. 306) because a reduction in negative emotions can be achieved through a greater sense of belonging when the ECT feels recognised as a member of a network or team. The addition of a structured professional learning community (PLC) and a school-based mentor was added to the RETAIN pilot programme as a way of enhancing ECT wellbeing, engagement with RETAIN and of creating networks for future support (Bolam et al., 2005).

The RETAIN pilot programme PLCs and professional learning reflected: DuFour's (2004) analysis of focused and meaningful PLCs; the 'taxonomy' of effective PLC approaches developed by Blankenship and Ruona (2007); and the effective development of 'mature' PLCs investigated by Owen (2016). In synthesising these perspectives, the RETAIN ECTs were participants in PLCs that intentionally modelled the key aspects of effective PLCs. ECTs were supported by the RETAIN team to critically consider these communities as part of their professional learning and career development planning. A school-based mentor (called a school champion), supported by the RETAIN team, also worked with each ECT as a support in understanding how learning from the RETAIN pilot programme was best applied in the school's context.

What are the key components of the RETAIN model?

The research just discussed informed the design of the RETAIN model for the pilot programme. Funded by the Education Endowment Foundation, who understood the significance of the rationale for considering CPD as a solution for ECT retention, the RETAIN pilot programme (2016/17) provided evidence-based and research-informed CPD to ECTs working in the most disadvantaged coastal and rural schools in Cornwall.

RETAIN had a specific focus on ECTs of children at the earliest stage of compulsory schooling (ages 5–7 years), and in particular on literacy as a driver for curriculum development (Shanahan & Barr, 1995; Danoff, 2006). The CPD content was developed through three modules to enhance ECTs' knowledge, understanding and skills in pedagogy and practice, to support children from persistently disadvantaged backgrounds and to develop their own careers. Each module was delivered through the key components identified later. All the research-informed resources or content, such as module handbooks, module research books and wider reading, for the pilot programme were available to schools and ECTs through an online platform.

The content (or the 'what' of the CPD) was supported by the design of delivery (or the 'how' of CPD), which had three main components:

1   Classroom – Taught workshops (six evening workshops changed to two full
      days per module to support attendance after module one) of research-informed

professional learning and development. This was supported in its application to practice through:

2   Collaboration – Professional Learning Communities (PLCs) established peer learning, peer lesson observations, peer discussions, peer action learning sets, all of which were supported by in-school champions (mentors); and

3   Coaching – In-school coaching *by an external coach* to enhance critically reflective practice of applied learning.

These components, based on a review of available evidence on effective CPD in schools, became the RETAIN model for delivery and were initially called the 3 Cs. As the concept of RETAIN developed, 4 Cs were used in order to focus the 3 component 'Cs' in delivery on what RETAIN hoped to achieve: the retention of more confident, research-informed teachers who will provide every *child* (the fourth C) with a high-quality learning experience (see Figure 5.1).

How a CPD programme is delivered was as important in the development and design of RETAIN as the *what* it delivers in terms of content. The literature on what makes CPD effective, outlined here, made the RETAIN team consider the *how* as essential to the pilot programme's promise for its theory of change (see the following section on how RETAIN was evaluated). The independent

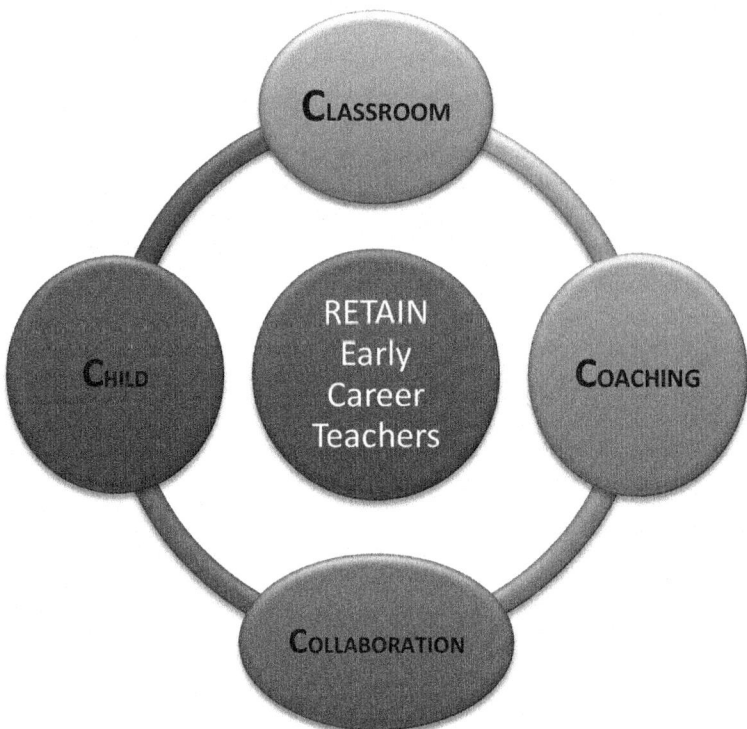

FIGURE 5.1   RETAIN 4 Cs – the RETAIN delivery model for effective CPD

evaluation of the RETAIN pilot programme identified the RETAIN model as the reason for the programme's promise (Maxwell et al., 2018). The novel contribution of RETAIN is the model: *how* the CPD is delivered through the combination of the three key components of classroom, collaboration and coaching. It means that the RETAIN 4 Cs can be applied to establish effective CPD for teachers to programmes with a range of content (*what*) and potentially in a range of countries, as the evidence base used for development was from international sources.

How was RETAIN evaluated?

Twelve primary schools were recruited for the pilot RETAIN programme, each having high numbers of pupils entitled to free school meals (known as 'Ever 6' Free School Meals in England – a proxy indicator of persistent disadvantage). Two schools withdrew from the programme the week it was due to commence and one ECT was removed from the programme in November 2016 due to non-attendance. In January 2017, RETAIN had engaged nine schools and ten ECTs, with all these ECTs completing the full programme.

A longitudinal theory-based evaluation (Rogers & Weiss, 2007) of the pilot RETAIN programme was undertaken by an independent evaluator appointed by the funder using multiple methods. As the evaluation was conducted alongside the pilot, insufficient time had elapsed by the end of the evaluation to meaningfully assess the impact on retention and other longer-term outcomes. However, the RETAIN team have tracked RETAIN ECTs' careers following completion of the programme, and all have remained in teaching at the time of writing, with all but one taking on leadership roles in their schools. The plausibility of the underpinning theory of change was assessed as a way of evaluating RETAIN over the pilot year. The RETAIN theory of change set out the steps, and theoretical and empirical rationale, for how and why the programme inputs were expected to lead to change via intermediate outcomes, such as improved knowledge and skills, self-efficacy and ability to engage in evidence-informed practice, to the final intended impact of retaining early career teachers in the profession.

To assess the plausibility of the theory of change, data was generated on: indicators of progress towards the intended impacts and longer-term outcomes; the perceived linkages between the key components and design features of RETAIN and the indicators of progress; and the contextual factors that influenced the effectiveness of RETAIN in meeting its aims. Data was gathered through repeated surveys of participating ECTs, which included ratings on the Teachers' Sense of Efficacy Scale (Tschannen-Moran & Woolfolk Hoy, 2001), 30 semi-structured individual interviews (14 with ECTs, ten with school champions and six with head teachers) and observations and focus groups at the launch workshop and end of programme workshop. For full details of the evaluation methods and findings, see Maxwell et al. (2018).

What were the findings of RETAIN?

ECT development on the RETAIN pilot programme

The surveys revealed broadly similar and moderately positive trends in ECTs' professional development over the duration of the programme. This included increased self-efficacy and knowledge and understanding, changes in practice with a particular focus on making greater use of evidence-informed strategies and techniques, stronger engagement in professional learning communities and an enhanced ability to plan and develop their careers. For example, there was a mean increase in score of +1.05 on the nine-point Teachers Sense of Efficacy Scale; on the five-point self-report scales for research use and knowledge and understanding, the mean increase in scores was +0.75 and +0.85, respectively. These increases demonstrate the positive change in the ECTs' self-efficacy, as well as in research use, and knowledge and understanding applied to their practice.

The findings on indicators of impact and longer-term outcomes were supported by the analysis of the qualitative data, which found that most ECTs attributed positive outcomes in relation to key components of the RETAIN model. However, some caution is needed as there were mixed views amongst school champions and headteachers on how the observed changes should be attributed, with some pointing to the effects of maturation as a teacher and the positive influence of school-related factors, such as support offered and in-school professional learning activities. The extent to which engagement in peer learning and support, coaching and using research to inform practice would be sustained after the end of the programme by the school or ECT was not part of the evaluation, although there was positive comment on the benefits of collaboration by all interviewees for ECT development.

Perceived links between the RETAIN key components and indicators of impact and longer-term outcomes

All interviewees perceived that it was the combination of the three key components of the RETAIN programme – the taught sessions (*classroom*), peer learning (*collaboration*) and in-school *coaching* by an external coach – together with the interweaving of research evidence that led to positive change. For example, some ECTs reported that the content and modelling of practices during RETAIN pilot programme workshops (*classroom*) helped them develop knowledge and understanding, while both the *coaching* and peer learning (*collaboration*) helped them contextualise that learning. In addition, peer discussion (*collaboration*) was perceived to help ECTs develop knowledge of practices in other schools which, together with the focus on disadvantage in the taught sessions (*classroom*), was recognised by some ECTs as significant in their changing beliefs about, and understanding of, how they as teachers could support children from disadvantaged backgrounds (*child*).

Coaching and peer discussions (*collaboration*), where ECTs realised that others on the programme faced similar issues to themselves, were perceived by ECTs to enhance their confidence. Positive pedagogical practice change was perceived to be supported by the combined influences of the taught modules (*classroom*), *coaching* and peer *collaboration*. Some ECTs noted that validation of their practices by the RETAIN team and the ability to cite research evidence (*classroom*) gave them confidence to experiment with their classroom practices, particularly but not exclusively in literacy (the subject focus of the RETAIN pilot programme). This, together with the *coaching* and peer learning (*collaboration*), was reported to lead to ECTs feeling more able to talk about their ideas in school and push for support to implement new pedagogical and curriculum practices, such as evidence-informed approaches for literacy, assessment and feedback.

Positive professional and career outcomes, such as progression into leadership roles for ECTs, were perceived to be supported by conversations with the RETAIN team and attendance at taught sessions (*classroom*) that provided the space to talk about career progression, as well as hearing others, particularly their peers, talk about their career pathways (*collaboration*). Therefore, while all interviewees made some links between the individual components of the RETAIN model and positive indicators of impact and longer-term outcomes, more often it was the 4 Cs of RETAIN (see Figure 5.1) in combination that were credited.

Could RETAIN offer promise in solving early career teacher retention?

The independent evaluation of RETAIN found evidence of promise that RETAIN could contribute to a solution for early career teacher retention (Maxwell et al., 2018). As discussed, the evaluation identified evidence of positive impact on ECTs over the course of the pilot programme, such as increased self-confidence, knowledge and skills. It also provided indicators of longer-term positive outcomes for ECTs and schools, such as using research to inform practice. Insights from supporting evidence demonstrated the ways in which the key components of the RETAIN model worked effectively together to effect a theory of change (Maxwell et al., 2018). However, for that promise to be realised, attention needs to be paid to the contextual influences that either act to support positive in-programme impact and longer-term outcomes or hinder their achievement.

The evaluation found that both individual and school factors acted to enable or impede successful outcomes. Those ECTs that demonstrated full engagement in the RETAIN pilot programme, and were keen to implement their learning in their classroom, tended to report gaining more from participating in RETAIN than ECTs who had more limited engagement due to other in-school commitments. At the school level, the majority of interviewees, including ECTs, school champions and head teachers, highlighted the necessity of a supportive school culture and openness to changes in school practice to enable ECTs to apply their learning in the classroom. Conversely, in a few schools, prescriptive pedagogical practices in curriculum delivery prevented ECTs from experimenting with evidence-informed practices, limiting their participation in implementing what they had learned in the RETAIN pilot programme. In a few schools, senior staff perceived that the content of some taught sessions and/or the coaching were not appropriate to their curriculum and/or pedagogy. These findings indicate that to maximise the impact of programmes that apply the RETAIN model, close working with school leaders is required to ensure that the content within the modules is understood and supported.

Is RETAIN a possible solution to the problem of early career teacher retention? The findings from the evaluation of the programme and the outcomes for ECT participants suggest that this research-informed model of CPD is promising and is a strong basis on which to model the *how* of future interventions aimed at reducing teacher attrition.

Note

1 The Research Schools Network in England is a collaboration between the Educational Endowment Foundation (EEF) and the Institute for Effective Education (IEE) to fund a network of schools, 32 Research Schools and seven Associate Research Schools, which supports the use of evidence to improve teaching practice.

References

Barmby, P. (2006). Improving teacher recruitment and retention: The importance of workload and pupil behaviour. *Educational Research, 48*(3), 247–265.

Blandford, S., & Knowles, C. (2013). *Achievement for all: Raising aspirations, access and achievement.* London: Bloomsbury.

Blandford, S., & Knowles, C. (2016). *Developing professional practice 0–7* (2nd ed.). Abingdon: Routledge.

Blankenship, S., & Ruona, W. (2007). *Professional learning communities and communities of practice: A comparison of models.* Unpublished literature review presented at Academy of Human Resource Development International Research Conference in the Americas.

Bolam, R., McMahon, A., Stoll, L., Thomas, S., Wallace, M., Greenwood, A., . . . Smith, M. (2005). *Creating and sustaining effective professional learning communities. Research Report 637.* London: DfES and University of Bristol.

Brill, S., & McCartney, A. (2008). Stopping the revolving door: Increasing teacher retention. *Politics & Policy, 36*(5), 750–774.

Caspersen, J., & Raaen, F. D. (2014). Novice teachers and how they cope. *Teachers and Teaching: Theory and Practice, 2*(2), 189–211.

Cochran-Smith, M. (2004). The problem of teacher education. *Journal of Teacher Education, 55*(4), 295–299.

Cordingley, P., Higgins, S., Greany, T., Buckler, N., Coles-Jordan, D., Crisp, B., . . . Coe, R. (2015). *Developing great teaching: Lessons from the international reviews into effective professional development.* London: Teacher Development Trust. Retrieved from Teacher Development trust website: https://tdtrust.org/wp-content/uploads/2015/10/DGT-Full-report.pdf

Danoff, S. (2006). *The golden thread: Storytelling in teaching and learning.* London: Storytelling Arts Press.

Department for Education [DfE]. (2018, May). *Department for education single departmental plan.* London: DfE. Retrieved from gov.uk website: www.gov.uk/government/publications/department-for-education-single-departmental-plan/may-2018-department-for-education-single-departmental-plan#schools

Department for Education [DfE]. (2019a). *Teacher retention and recruitment strategy.* London, DfE. Retrieved from gov.uk website: https://assets.publishing.service.gov.uk/government/uploads/system/uploads/attachment_data/file/786856/DFE_Teacher_Retention_Strategy_Report.pdf

Department for Education [DfE]. (2019b, January). *Early career framework.* London. DfE. Retrieved from gov.uk website: https://assets.publishing.service.gov.uk/government/uploads/system/uploads/attachment_data/file/773705/Early-Career_Framework.pdf

Dimmock, C. (2012). *Leadership, capacity building and school improvement: Concepts, themes and impact.* Leadership for Learning Series. London: Routledge. ISBN 9780415404365.

DuFour, R. (2004). What is a professional learning community? *Educational Leadership, 61*(8), 6–11.

Education Act. (2002). *Amendment to regulation The Education (School Teachers) (Qualifications and Specified Work) (Miscellaneous Amendments) (England) Regulations 2012.* Statutory Instruments 2012, No. 1736. Retrieved from legislation.gov.uk website: www.legislation.gov.uk/uksi/2012/1736/made#f00003

Education Endowment Foundation [EEF]. (2016). *RETAIN: Early career teachers CPD.* Retrieved from EEF website: https://educationendowmentfoundation.org.uk/our-work/projects/cornwall-college-retain

Feiman-Nemser, S. (2003). What new teachers need to learn. *Educational Leadership, 60*(8), 25–29.

Foster, D. (2019, December 16). *Teacher recruitment and retention in England.* House of Commons Briefing Paper, number 7222. London: House of Commons. Retrieved from the House of Commons Library on the parliament.uk website: https://researchbriefings.parliament.uk/ResearchBriefing/Summary/CBP-7222

Haggarty, L., Postlethwaite, K., Diment, K., & Ellins, J. (2011). Improving the learning of newly qualified teachers in the induction year. *British Educational Research Journal, 37*(6), 935–954.

Harrison, J., Lawson, T., & Wortley, A. (2005). Facilitating the professional learning of new teachers through critical reflection on practice during mentoring meetings. *European Journal of Teacher Education, 28*(3), 267–292.

Hobson, A. (2010). On being bottom of the pecking order: Beginner teachers' perceptions and experiences of support. *Teacher Development, 13*(4), 299–320.

Høigaard, R., Giske, R., & Sundsli, K. (2012). Newly qualified teachers' work engagement and teacher efficacy influences on job satisfaction, burnout, and the intention to quit. *European Journal of Teacher Education, 35*(3), 347–357.

Johnson, B., Down, B., Le Cornu, R., Peters, J., Sullivan, A., Pearce, J., & Hunter, J. (2014). Promoting early career teacher resilience: A framework for understanding and acting. *Teachers and Teaching: Theory and Practice, 20*(5), 530–546.

Jones, N. (2018, June 8). Has a solution to retention been found? [blog]. *Research Schools Network.* Retrieved from Research Schools Network website: https://researchschool.org.uk/sandringham/news/has-a-solution-to-retention-been-found/

Kennedy, A., McKay, J., Clinton, C. Fraser, C., McKinnery, S., & Welsh, M. (2008, September). *Early professional development in Scotland: Teachers in years 2–6.* Strathclyde:

University of Strathclyde. Retrieved from https://core.ac.uk/download/pdf/9030 579.pdf

Kitching, K., Morgan, M., & O'Leary, M. (2009). It's the little things: Exploring the importance of commonplace events for early-career teachers' motivation. *Teachers and Teaching: Theory and Practice, 15*(1), 43–58.

Korthagen, F. A., Kessels, J., Koster, B., Lagerwerf, B., & Wubbels, T. (2001). *Linking practice and theory: The pedagogy of realistic teacher education.* London: Routledge.

Maxwell, B., Clague, L., Byrne, E., Culliney, M., Coldwell, M., Hobson, A., & Glentworth, A. (2018, May). *Retain: CPD for early career teachers of KS1 Pilot report and executive summary.* Millbank: Education Endowment Foundation. Retrieved from the EEF website: https://educationendowmentfoundation.org.uk/public/files/Projects/ Evaluation_Reports/Retain.pdf

McCann, T. M., & Johannessen, L. R. (2004). Why do new teachers cry? *The Clearing House: A Journal of Educational Strategies, Issues and Ideas, 77*(4), 138–145.

Menzies, L. (2019, January 28). The DfE's recruitment and retention strategy: The good the bad and the ugly [blog]. *The Centre for Education & Youth.* Retrieved from https://cfey.org/2019/01/the-dfes-recruitment-and-retention-strategy-the-good-the-bad-and-the-ugly/

Menzies, L., Parameshwaran, M., Trethewey, A., Shaw, B., Baars, S., & Chiong, C. (2015). *Why teach?* London: LKMco. Retrieved from http://whyteach.lkmco.org/ wp-content/uploads/2015/10/Embargoed-until-Friday-23-October-2015-Why-Teach.pdf

National Association of Schoolmasters and Union of Women Teachers [NASUWT]. (2017). *The big question 2017.* Retrieved from NASUWT The Teachers' Union website: www.nasuwt.org.uk/uploads/assets/uploaded/7649b810-30c7-4e93-986b363487 926b1d.pdf

National Association of Schoolmasters and Union of Women Teachers [NASUWT]. (2019). *The big question 2019.* Retrieved from NASUWT The Teachers' Union website: www.nasuwt.org.uk/uploads/assets/uploaded/981c20ce-145e-400a-805969e77 7762b13.pdf

Ofsted. (2019, May) *The education inspection framework. Ref. 190015.* London: Ofsted. Retrieved from gov.uk website: https://assets.publishing.service.gov.uk/government/ uploads/system/uploads/attachment_data/file/801429/Education_inspection_ framework.pdf

Ovenden-Hope, T., & Passy, R. (2019). *Educational isolation: A challenge for schools in England.* Plymouth: Plymouth Marjon University and University of Plymouth. Retrieved from Marjon University website: www.marjon.ac.uk/educational-isolation

Owen, S. (2016). Professional learning communities: Building skills, reinvigorating the passion, and nurturing teacher wellbeing and "flourishing" within significantly innovative schooling contexts. *Educational Review, 68*(4), 403–419.

Rogers, P., & Weiss, C. (2007). Theory-based evaluation: Reflections ten years on: Theory-based evaluation: Past, present, and future. *New Directions for Evaluation, 114,* 63–81. https://doi.org/10.1002/ev.225

Sabar, N. (2004). From heaven to reality through crisis: Novice teachers as migrants. *Teaching and Teacher Education, 20*(2), 145–161.

Schön, D. (1983). *The reflective practitioner: How professionals think in action.* New York: Basic Books.

Shanahan, T., & Barr, R. (1995). Reading recovery: An independent evaluation of the effects of an early instructional intervention for at-risk learners. *Reading Research Quarterly, 30*(4), 958–996. https://doi.org/10.2307/748206.

Swafford, J. (2000). Teachers supporting teachers through peer coaching. In B. Moon, J. Butcher, & E. Bird (Eds.), *Leading professional development in education*. London: Routledge.

Tonna, M. A., Bjerkholt, E., & Holland, E. (2017). Teacher mentoring and the reflective practitioner approach. *International Journal of Mentoring and Coaching in Education*, *6*(3), 210–227. https://doi.org/10.1108/IJMCE-04-2017-0032

Tschannen-Moran, M., & Woolfolk Hoy, A. (2001). Teacher efficacy: Capturing an elusive concept. *Teaching and Teacher Education*, *17*(7), 783–805. https://doi.org/10.1016/S0742-051X(01)00036-1

Veenman, S. (1984). Perceived problems of beginning teachers. *Review of Educational Research*, *54*(2), 143–178.

Ward, J. R., & McCotter, S. S. (2004). Reflection as a visible outcome for preservice teachers. *Teaching and Teacher Education*, *20*(3), 243–257.

Worth, J., Lynch, S., Hillary, J., Rennie, C., & Andrade, J. (2018, October). *Teacher workforce dynamics in England*. Slough: National Foundation for Educational Research. Retrieved from NFER website: www.nfer.ac.uk/media/3111/teacher_workforce_dynamics_in_england_final_report.pdf

6

UNDERSTANDING THE CONTRIBUTION OF PROFESSIONAL COMMUNITIES OF PRACTICE IN EDUCATION TECHNOLOGY IN INFLUENCING TEACHER RECRUITMENT AND RETENTION

Sarah Younie and Christina Preston

Introduction

> at a time when there are more pupils in our schools than ever before, we need to be attracting and keeping great people in teaching.
>
> (DfE, 2019a, p. 3)

And yet,

> it is becoming increasingly difficult to recruit and retain staff of the calibre required.
>
> *(DfE, 2019a, p. 4)*

These two extracts from the Department of Education (DfE) teacher recruitment and retention strategy (DfE, 2019a) acknowledge the problems of teacher overload and the challenges for teacher recruitment and retention in England.

The background is that fundamental changes had been made to education technology as a subject in school in 2012. This change consisted of the information and communications technology (ICT) curriculum being reduced from three strands: digital literacy; information technology; and computer science. Only one strand was retained, computer science, which was characterised by greater emphasis on coding. The challenges in recruitment and retention began to emerge after this curriculum change and were indicated by a shortfall of 8,000 computing teachers in England (National Audit Office, 2016).

In anticipation of a teacher shortfall as a consequence of the curriculum change (and by proxy the additional skills being required of ICT teachers), the government tasked the British Computer Society and Microsoft to select computer science graduates who were willing to teach in schools. These graduates were paid a bursary of £28,000 by the government (BCS, 2018). The grant did not tempt enough computer graduates, and too many of those who did the one-year training in school left at the end (Hammond, 2017). Yet in 2018, the DfE pledged a further £84 million towards these grants to train new computing teachers to be distributed by a new National Centre for Computing Education (Staufenberg, 2018).

Although there are no official figures since 2016 specifically on computer science teachers, Seith published an article in November 2019 entitled, 'Are computer science teachers as rare as unicorns?'. Her evidence from discussion with schools suggests that the recruiting problems have become worse since 2016. In 2020, Mee reported that some schools were dropping the subject in the face of the challenges to recruit and retain teachers.

Suggesting recruitment and retention strategies to the Department for Education

As authors, we are reviewing the retention and recruitment issues from the perspective of the two professional organisations that we represent. The first, the Technology, Pedagogy and Education Association (TPEA[1] – formerly the Information Technology and Teacher Education (ITTE) Association) stretches back to the introduction of computers into schools in the 1980s. This subject association represents a wide range of education technology (EdTech) expertise, including teacher educators, advisory independent consultants, school leaders, classroom teachers and researchers, who all share an interest in improving learning through the application of digital technology in teaching. Members of TPEA publish widely in professional journals, as well as edit their own international academic journal *Technology, Pedagogy and Education,*[2] published by Taylor & Francis. They also contribute to, as well as edit, the leading teacher training textbooks used in initial teacher education over many years, such as those by Leask, Litchfield, and Younie (2005), Younie and Bradshaw (2018), and Capel, Leask, and Younie (2019).

The second organisation, the MirandaNet Fellowship (MF),[3] serves a similar cross-section of educators. However, their membership also includes the education representatives of EdTech companies who fund practice-based research with teachers in the classroom. The website archives teachers' publications, dating back to 1994, which provides a research-informed evidence base that other teachers can harvest and build on. In addition, teachers and trainee teachers can also gain awards from this community of practice (CoP) for sharing their research and professional practice in the form of short articles, blogs, talking heads, conference presentations and delivering practitioner workshops.

Problems with recruitment and retention of computing teachers stemmed from 2010, when Gove was elected the Secretary of State for Education. Working with his adviser, Dominic Cummings, Gove, in his first week in power, closed the British Education and Communications Technology Agency (Becta), which was the government agency covering EdTech in schools and colleges. The members of TPEA and MF were astounded at this political decision, particularly because many members had been engaged in working with this agency and conducting research on their behalf. Their research publications covered topics from developing the curriculum to establishing effective training models, such as those of Preston (2004), Leask and Preston (2009), Pachler, Preston, Cuthell, Allen, and Torres (2011) and Allen, Preston, Payton, and Pickering (2011). The Becta research reports and resources were moved to the National Archive[4] where searching became problematic, with broken links and lack of effective search facilities on the site, so the resources were also reassembled by members of MF (MirandaNet, 2010).

The two professional organisations, TPEA and MF, were not consulted between 2010 and 2019 as the recruitment and retention crisis deepened. In 2017, The Royal Society of Arts (RSA) warned in their report, 'After the Reboot – Computing Education in UK Schools', that this lack of government consultation with the experts might have exacerbated the problems that had arisen from the fundamental change from the ICT curriculum to the computing curriculum. The RSA reporting team indicated that the long-term memory and experience of a CoP, also called a 'learned society', can be valuable to government decision-making on policy change. Then late in 2019, perhaps as a result of the RSA recommendation, both of our CoPs were asked to comment on teacher recruitment and retention by the new Secretary of State for Education, Damien Hinds. He had also promised £10 million to be invested in solutions to the overall recruitment and retention crisis (DfE, 2019b).

Members of TPEA and MF were tasked with responding to the DfE request for comment on computing teacher recruitment and retention. Working together in focused meetings and online, the membership developed advice about how digital technologies might be deployed effectively across the curriculum to ease the shortfall in computing teachers. They also tackled teacher workload and the recruitment and retention challenges facing the profession more generally.

The TPEA/MF report was entitled 'Digital Technologies and the Teaching Profession'. How can education technology improve recruitment, reduce workload and support teacher retention (Younie & Preston, 2019)? Thirty-three members provided expert detailed advice online and 20 members attended three focus groups, providing a total of 53 member contributions. The key points in this report have been summarised later under the headings: workload issues; ensuring continuing professional development (CPD) entitlement; and joining a professional community. These members of TPEA/MF also identified topics for research through their experience of workload issues and retention and recruitment as practicing teachers in the digital technology.

Workload issues

In 2019, the DfE offered guidance (2019b) on ways of working digitally to reduce teacher workload. However, our members pointed out that, from experience, this advice about working digitally did not take account of managerial practice. Sometimes digital solutions can themselves negatively impact on workload. For example, the time spent online for teaching preparation and for marking is often not adequately accounted for in teachers' workloads. Therefore, careful estimates of the impact of any EdTech solutions on workload are essential, as is training teachers to use digital tools efficiently.

The TPEA/MF report (Younie & Preston, 2019) identified that the web offers unprecedented access to high-quality resources that can improve the quality of teachers' work. The members who have themselves developed websites to disseminate peer-reviewed resources think there is a continued need to develop online resources and make them widely available. However, TPEA/MF members cautioned about the simplicity of the idea that teachers can just download lessons from the web without being critical. The concern was that not only do online publishers benefit by making money from this approach, but also that teachers need the skills to plan schemes of work first, then how to find and evaluate appropriate resources and finally to adapt them to the context.

Members suggested that without careful planning and attention to long-term sustainability, the profession risks wasting precious effort and resource on digital solutions. The archiving of the Becta resources that has been mentioned already is a case in point. These resources carried a range of deliverables, like research into the impact of EdTech, advice on purchasing EdTech, recommended curricula, guidance for teachers and an extensive range of online resources for teachers and pupils. When they were withdrawn, there was protest not only in the UK but also by teachers and advisers internationally who were using the free resources, too (Blamires, 2015). Although they were archived (see note 4), the lack of technical updating in the archives has made many resources inaccessible.

Another resource developed by TPEA/MF members that was archived at the same time was the Teacher Training Resource Bank (TTRB). Like the Becta resources, the links have become broken, so without knowing the filename for the resource to enable its location and access, teachers cannot find what they are looking for (Blamires, 2015). This is too large a task for volunteers, so the resources are lost. Members report an international issue about the government withdrawing national resources, used not only in the UK but across the world. Consequently, the TPEA/MF report (Younie & Preston, 2019) advises that a clear strategy is needed by professionals globally to ensure the sustainability of their work on websites remains independent of political changes.

Ensuring continuing professional development entitlement

TPEA/MF members pointed out that there is increasing evidence that effective, continuing professional development (CPD) and collegial support have a significant impact on teacher retention as highlighted by the IRIS Connect research (IRIS, 2018). Regular opportunities for high-quality professional learning motivate and inspire teachers, so ensuring an entitlement to continuing professional development could improve retention. The DfE have reported on improving early career opportunities and asked the CPD Expert Group to reconvene to explore how to help all schools improve the provision of professional development to all staff (DfE, 2019c). With such a wide remit, our members pointed out that the DfE could fund the creation of specific online CPD packages by professional organisations. These should be academically rigorous, taught at master's level and provide teachers with opportunities to engage with current thinking, research and different models of CPD. However, careful arrangements should be made about where they are held. Websites independent of governments are suggested.

TPEA/MF members proposed CPD opportunities could include online support systems, for example, lesson video and coaching, and online support from more experienced teachers. The TPEA/MirandaNet report also suggested that any CoP specialising in EdTech resources could support teachers' CPD with strategies for developing teachers' digital literacy, including efficient navigation, online harvesting and understanding the provenance of content. In addition, teachers should be given more guidance in using web content wisely through focused CPD activities to increase greater competence and proficiency in these digital skills (Younie & Bradshaw, 2018). Many of our members have experience with designing Specialist Open Online Courses (SPOCs), Massive Open Online Courses (MOOCs) and more specifically Community Open Online Courses (COOCs) that they would like to pass on. But staff workloads, in our experience, no longer make voluntary development of courses a realistic possibility.

FutureLearn from the Open University is another example of an online platform that is universally available, can provide a robust infrastructure with clear pedagogical design and would be a relatively low-cost solution to online learning. FutureLearn partner status could be acquired by an appropriate body such as professional subject associations with the aim of providing an easily accessible, well-supported platform geared towards initial teacher training and professional development with a range of educational outcomes: certified/non-certified, accredited/non-accredited and so on. But the time required to do this is not inconsiderable.

MF/TPEA members also drew on their experience of the use of online records or eportfolios of professional development for teachers. Some members made effective use of digital technologies for collecting, storing and updating of evidence. Taking this approach further, they suggested that the use of eportfolios could aid retention as teachers would have a record of evidence of how much they have achieved, thereby restoring professional worth and esteem. This could be linked to the teacher standards pertaining to the commitment to continue learning across an entire career. For example, Donaldson, Finn and Hamilton (2012) argue that standards should address: first, a commitment to keep learning and improving throughout a teacher's career; second, a commitment to collaborate with other professionals; and third, aspiring to achieve optimal performance. All of this could be effectively recorded in an online professional portfolio, which could lead on from the professional development portfolio (PDP) used in initial teacher education to a completely accessible online career-long PDP. As Finn argues, it is 'not sufficient for teachers simply to reach an early professional standard; there is also a need to maintain and improve standards throughout a career' (Finn, 2017, p. 153).

Another means of supporting CPD entitlement would be to provide better access to research and evidence-based practice to support teachers. Given the increasing emphasis on basing professional practice on research evidence, the TPEA/MF strategy was to recommend greater access for teachers in England to education research journals. However, just providing access to research is insufficient: understanding and interpreting research for professional practice has to be an element of the process. Teachers would benefit from robust, evidence-informed research summaries that demonstrate ways of translating research into classroom practice. This approach to application is known as 'translational research' (TR) and is literally translating research findings into professional practice.

TR provides a bridge between research and practice, which originally was developed in the field of science and medicine, but is less established in education (Jones, Procter, & Younie, 2015). There is an education translational research initiative called MESH, which stands for Mapping Educational Specialist know-How.[5] The MESH project is a knowledge mobilisation initiative that provides research summaries (TR) for teachers, available to all and free at point-of-access. The MESHGuides are published online as flowcharts that allow teachers to access the most up-to-date research and pedagogy in their subject. An independent evaluation and impact study on the early years MESHGuides carried out in the Rohingya refugee camps in Bangladesh showed a high level of impact and effect on users (VSO, 2019, pp. 14–15). The analysis of the MESH website statistics in the first two months of 2020 showed 250,000 visitors from more than 200 countries and 60,000 users and rising each month. There is clearly a need in CPD being identified through user and visitor numbers by this online TR resource.

The TPEA/MF members indicated supporting the teaching standards could also be achieved by giving teachers access to research. This would be a means of enhancing teachers' professional identity, with their ongoing development recognised as an element of the teacher's professional commitment (Finn, 2017). This in turn could engender greater commitment and potentially aid retention in the profession. In this way, MESHGuides address key areas of teacher professional knowledge, both general pedagogic knowledge (the broad principles of teaching and learning that apply irrespective of the curriculum subject) (Shulman, 1986, 1987), pedagogical content knowledge (knowing what constitutes effective teaching and learning in relation to specific curriculum content, including effective teaching of threshold concepts) (Shulman, 1986, 1987; Meyer & Land, 2003), troublesome knowledge (knowledge that is conceptually difficult, counter-intuitive or 'alien') (Perkins, 1999) and knowledge of learners and their characteristics (such as how learners develop with age; their cognitive development and knowledge of their learning needs) (Shulman, 1986, 1987). Acknowledging the depth and richness of the different types of knowledge teachers need highlights how teaching is indeed a profession (Younie, 2007).

In this context, retention and recruitment of teachers might be supported in their development if more mentoring took place in CoPs. Professor Rachel Lofthouse has set up a relevant CoP, CollectivED, the Centre for Mentoring, Coaching and Professional Learning,[6] which is a Research and Practice Centre based in the Carnegie School of Education, Leeds Beckett University (Lofthouse, 2019). In this CoP, members share similar concerns to TPEA and MF about giving teachers access to the knowledge they need for their professional practice and ongoing development.

Given the lack of funding for CPD, the MF members recommended their own strategy of involving EdTech companies in providing affordable CPD. However, MF members said that innovation should not be led by company products or their technologies in isolation, but with teachers and how they can use these technologies to support their core professional obligations and aid learning and teaching. In the MF model, EdTech companies take responsibility for research into the efficacy of their own products. MF has worked alongside a number of companies to evaluate their technologies, working collaboratively with teachers on practice-based research projects (Preston, 2013, 2016a, 2016b; Preston & Younie, 2015, 2017; Younie & Cheema, 2015; Preston & Dady, 2018). In these projects, companies working alongside teachers through small-scale, school-based research projects provide teachers and their leaders with in-classroom opportunities to reflect, often with the involvement of pupils and parents as well. MF members suggested that the DfE could also work with these companies to ensure that they are focused on addressing the issues of teachers' workload, recruitment and retention and could support small-scale projects to evaluate potential impacts.

Joining a professional community of practice: teachers building resilience together

Groups of professionals working together have a long tradition that started with the medieval trade guilds in England. In education circles, Wenger, DerMott and Synder interpret this phenomenon as 'communities of practice (CoPs)': 'groups of people who share a concern, a set of problems or a passion about a topic, and who deepen their knowledge and expertise in this area by interacting on an ongoing basis' (Wenger et al., 2002, p. 4). The TPEA/MF membership's view was that membership of CoPs could be very important in reducing stress. When there is an overloaded curriculum with excessive workloads, the greatest threat is one of losing a sense of worth as a professional, with an increased risk of tiredness and burnout that can lead to high rates of teacher attrition.

The members recommended joining an appropriate CoP offering to provide collaborations where like-minded teachers can support each other. Many CoPs have spanned members' entire careers and over the years have provided the voice of professional reason in both face-to-face and online contexts. Groups in the community coalesce around shared interests and subject areas, which provide professional support. Interestingly, digital technologies also support these groups through the innovative uses of social media, such as Twitter, Google discussion groups and online blogs. As Hynes and Younie (2018) argue, these 'are fast and effective communication channels, which inform teachers of evolving [practices], often written by teachers to share and disseminate ideas with other teachers' (p. 156). These are also referred to as professional learning networks (PLNs), which enable teachers to reach out, support and learn from one another. The need to reach out can be forgotten in an academic approach to issues like workload, recruitment and retention. We believe that there is a danger of sanitising the pain that conscientious teachers can suffer when they are not able to do all that has been required of them.

But the members of the TPEA/MF report for the DfE (Younie & Preston, 2019) have seen the reality of the situation: nearly half of teachers planned to leave the profession within five years because they were 'at breaking point', listing pressures such as: increasing bureaucracy around the recording of pupil progress; the need to keep data related to staff performance; and increased time devoted to marking (Lightfoot, 2016). Despite a change in focus from 2019, with the Ofsted framework examining the curriculum, we argue the same challenges still remain.

Conclusions

As the leaders of two EdTech professional associations, we make no claims for easy solutions or quick technological fixes to difficult problems. However, the conclusions we drew from the TPEA/MF members' report to the DfE (Younie & Preston, 2019) that we have covered in this chapter suggest that there are opportunities to make more effective use of technology to support teachers and reduce retention and recruitment issues. This will take time to implement and evaluate and will require an agile approach to educational innovation that is dynamic, interactive and responsive to an alignment between solution and problem.

We must be cautious, however, about assuming that solutions that work locally for some will work at a scale sufficient to help solve professional problems that are regional or national in scope. Of the proposals outlined in this chapter, each would need to be accompanied by a programme of rigorous research and evaluation to ensure maximising impact and to aid teachers in their professional roles, and thereby keep them in the profession.

Meanwhile, more research is needed about how effective planning and usage of EdTech can reduce a teacher's workload, enhance the establishment and recognition of CoPs and, thereby, grow teacher's self-efficacy and sense of worth: these strategies will improve recruitment and ensure retention of trained teachers and leaders. The use of eportfolios is another potential research area in terms of retention. Research of this kind would seek to identify the benefits as well as the challenges of using EdTech and the forms of continuing professional development that are most effective. Clearly the evidence published by TPEA/MF members in the report to the DfE covered in this chapter suggests that joining a CoP is one of the most effective ways of supporting continual professional learning and also maintaining professional pride in difficult circumstances.

Notes

1 Technology, Pedagogy and Education Association: www.tpea.org.uk
2 *Technology, Pedagogy and Education* journal: www.tandfonline.com/toc/rtpe20/current
3 MirandaNet Fellowship: https://mirandanet.ac.uk
4 National Archive (2010) www.nationalarchives.gov.uk/
5 MESH www.meshguides.org
6 CollectivED. Working papers can be found at www.leedsbeckett.ac.uk/carnegie-school-of-education/research/working-paper-series/collectived/

References

Allen, A., Preston, C., Payton, M., & Pickering, S. (2011). *Safeguarding learners in a digital world: e-Safety module information for further education & skills providers & learners.* Coventry: Becta.

Blamires, M. (2015). Building portals for evidence-informed education: Lessons from the dead. A case study of the development of a national portal intended to enhance evidence informed professionalism in education. *Journal of Education for Teaching: International Research and Pedagogy, 41*(5) [Special Issue], 597–607.

British Computing Society [BCS]. (2018). *Computer teacher scholarships.* London: British Computing Society. Retrieved from BCS website: www.bcs.org/get-qualified/certification-and-scholarships-for-teachers/bcs-computer-teacher-scholarships/

Capel, S., Leask, M., & Younie, S. (Eds.). (2019). *Learning to teach in the secondary school: A companion to school experience* (8th ed.). Abingdon: Routledge.

Department for Education [DfE]. (2019a). *Teacher recruitment and retention strategy.* London: DfE. Retrieved from gov.uk website: https://assets.publishing.service.gov.uk/government/uploads/system/uploads/attachment_data/file/786856/DFE_Teacher_Retention_Strategy_Report.pdf

Department for Education [DfE]. (2019b). *Realising the potential of technology in education: A strategy for education providers and the technology industry.* London: DfE. Retrieved from gov.uk website: https://assets.publishing.service.gov.uk/government/uploads/system/uploads/attachment_data/file/791931/DfE-Education_Technology_Strategy.pdf

Department for Education [DfE]. (2019c). *Supporting early career teachers.* London: DfE. Retrieved from gov.uk website: www.gov.uk/government/publications/supporting-early-career-teachers

Donaldson, G., Finn, A., & Hamilton, H. (2012). *Leading systems change in Scotland – Challenges of implementation.* General Teaching Council Scotland Professional update: A GTC Scotland Position Paper. Edinburgh: GTCS.

Finn, A. (2017). The professional standing of teaching in Europe: regulation or relegation? In B. Hudson (Ed.), *Overcoming fragmentation in teacher education: Implications for policy, practice and future research.* Cambridge: Cambridge University Press.

Hammond, P. (2017, November 22). *Autumn Budget Statement* [speech]. London: House of Commons. Retrieved from gov.uk website: www.gov.uk/government/speeches/autumn-budget-2017-philip-hammonds-speech

Hynes, P., & Younie, S. (2018). BYOD: Bring your own device. In S. Younie & P. Bradshaw (Eds.), *Debates in computing and ICT education*. London: Routledge.

IRIS. (2018). *Shaping the future of CPD: Recruit, train, develop, retain* [report: Teacher recruitment and retention]. Retrieved from IRIS website: https://discover.irisconnect.com/shaping-the-future-of-cpd-report

Jones, S., Procter, R., & Younie, S. (2015). Participatory knowledge mobilization: An emerging model for translational research in education. *Journal of Education for Teaching: International Research and Pedagogy, 41*(5) [Special Issue], 555–574.

Leask, M., & Preston, C. (2009). *E-tools for future teachers*. Coventry: Becta with Brunel University.

Leask, M., Litchfield, P., & Younie, S. (2005). Using ICT in your particular subject. In M. Leask & N. Pachler (Eds.), *Learning to teach using ICT in the secondary school* (2nd ed., pp. 4–16). London: Routledge.

Lightfoot, L. (2016, March 22). Nearly half of England's teachers plan to leave in the next five years. *The Guardian*. Retrieved from Guardian website: www.theguardian.com/education/2016/mar/22/teachers-plan-leave-five-years-survey-workload-england

Lofthouse, R. (2019, May). *Editorial*. CollectivED Working Papers. Leeds: Carnegie School of Education, Leeds Beckett University.

Mee, A. (2020, February). *Computing in the school curriculum: A survey of 100 teachers*. London: University College London. Retrieved from ResearchGate: www.researchgate.net/publication/339536481_Computing_in_the_school_curriculum_a_survey_of_100_teachers

Meyer, J. H. F., & Land, R. (2003). Threshold concepts and troublesome knowledge 1 – Linkages to ways of thinking and practising. In C. Rust (Ed.), *Improving student learning – Ten years on*. Oxford: OCSLD.

MirandaNet. (2010). *Becta Reassembled*. Retrieved from https://mirandanet.ac.uk/becta-reassembled/

National Audit Office [NAO]. (2016). *Training new teachers*. London: NAO. Retrieved from NAO website: www.nao.org.uk/press-release/training-new-teachers/

Pachler, N., Preston, C., Cuthell, J. P., Allen, A., & Torres, P. (2011). *The ICT CPD landscape in England*. London: Becta. Retrieved from MirandaNet website: https://mirandanet.ac.uk/external-publications-by-mirandanet-members/

Perkins, D. (1999). The many faces of constructivism. *Educational Leadership, 57*(3), 6–11.

Preston, C. (2004). *Learning to use ICT in classrooms: Teachers' and trainers' perspectives: An evaluation of the English NOF ICT teacher training programme (1999–2003)*. London: MirandaNet.

Preston, C. (2013). The price of beauty and usefulness in learning: A study of value for money in nursery setting. *MirandaNet Fellowship*. Retrieved from MirandaNet website: https://mirandanet.ac.uk/about-associates/associates-research/

Preston, C. (2016a). Developing working memory with Meemo. *MirandaNet*. Retrieved from MirandaNet website: https://mirandanet.ac.uk/about-associates/associates-research/rising-stars-research-page/

Preston, C. (2016b). *Innovations in professional development: Real-time, in-ear*. Retrieved from https://mirandanet.ac.uk/wp-content/uploads/2019/06/Innovations-in-PD-V9-1final-9th-Dec-2016.pdf

Preston, C., & Dady, B. (2018). *Three cases for education technology across the curriculum: Inspiring tomorrow's leaders of creativity – Improving reading standards using e-readers – Moving from a Computing to a Digital Media curriculum.* Retrieved from MirandaNet website: https://mirandanet.ac.uk/about-associates/associates-research/

Preston, C., & Younie, S. (2015). *Innovation in teaching and learning: Using web-enabled video technology to build professional capital through reflective practice, coaching and collaboration.* Retrieved from IRIS website: http://irisconnect.co.uk/wp-content/uploads/2014/08/Innovation-in-teaching-and-learning-research-report.pdf

Preston, C., & Younie, S. (2017). Taking the tablets: Has the long-predicted revolution in teaching and learning finally arrived? In A. Marcus-Quinn & T. Hourigan (Eds.), *Handbook on digital learning for K-12 schools* (pp. 147–171). New York: Springer. https://doi.org/10.1007/978-3-319-33808-8_10

Royal Society of Arts. (2017, November). *After the reboot: Computing education in the UK.* London: Royal Society. Retrieved from Royal Society website: https://royalsociety.org/~/media/policy/projects/computing-education/computing-education-report.pdf

Seith, E. (2019, November 15). Are computer science teachers as rare as unicorns? *Times Education Supplement.* Retrieved from TES website: www.tes.com/news/are-computer-science-teachers-rare-unicorns

Shulman, L. S. (1986). Those who understand: Knowledge growth in teaching. *Educational Researcher, 57,* 4–14.

Shulman, L. S. (1987). Knowledge and teaching: Foundations of the new reform. *Harvard Educational Review, 57,* 1–22.

Staufenberg, J. (2018, November 7). *BCS among 3 firms chosen to run £84m National Centre for Computing Education.* Retrieved from Schools Week website: https://schoolsweek.co.uk/bcs-among-3-firms-chosen-to-run-84m-national-centre-for-computing-education/

Voluntary Service Overseas [VSO]. (2019). Inclusive education. In *Leave no one behind: Annual report and account 2017/18* (pp. 14–15). London: VSO. Retrieved from VSO website: www.vsointernational.org/sites/default/files/VSO-Annual-Report17-18.pdf

Wenger, E., McDermott, R., & Synder, W. (2002). *Cultivating communities of practice: A guide to managing knowledge.* Cambridge, MA: Harvard Business School Press.

Younie, S. (2007). *Integrating ICT into teachers' professional practice: The cultural dynamics of change.* PhD thesis, De Montfort University, Leicester.

Younie, S., & Bradshaw, P. (Eds.). (2018). *Debates in computing and ICT education.* London: Routledge.

Younie, S., & Cheema, R. (2015). *Investigating the use of eye tracking technology in the assessment of learning: A case study of research and innovation at Netherhall Special School.* Research Report to Leicester City Council.

Younie, S., & Preston, C. (2019). Digital technologies and the teaching profession: How can education technology improve recruitment, reduce workload, and support teacher retention? *MirandaNet Fellowship.* Retrieved from https://mirandanet.ac.uk/wp-content/uploads/2019/06/DFE-retention-and-recruitment.pdf

7

UNDERSTANDING SCHOOL CONTEXT IN COASTAL COMMUNITIES

*Lucy Stokes, Jake Anders, Michele Bernini
and Helen Gray*

Introduction

Regional differences in school performance have attracted increasing attention in recent years. Ofsted, the national school inspection body, have highlighted a growing gap between schools in the North and South of England, with secondary schools in the North and Midlands less likely to be judged as 'good' or 'outstanding' than those located in the South (Ofsted, 2015).

One dimension of regional variation that has raised particular concern is the performance of schools in coastal areas. There is also increasing recognition of the broader challenges faced by some coastal communities, with many experiencing greater levels of deprivation, lower rates of employment and lower average earnings compared with the rest of England (Beatty, Fothergill, & Wilson, 2008, 2011). In 2007, the Communities and Local Government Select Committee report (2007) identified a number of common challenges for coastal towns, including physical isolation; higher levels of deprivation; inward migration of older people; outward migration of younger people; and poor-quality housing. Compared with the rest of England, seaside towns have been shown to have lower average employment rates, lower average earnings, a higher proportion of benefit claimants and greater deprivation levels, although there is considerable variation between different seaside towns (Beatty et al., 2008, 2011). Similarly, Humby (2013) finds larger seaside destinations were typically more deprived than the rest of England, although with some exceptions.

Using a broader definition of coastal communities, including not only seaside destinations but also residential and industrial coastal areas, the Office for National Statistics [ONS] (2014) show that coastal communities differ from other communities, typically having a higher proportion of older residents, a higher proportion of individuals with health problems, a higher proportion of individuals from White ethnic backgrounds and lower average employment rates. However, there were also notable differences in terms of these characteristics between coastal communities.

Existing analyses of secondary school performance in coastal areas have identified poorer performance compared with non-coastal schools (e.g. Hannay, 2015; Thomson, 2015). While differences in school performance have partly been attributed to the higher proportion of disadvantaged pupils in coastal schools, there is some evidence to suggest that such pupils fare worse than disadvantaged pupils in other geographical areas (Ofsted, 2013).

Teacher recruitment and retention issues are one potential explanation put forward to account for poorer performance in coastal schools (Ovenden-Hope & Passy, 2015). As discussed throughout this book, teacher shortages, recruitment and retention present a serious challenge for the school education system in England and beyond. Within England, regional variation in recruitment and retention issues have also been acknowledged; the National Audit Office (2017), for example, reports that while all regions in England had seen an increase in the percentage of schools with at least one vacancy between 2010 and 2015, schools in London are most likely to report having at least one vacancy, while those in the North East are the least likely. Teachers in London are also more likely than those in other regions to leave the teaching profession (Worth, Lynch, Hillary, Rennie, & Andrade, 2018). Indeed, differences in regional circumstances led the Social Mobility Commission (2017) to recommend that there should be region-specific strategies for the training and development of the teaching workforce. Ofsted (2015) have suggested schools in coastal areas can experience particular recruitment difficulties as a result of location, performance and pupil intake.

In this chapter, we examine the performance of coastal schools using administrative data on state-funded schools in England. We consider both primary and secondary schools and explore possible reasons for the observed differences in performance between coastal and non-coastal schools. We begin by describing how we identify coastal schools and the data used in our analysis. We then present a descriptive account of differences in performance between coastal and non-coastal schools. The next section explores the extent to which these differences are accounted for by differences in school and pupil characteristics. We compare school performance in coastal areas with those in statistically matched non-coastal areas, in order to explore whether there is a distinct coastal schools problem, or whether it is simply a result of challenges seen in other areas with similar levels of deprivation. Finally, we explore vacancy rates for coastal and non-coastal schools, as a proxy for recruitment issues, before concluding with a discussion of our findings. This examination of the coastal community context aims to help set the scene for further consideration of recruitment and retention challenges faced by coastal schools.

Identifying coastal schools

There are various alternative approaches to defining coastal areas and therefore in identifying coastal schools. We use the coastal communities classification developed by the ONS (2014). This classification is based on information collected in the 2011 census, and it identifies 274 coastal communities in England and Wales. Of these, 217 coastal communities are located in England, and all but 11 of these communities have at least one school.

This definition includes all coastal communities, regardless of whether they are focused on the tourist industry or are mainly industrial or residential, enabling us to capture a broader range of coastal communities than classifications which focus solely on seaside towns or destinations. One potential limitation of adopting a broader definition of coastal communities is that the heterogeneity across coastal communities may make it more difficult to identify common socio-economic characteristics. An alternative approach would be to identify schools based on distance from the coast, as adopted by Hannay (2015) and Thomson (2015). However, this does not necessarily reduce variation in the characteristics of the coastal areas and raises issues as to what the appropriate distance should be.

We use the 2015 School Census to identify state-funded primary and secondary schools within England. ONS (2013) define coastal communities on the basis of built-up-areas (BUA) and built-up-area subdivisions (BUASD); we identified the BUA or BUASD in which each school was located using school postcodes. The vast majority (93 per cent) of schools were located in a BUA or BUASD; the remaining 7 per cent of schools within the School Census were either cross-border schools, or were not located in a BUA or BUASD. These are typically schools located in small rural areas; these schools are excluded from our analysis.[1] In total, 1,575 schools were located in coastal communities, of which 1,219 were primary schools and 356 were secondary schools.

Information on attainment was obtained from the Department for Education [DfE] 2015 Performance Tables (DfE, 2016). Further information on composition of pupils within schools was obtained from the pupil-level census within the National Pupil Database [NPD] (DfE, 2015a), as this allowed us to construct measures of the proportion of pupils within each school who were White British and eligible for free school meals. Eligibility for free school meals is commonly used in analyses of the English education system as a proxy indicator for socio-economic disadvantage, or low family income (Hobbs & Vignoles, 2010). This was important given previous evidence indicating that much of the difference between coastal and non-coastal schools in progress among pupils eligible for the pupil premium was explained by the greater proportion of White British disadvantaged pupils in coastal schools (Thomson, 2015). Information on teacher vacancy rates is obtained from the 2014 School Workforce Census (DfE, 2015c).

School performance in coastal communities: a descriptive overview

Existing studies have shown lower average attainment levels in secondary schools in coastal areas. Hannay (2015) finds coastal schools have shown poorer performance at GCSE level, the main exams taken at the end of compulsory schooling in England, compared with inland schools throughout the period 2011/15.[2] This poorer performance is found to correlate with deprivation measured in terms of eligibility for free school meals. While on average coastal schools performed less well than inland schools, there was considerable variation by area, and some areas where coastal schools did better than inland schools. Thomson (2015) explores performance of the pupil premium group in coastal secondary schools, finding that pupils eligible for the pupil premium fared worse in terms of Progress 8 than their peers in non-coastal schools; Progress 8 aims to capture the progress pupils make between the end of primary school, at age 11, and the end of secondary school, at age 16. Further exploration suggests that much of this gap is explained by differences in the composition of the pupil premium group, namely the greater proportion of White British pupils eligible for the pupil premium in coastal schools. Little difference remains between coastal and non-coastal schools when focusing solely on progress among White British pupils within the pupil premium group.

Both studies outlined identify coastal schools on the basis of distance to the coastline. We find the same applies for schools located in coastal communities: Table 7.1 shows the lower average attainment at Key Stage 4 (KS4 – that is, at the end of compulsory schooling when pupils take their GCSE exams) among coastal schools compared with non-coastal schools, based on data for 2014/15, and across a range of attainment measures. In this year, the percentage of pupils achieving five or more GCSEs or equivalent at grades A*-C, including English and maths, formed a headline measure against which secondary school performance

TABLE 7.1 Attainment at KS4, 2014/15, coastal and non-coastal schools

	Coastal schools	Non-coastal schools
Average percentage of pupils attaining 5 or more A*-C GCSEs (or equivalent), including English and maths	53.6	58.0
Average percentage of pupils attaining the English Baccalaureate	20.0	24.9
Average percentage of pupils making expected progress in English	69.1	72.5
Average percentage of pupils making expected progress in maths	63.5	67.9
Average Best 8 value added score	991.8	999.9
Number of schools	325	2,668

TABLE 7.2 Attainment at KS2, 2014/15, coastal and non-coastal schools

	Coastal schools	Non-coastal schools
Average percentage of pupils achieving level 4B or above in reading and maths test and level 4 in writing teacher assessment	68.1	70.5
Average percentage of pupils achieving level 4B or above in maths	76.6	78.3
Average percentage of pupils achieving level 4B or above in reading	80.5	81.9
Average percentage of pupils achieving level 4 or above in writing teacher assessment	87.2	88.1
Number of schools	1,122	12,156

was judged. The average percentage of pupils achieving this benchmark stood at 53.6 per cent among schools in coastal communities, compared with 58.0 per cent among schools in non-coastal communities. This lower attainment was also apparent across a range of other key measures, with coastal schools also faring less well in terms of the percentage of pupils attaining the English Baccalaureate (which measures achievement of GCSEs in a specified set of subjects), the percentage making the expected level of progress in English and maths, and in terms of Best 8 value added (a measure aiming to reflect progress from end of primary school to end of secondary school).

Average attainment at the end of primary school (also known as the end of Key Stage 2 [KS2]), when pupils are typically aged 11 years old, was also lower in coastal schools. On average, in 2014/15, the percentage of KS2 pupils achieving Level 4B or above in reading and maths, along with at least Level 4 in writing (the expected standards for this age), was lower among schools in coastal communities, standing at 68.1 per cent for coastal schools compared with 70.5 per cent among non-coastal schools (Table 7.2). This difference was also evident when looking at attainment for each subject separately. Thus, a difference in average performance between coastal and non-coastal schools is already evident at the end of primary school.

What factors account for differences in performance between coastal and non-coastal schools?

The descriptives presented here indicate that average attainment in coastal schools is typically lower, at both KS2 and KS4, than in non-coastal schools. In this section, we use multiple regression analyses to explore whether differences between coastal and non-coastal schools remain, once controlling for a range of school characteristics.[3]

Attainment at KS4

Figure 7.1 summarises the impact of controlling for school characteristics on the difference in KS4 attainment between coastal and non-coastal schools. Here we focus on attainment in terms of the percentage of pupils in each school achieving five or more GCSEs or equivalent at grades A*-C, including English and maths. As reported in Table 7.1, there was a 4.4 percentage point difference in attainment on this measure between coastal and non-coastal schools, before controlling for any other factors (average attainment stood at 53.6 per cent in coastal schools and 58 per cent in non-coastal schools). This is represented by the first bar in Figure 7.1.

Once we control for school type and school size (number of pupils), this gap narrows to 2.3 percentage points, although it remains statistically significant (second bar, Figure 7.1). Additionally, including controls for the proportion of boys, the proportion of pupils with special educational needs and the proportion

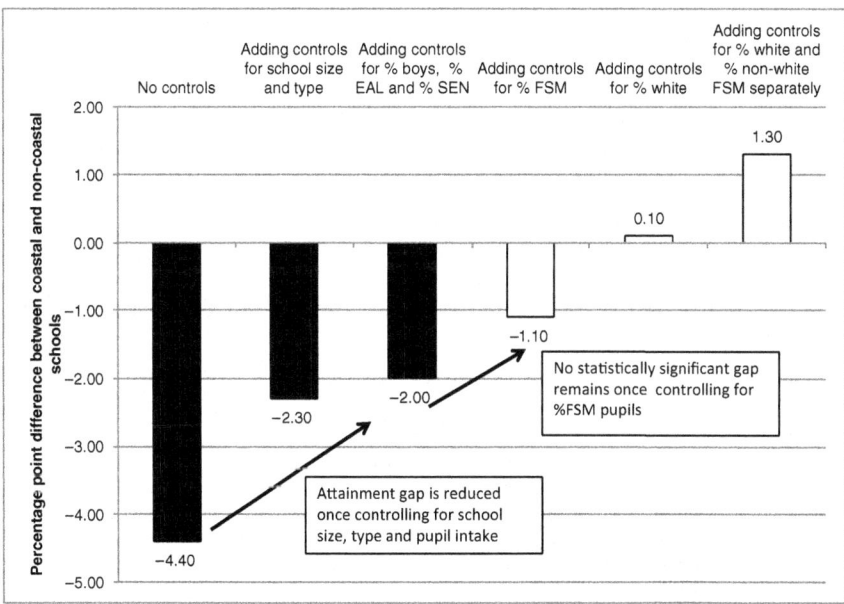

FIGURE 7.1 Attainment gap between coastal and non-coastal schools, KS4

Note: the shading of the bars in the chart represents statistical significance, with the dark bars indicating statistically significant differences at the 5 per cent level of significance; light bars indicate no statistically significant difference. Each bar in the chart represents the average difference in attainment between coastal and non-coastal schools (as indicated by the size of the coefficient on the variable indicating whether a school is coastal from the regression models). Moving from left to right, each set of controls is included in addition to those in the previous column, with the exception of the final column, where instead of controlling for the per cent of pupils eligible for FSM, this is replaced with separate controls for the per cent of White British pupils eligible for FSM and the per cent of non-White British pupils eligible for FSM.

of pupils for whom English is an additional language, the gap in attainment remains similar at 2.0 percentage points.

However, once controlling for the proportion of pupils eligible for free school meals (FSM), the gap in attainment between coastal and non-coastal schools is no longer statistically significant, and the gap disappears once controlling for the proportion of pupils of White British origin. Therefore, it appears that much of the difference in average KS4 attainment between coastal and non-coastal schools is explained by the higher proportion of pupils eligible for FSM in coastal schools.

Furthermore, once we distinguish between White British pupils eligible for FSM and pupils from other ethnic backgrounds eligible for FSM, it is pupils in schools with a higher proportion of White British FSM children that fare worse in terms of attainment. This implies that the apparent gap in KS4 attainment between coastal and non-coastal schools is largely accounted for by the higher proportion of White British pupils eligible for FSM in coastal schools. Among coastal secondary schools, on average 14 per cent of pupils were White British and eligible for FSM, compared with 9 per cent in non-coastal schools.

The same patterns are also evident when considering attainment in terms of progress (as measured by Best 8 value added) (Figure 7.2). Again, the difference in average value added between coastal and non-coastal schools reduces once controlling for school type and pupil composition, and it is no longer evident

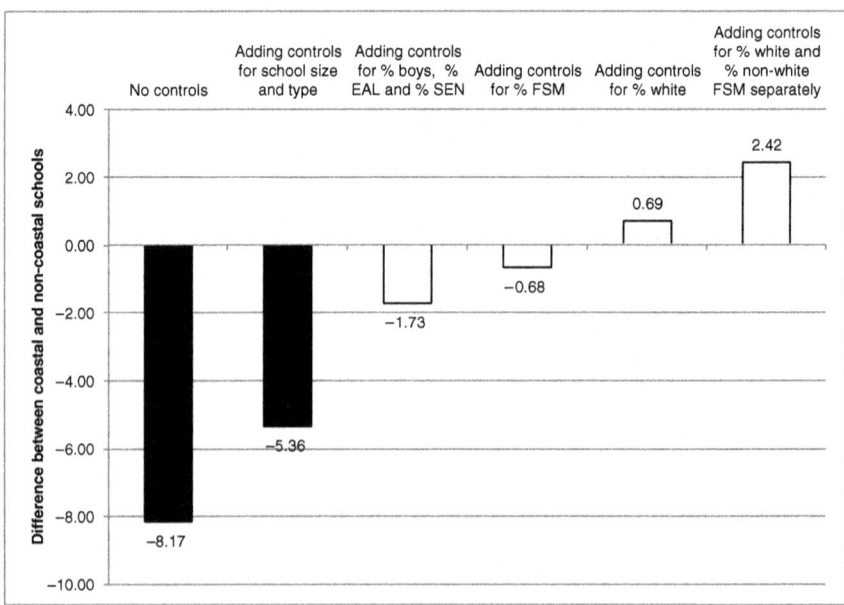

FIGURE 7.2 Attainment gap between coastal and non-coastal schools, Best 8 value added

once accounting for the proportion of pupils who are eligible for FSM. Again, within this group, it is the proportion of pupils who are White British and eligible for FSM that is associated with lower value added.

Attainment at KS2

Broadly similar patterns are apparent for attainment at KS2 (Figure 7.3). Before controlling for other factors, mean attainment in coastal schools was 2.4 percentage points lower than in non-coastal schools, based on the percentage of pupils achieving Level 4B or above in reading and maths, along with at least Level 4 in writing. This attainment gap remains evident when controlling for school size, type and pupil composition in terms of the proportion of boys, the proportion of pupils with special educational needs and the proportion of pupils for whom English is an additional language.

Controlling for the proportion of all pupils that are eligible for FSM, the attainment gap between coastal and non-coastal schools reduces. Once controlling for the proportion of pupils that are White British, the gap between coastal and non-coastal schools is no longer statistically significant at either the 5 per cent or 10 per cent level. Again, as for attainment at KS4, once we distinguish by ethnicity between pupils eligible for FSM, we find it is schools with higher proportions of White British pupils eligible for FSM where attainment is lower.

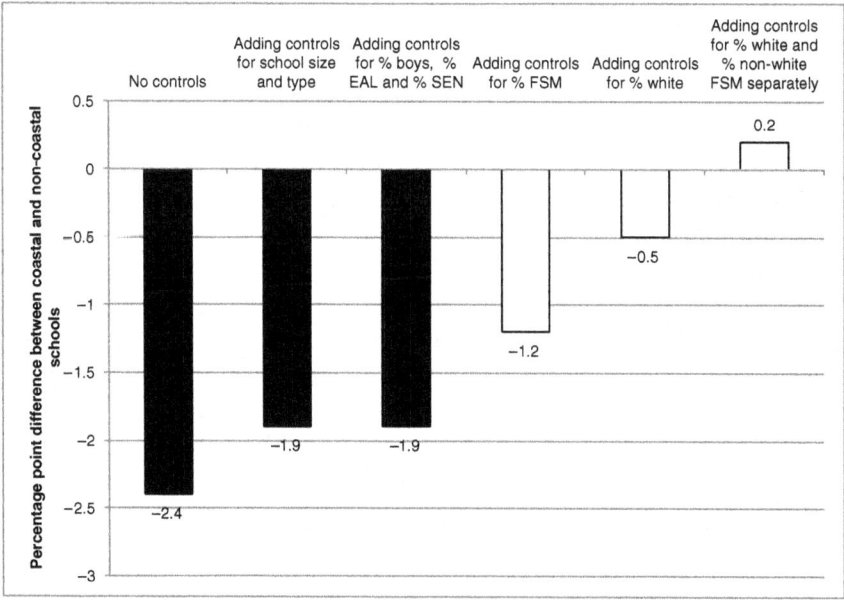

FIGURE 7.3 Attainment gap between coastal and non-coastal schools, KS2

At both KS2 and KS4, therefore, the apparent gap in average attainment between coastal and non-coastal schools is largely accounted for by the higher proportion of White British pupils eligible for FSM in coastal schools.

Attainment in similar schools

The analysis here has suggested that much of the difference in average performance between coastal and non-coastal schools can be explained by the typically higher proportion of disadvantaged pupils in coastal schools, suggesting differences between coastal and non-coastal schools reflect the more disadvantaged nature of coastal areas. One limitation of the analysis presented so far is that it compares schools in coastal communities with schools in *all* other non-coastal communities, yet we know from existing evidence that coastal areas differ in their economic and social characteristics from other areas. In order to investigate more closely whether there is a distinct coastal schools issue, we identify a subset of non-coastal areas which are more similar in their characteristics to coastal areas. We then explore whether differences in attainment between coastal and non-coastal schools remain when undertaking the comparison based on this more comparable subset of areas.

A range of area characteristics, based on the 2011 census, were used to identify non-coastal areas which were similar to the coastal communities (ONS, 2014). This included demographic, economic and social characteristics.[4] For each coastal community, the aim was to identify the most comparable non-coastal community, on the basis of these characteristics (using one-to-one propensity score matching). The group of non-coastal areas used as potential 'matches' for the coastal areas was restricted to those non-coastal areas in which schools were located. For some coastal areas, it was necessary to match with the same non-coastal area multiple times, due to a shortage of areas with similar characteristics, and for two coastal areas it was not possible to obtain any match. This is consistent with at least some coastal communities differing substantially from non-coastal areas.

Notwithstanding these issues, we then run our analysis based on this subsample of more comparable areas. We exclude a small number of coastal and non-coastal areas that had a very high number of schools to ensure a more comparable distribution between coastal and non-coastal communities.[5] Comparing average attainment between coastal and non-coastal schools on this subset of areas, there was no statistically significant difference in attainment at either KS2 or KS4 (Table 7.3). This remained the case when additionally controlling for school and pupil characteristics.

These results indicate that once coastal schools are compared with schools located in similar non-coastal areas, coastal schools do not, on average, show lower attainment. This provides further support for the idea that differences in average attainment between coastal and non-coastal schools reflect the typically more

TABLE 7.3 Regression results, KS2 and KS4 attainment, matched coastal and non-coastal areas

	KS2		KS4	
	No controls	*With controls*	*No controls*	*With controls*
Coastal school	0.030	0.015	−0.012	−0.017
	(0.020)	(0.017)	(0.045)	(0.026)
Number of observations	1,241	1,236	340	330
R-squared	0.008	0.165	0.001	0.555

Notes: Models estimated using OLS. Standard errors in parentheses. No statistically significant differences between coastal and non-coastal schools were evident in any of these specifications.

Controls: number of pupils; proportion male; proportion EAL (English as additional language); proportion with SEN; proportion White British; proportion non-White British FSM; proportion White British FSM; and school type.

disadvantaged nature of many coastal communities, and among similarly disadvantaged coastal and non-coastal communities, performance is no worse in coastal schools.

Recruitment challenges in coastal and non-coastal schools

Recruiting and retaining teachers can be particularly challenging for schools located in disadvantaged areas, especially for certain subjects (Social Mobility Commission, 2017). While some concerns around the teaching workforce focus on high rates of teacher turnover, it has been argued that coastal (and rural) areas can also experience issues through a lack of turnover – with a more limited number of schools in the area and fewer non-teaching employment opportunities meaning fewer new teachers joining schools (Ovenden-Hope & Passy, 2019; Social Mobility Commission, 2017). This is consistent with evidence from the School Workforce Census showing that teachers in coastal areas are slightly less likely to leave the profession (DfE, 2017). A lack of new entrants can potentially limit opportunities for schools to benefit from fresh ideas.

Data on teacher vacancies at school level are published in the annual School Workforce Census statistics. In November 2014, for England as a whole, the vacancy rate stood at 0.3 per cent and the percentage of temporarily filled posts at 0.9 per cent (DfE, 2015b).[6] Exploring figures for coastal and non-coastal schools reveals some differences for primary and secondary schools (Table 7.4). On average, vacancy rates are higher in coastal secondary schools compared with non-coastal secondary schools, while the reverse applies for primary schools. These results are relatively unchanged if schools located in London are excluded.

TABLE 7.4 Full-time vacant posts and temporarily filled posts, coastal and non-coastal schools, 2014

	Primary		Secondary	
	Coastal	Non-coastal	Coastal	Non-coastal
Per cent full-time posts vacant	0.09	0.20	0.37	0.22
Per cent full-time posts temporarily filled	0.86	1.06	0.86	0.76
Number of schools	1,341	15,385	330	2,895

Source: Authors' calculations using the 2014 School Workforce Census (DfE, 2015c).

Discussion

In line with existing evidence, we find on average attainment is lower in coastal schools than in non-coastal schools. This is apparent not only at KS4 but is already evident at KS2. For both primary and secondary schools, the gap in average attainment between coastal and non-coastal schools is reduced once we account for differences in terms of school type, size and pupil intake in terms of the proportion of pupils who are boys, the proportion with English as an additional language and the proportion with special educational needs. Once we account for the proportion of pupils who are eligible for free school meals, there is no longer a statistically significant difference in average attainment between coastal and non-coastal schools. Furthermore, once we distinguish between White British pupils who are eligible for free school meals, and pupils from other ethnic backgrounds who are eligible for free school meals, it is schools with higher proportions of White British pupils eligible for free school meals that show lower average attainment. This implies that the apparent gap in attainment between coastal and non-coastal schools is largely accounted for by the higher proportion of White British pupils eligible for free school meals in coastal schools, possibly reflecting the greater disadvantage seen in many coastal areas.

Furthermore, once coastal schools are compared with schools located in similar non-coastal areas, coastal schools do not, on average, show lower attainment. The fact that much of the difference in average attainment between coastal and non-coastal schools seems to reflect the greater level of disadvantage faced by many coastal communities does not mean that the attainment of coastal schools is not cause for concern. Strategies to raise attainment in coastal schools may well need to take account of the specific context of the areas in which they are located.

On average, teacher vacancy rates in secondary schools are slightly higher in coastal than in non-coastal schools, although the reverse applies for primary schools. While there are limitations to using vacancy rates to capture recruitment issues, this suggests that difficulties in recruitment for coastal schools are more likely to affect secondary schools. It is also important to note that, in general, recruitment and retention issues in schools have intensified since the period of our analysis. Given the evidence on the particular importance of high-quality teaching for disadvantaged pupils, and the typically greater levels of disadvantage in coastal areas, a deeper understanding of recruitment and retention challenges faced by coastal schools would be valuable. Qualitative research on these issues is likely to be of particular value in obtaining more detailed insights into the experiences of schools and their staff.

Finally, it is worth noting that there is considerable variation in performance among coastal schools. This variation is in part related to differences in pupil composition. Even so, there are some coastal schools which manage to achieve above-average attainment despite having higher proportions of disadvantaged pupils. In order to understand more about what works in improving attainment in coastal schools with high levels of disadvantage, it may be useful to explore in greater depth, through both quantitative and qualitative approaches, the characteristics of these schools and the strategies they have adopted, including approaches to staff recruitment and retention.

Acknowledgements

This chapter is based on work originally undertaken for the Regional Schools Commissioner South East and South London, through the Department for Education Analytical Associate Pool. The remit, and thus context, of the original work was shaped specifically by the needs and interests of Regional Schools Commissioner South East and South London colleagues to support the development of an approach/strategy to improve the performance of schools across their region. Further work with schools in the area aimed to develop an understanding of 'what works' in these contexts and what effective support could be offered. We thank the Department for Education for granting access to data from the National Pupil Database. All errors and omissions remain the sole responsibility of the authors.

Notes

1 This is because we make use of area characteristics at BUA/BUASD level, and by definition these are not available for schools not located in a BUA/BUASD.
2 GCSE stands for General Certificate of Secondary Education.
3 All models are estimated using Ordinary Least Squares (OLS) regression.
4 These were: all usual resident population; percentage of resident population aged under 15, aged 16–64 and aged 65 or more; percentage of resident population aged 16–64 with a health problem that affects them a lot; percentage of resident population in private rented accommodation; percentage of household spaces with no usual residents; percentage of resident population UK born, born overseas and moved to the UK before 2001, and born overseas and moved to the UK after 2000; resident population unemployed as a percentage of those aged 16 or more who are economically active; resident population inactive as a percentage of those aged 16–64 who are economically active; percentage of employees aged 16–64 who work part time; percentage of those aged 16 or more who are

homeworkers; percentage of resident population employed in manufacturing industry, in wholesale and retail trade, in transport and storage, in accommodation and food service activities, in professional, finance and information, in public administration, health and education, and in other industries; percentage of employed residents working within area.

5 Nine coastal areas and five non-coastal areas were removed from the analysis for primary schools; seven coastal areas and five non-coastal areas were removed from the analysis for secondary schools.

6 We use data from November 2014 for consistency with the time period used in our attainment analysis.

References

Beatty, C., Fothergill, S., & Wilson, I. (2008, November). *England's seaside towns: A 'benchmarking' study*. Report to the Department for Communities and Local Government.

Beatty, C., Fothergill, S., & Wilson, I. (2011). *England's smaller seaside towns: A benchmarking study*. Report to the Department for Communities and Local Government. London: HMSO. Retrieved from gov.uk website: www.gov.uk/government/publications/englands-seaside-towns-benchmarking-study

Communities and Local Government Select Committee. (2007). *Coastal towns: Second report of session 2006–07*. (HC 351, 2006–07). London: HMSO. Retrieved from parliament.uk website: www.publications.parliament.uk/pa/cm200607/cmselect/cmcomloc/351/351.pdf

Department for Education (DfE). (2015a). *School census*. National Pupil Database.

Department for Education [DfE]. (2015b). *School workforce in England: November 2014*, Statistical First Release, SFR 21/2015. London: DfE. Retrieved from gov.uk website: www.gov.uk/government/statistics/school-workforce-in-england-november-2014

Department for Education [DfE]. (2015c). *School workforce in England: November 2014*, Underlying data. London: DfE. Retrieved from gov.uk website: www.gov.uk/government/statistics/school-workforce-in-england-november-2014

Department for Education [DfE]. (2016). *School and college performance tables in England: 2014 to 2015*. London: DfE. Retrieved from gov.uk website: www.gov.uk/government/statistics/school-and-college-performance-tables-in-england-2014-to-2015

Department for Education [DfE]. (2017, May). *Analysis of teacher supply, retention and mobility*. London: DfE. Retrieved from gov.uk website: www.gov.uk/government/statistics/teachers-analysis-compendium-2017

Hannay, T. (2015, November 2). Beside the seaside [blog]. *SchoolDash*. Retrieved from SchoolDash website: www.schooldash.com/blog-1511.html#20151102

Hobbs, G., & Vignoles, A. (2010). Is children's free school meal "eligibility" a good proxy for family income? *British Educational Research Journal*, *36*, 673–690. https://doi.org/10.1080/01411920903083111

Humby, P. (2013, August 21). *A profile of deprivation in larger English seaside destinations, 2007 and 2010*. Office for National Statistics. Retrieved from Coastal Communities Alliance website: www.coastalcommunities.co.uk/wp-content/uploads/2015/07/A_Profile_of_Deprivation_in_Larger_English_Seaside_Destinations.pdf

National Audit Office [NAO]. (2017, September 12). *Retaining and developing the teaching workforce*. Report by the Comptroller and Auditor General. (HC 307, 2017–19). Retrieved from NAO website: www.nao.org.uk/report/supporting-and-improving-the-teaching-workforce/

Office for National Statistics [ONS]. (2013, June). *2011 Built-up areas – Methodology and guidance*. Office for National Statistics.

Office for National Statistics [ONS]. (2014). *2011 census: Coastal communities*. Office for National Statistics.

Ofsted. (2013). *Unseen children: Access and achievement 20 years on. Evidence report*. Ofsted. Retrieved from gov.uk website: www.gov.uk/government/speeches/unseen-children

Ofsted. (2015). *Ofsted annual report 2014/15: Education and skills*. (HC 616). London: HMSO. Retrieved from gov.uk website: www.gov.uk/government/publications/ofsted-annual-report-201415-education-and-skills

Ovenden-Hope, T., & Passy, R. (2015). *Coastal academies: Changing school cultures in disadvantaged coastal regions in England* [report by Plymouth University and The Cornwall College Group]. Retrieved from University of Plymouth website: www.plymouth.ac.uk/uploads/production/document/path/11/11623/Coastal_Academies_Report_2015_final_2_Tanya_Ovenden-Hope_and_Rowena_Passy.pdf

Ovenden-Hope, T., & Passy, R. (2019). *Educational Isolation: A challenge for schools in England* [report by Plymouth Marjon University and University of Plymouth]. Retrieved from University of Plymouth website: www.plymouth.ac.uk/uploads/production/document/path/13/13574/Education_Isolation_Report.pdf

Social Mobility Commission. (2017, November). *State of the nation 2017: Social mobility in Great Britain*. London: Social Mobility Commission. Retrieved from gov.uk website: https://assets.publishing.service.gov.uk/government/uploads/system/uploads/attachment_data/file/662744/State_of_the_Nation_2017_-_Social_Mobility_in_Great_Britain.pdf

Thomson, D. (2015, April 27). The pupil premium group in coastal schools: Is their rate of progress really any different to schools with similar intakes? [blog] *Education Datalab*. Retrieved from Education Datalab website: https://ffteducationdatalab.org.uk/2015/04/the-pupil-premium-group-in-coastal-schools-is-their-rate-of-progress-really-any-different-to-schools-with-similar-intakes/

Worth, J., Lynch, S., Hillary, J., Rennie, C., & Andrade, J. (2018, October). *Teacher workforce dynamics in England*. Slough: NFER. Retrieved from National Foundation for Educational Research website: www.nfer.ac.uk/media/3111/teacher_workforce_dynamics_in_england_final_report.pdf

8

UNDERSTANDING THE CHALLENGES OF TEACHER RECRUITMENT AND RETENTION FOR 'EDUCATIONALLY ISOLATED' SCHOOLS IN ENGLAND

Tanya Ovenden-Hope and Rowena Passy

Introduction

Educational isolation is complex, grounded in location and situated in access to resources. In this chapter, we draw on our research and school-based intervention work with coastal, rural and urban schools over the last ten years to demonstrate how the challenges of 'educational isolation' interact to limit access to resources for school improvement. We identify the challenges of educational isolation as geographical remoteness, socio-economic deprivation and cultural isolation, which, when experienced by a school together, act to the detriment of schools serving persistently disadvantaged pupils. We recognise that, for these pupils, the quality and continuity of good teaching makes a considerable difference to their attainment (Higgins, Cordingley, Greany, & Coe, 2015), and that the quality of teaching is central to their school experience. Our focus in this chapter is therefore on the way that educational isolation affects the recruitment and retention of high-quality teachers.

Educational isolation is a relatively neglected research area, partly because the British Government's emphasis has primarily been on densely populated and often disadvantaged areas which, in turn, has encouraged educational researchers to tread the same path. This is changing, as research has begun to show how persistently disadvantaged pupils from schools in isolated areas have performed less well in examinations than those in more populated areas. A study by the Future Leaders Trust (2015a, p. 1), which resulted from working with the authors on applying the early concept of educational isolation to schools in their trust (Future Leaders Trust, 2015b), found that as schools' relative isolation increased, so the average attainment of disadvantaged pupils decreased, a finding supported by Odell (2017). A more recent report from the Department for Education (DfE) (2019a) commented that, 'For a given level of deprivation, the attainment levels of [secondary] pupils living in rural areas were lower than for pupils living in urban areas with a similar level of deprivation' (p. 5).

Hannay (2020) argues that the relationship between geographical isolation and socio-economic deprivation is realised in Ofsted judgements of school performance, particularly in secondary schools in England, where 'poverty and isolation seem to act in concert. Among the relatively small number of secondary schools with high levels of both, two-thirds are rated "Requires Improvement" or "Inadequate"' (para. 1, bullet 2).

Hannay (2020) also argued a geopolitical element in his findings on school performance and geographical remoteness/poverty, in that 'the areas in which these schools are located showed high levels of support for Brexit and large swings towards the Conservatives in the 2019 general election' (para. 1, bullet 3). We would suggest that this is a reflection of the cultural position of these schools identified in our conceptualisation of educational isolation.

The Key (2018) examined the situation of rural school leaders, and found a complex situation relating to disadvantage that is 'closely linked to wider socio-economic and infrastructural issues' (p. 3), a finding given an international dimension by Fowles, Butler, Cowen, Streams, & Toma (2014), who found similar problems in schools in the United States, as did Halsey and Drummond (2014) in Australia. Our research explores these issues in detail, and it offers a conceptualisation of educational isolation that supports a deeper understanding of its challenges and consequences.

Conceptualising education isolation

We began exploring educational isolation in 2010 as a response to the specific challenges observed in coastal schools in England. Building on the body of work with different projects enabled us to consider the concept of 'educational isolation' from a range of different perspectives. The common thread in all of our research and developed interventions with schools was the way in which the place-based challenge of geographical isolation interacted with other specific contextual factors to increase difficulty for school improvement.

Coastal schools research and continuing professional development

The first project, *Coastal Schools Research*, was conducted between 2010 and 2017. This consisted of four linked but separate studies that used a qualitative longitudinal research approach to examine leadership in six secondary schools located up to five miles from the coast in areas of long-standing socio-economic deprivation (indicated by multiple indices of deprivation). Schools were recruited from those that had converted to academy status during the time of – or shortly after – the Labour administration, in line with their academisation programme introduced in 2008. The government's ambition was that all mainstream secondary schools in England had a minimum of 30 per cent of pupils passing five or more equivalent GCSE passes at grades A★-C, including maths and English at the age of 16. Those schools that were not achieving the expected standard and did not improve their examination results quickly could be closed and re-opened as academies or trust schools (DCSF, 2008, pp. 14–16). This meant that the school would be managed by a team of independent co-sponsors rather than the local authority (educational administration), and this was expected to generate the type of entrepreneurial leadership that was more generally associated with private sector business (Woods, Woods, & Gunter, 2007, p. 239).

The converter academies within our Coastal Schools Research project had the expectation that the new structure and leadership would rapidly improve examination results. All the schools in these studies therefore had a long history of pupil underperformance in examinations and had experienced new leadership teams following academisation. Pupils were drawn from populations that were predominantly White working class, were located in communities that had many cases of multi-generational, low, un- or seasonal employment and that had a wide range of social problems that included inadequate housing and/or high levels of poor health. Details of our findings relating to how school leaders faced these challenges – which included as a key issue teacher and leader recruitment and retention – their ways of mitigating these challenges, and a discussion of the research methodology can be found in earlier publications (Ovenden-Hope & Passy, 2015; Passy & Ovenden-Hope, 2017; Passy & Ovenden-Hope, 2019). Central to this project was the establishment of geographical, economic and cultural isolation as contributing factors for educational isolation and in turn the context for limiting school access to high-quality teachers (Ovenden-Hope & Passy, 2015).

The project's findings and recommendations were explored further in a series of case studies with the Future Leaders Trust, and resulted in a report that illustrated how coastal school leaders had responded to: the factors of educational isolation identified in our 2015 study; the challenges, such as difficulties in teacher recruitment and retention, that these factors had caused; and the strategies they had used to address them (Future Leaders Trust, 2015b). Our finding, that all principals in our study reported recruiting staff was a challenge and attributed this to their coastal location (characterised by geographical isolation, poor transport links, limited employment prospects for partners of teachers and long commutes from more affluent areas) (Ovenden-Hope & Passy, 2015), was a key area examined by the Future Leaders Trust (2015b). The solutions headteachers of coastal schools found for their workforce supply issues were considered and pragmatic:

> Headteachers cannot build railway lines but they can reduce the impact of geographical isolation by taking students to important locations (universities, museums, historical sites) and bringing important artefacts to the students (public figures, touring events). They can extend recruitment

activity (onto social media, using inspiring messages or targeting national training institutions) and work to raise the reputation of the school across the region.

(Future Leaders Trust, 2015b, p. 11)

The work undertaken on coastal schools led to Ovenden-Hope developing and leading the Educational Endowment Foundation-funded RETAIN project between 2015/17. The RETAIN pilot programme was a continuing professional development (CPD) for early career teachers in coastal-rural primary schools in Cornwall with the highest levels of persistently disadvantaged pupils with the aim of improving early career teacher retention (see Chapter 5 in this volume). During this period, Ovenden-Hope was invited to work with coastal-rural school leaders in Cornwall as part of their CPD. This CPD used findings and recommendations from the coastal schools project and RETAIN to establish and implement solutions for the challenges experienced by these school leaders. A key challenge was the recruitment of early career teachers and school leaders. The school leaders shared the same pragmatism as the headteachers who took part in the Future Leaders Trust case studies (Future Leaders Trust, 2015b) and implemented strategies that were within their control, such as providing opportunities for early career teachers to meet and socialise with other early career teachers within the county. This connecting of teachers in remote schools in Cornwall, as a way of keeping teachers in teaching, was recognised as good practice in the Social Mobility Commission State of the Nation Report (2017, p. 51).

The combination of our longitudinal research with coastal schools that had an established history of disadvantage, and of the CPD with schools located in coastal-rural isolated areas, sensitised us to the multiple challenges that coastal and rural schools faced. We had identified in 2015 that geographical isolation was one – highly important – factor that affected school improvement, but that economic and cultural factors were important, too (Ovenden-Hope & Passy, 2015). We therefore shifted the focus for our next research project into a more detailed investigation into the ways in which school leaders experienced what we were beginning to term 'educational isolation'.

Educational Isolation Project

In the *Educational Isolation Project* (EIP) (2017/19), we collected data using an online questionnaire and case study semi-structured interviews. Once our ethics application, in which we set out project principles of voluntary participation, right to withdraw, anonymity, confidentiality and data security, was approved, an invitation to participate in the research (questionnaire and interview) was sent to 'partner' school leaders via email. There were the partner schools working in partnership with the research teams', and other institutions', teacher education programmes. We also invited participation more generally through social media (Twitter). From the estimated sample size of 1,800 (1,500 via email and 300 via

Twitter), 61 responses were returned from all the regions in England apart from the North East; eight school leaders for the case study interviews came from six different institutions as a follow-up from the questionnaire. For a full report on this research, see Ovenden-Hope and Passy (2019).

The questionnaire invited school leaders to indicate their location (urban; coastal-urban; rural and coastal) and to answer a series of 38 questions related to pupil deprivation, examination scores and future prospects; teacher and leader professional development; levels of parent and community involvement; and challenges that the school and its leaders experienced. School leaders were invited to comment on their responses to each section. The penultimate question asked respondents if they considered themselves to be isolated from 15 different elements of isolation (EoI) that included employer engagement, government initiatives, workforce supply (teacher retention and recruitment), and cultural and social opportunities. Participants were offered the option of 'no isolation'. Case study interviews focused on how school leaders experienced the different elements of isolation, and ways in which they responded to mitigate its effects.

Although from a relatively small sample, the detail in this research enabled us to establish and examine how the different aspects of educational isolation interact with one another to affect school improvement in schools that have high levels of persistent disadvantage, and to build a more robust conceptualisation of educational isolation than one based purely on location (e.g., Odell, 2017). Table 8.1 shows that leaders from coastal and rural schools indicated that their school experienced the highest number of EoI, with an average of seven and a small proportion of respondents indicating 11–15. This confirmed our perception that location or place was the fundamental element of educational isolation.

We analysed the numerical data with the commentary provided from both the questionnaires and the case study interviews, enabling us to conceptualise educational isolation as a complex phenomenon in which specific factors of location interact to restrict the school's capacity to access the resources it needs to succeed against national standards. We therefore define educational isolation in its broadest sense as: 'a school experiencing limited access to resources for school improvement, resulting from challenges of school location' (Ovenden-Hope & Passy, 2019, p. 4).

TABLE 8.1 Elements of isolation

	No EoI	1–5 EoI	6–10 EoI	11–15 EoI	Average
Urban*	5 (23%)	14 (64%)	3 (14%)	0	3
Coastal-urban**	2 (33%)	3 (50%)	1 (17%)	0	2
Rural and coastal***	0	14 (42%)	13 (39%)	6 (18%)	7

*n = 22; **n = 6; ***n = 33. Percentages are calculated as the proportion of each of these three categories and are rounded to the nearest full number.

Source: Ovenden-Hope & Passy, 2019, p. 14.

To add to the conceptualisation of educational isolation, we identified from the findings three key locational/place-based challenges: geographic location, socio-economic conditions and cultural opportunities and diversity. We argue that a school in a location with geographic, socio-economic and cultural isolation has limited access to a high-quality school workforce, funded school improvement interventions and school support (Ovenden-Hope & Passy, 2019). This is shown graphically in in Figure 8.1.

The complexity of the interaction between the different locational factors means that educational isolation is experienced in different ways by different schools, with some resources more limited than others. All, however, are limited in comparison to urban schools' access to these resources. Rather than a formula for measuring the level of educational isolation, our conceptualisation suggests that the presence of these place-based challenges can limit a school's access to educational resources that support school improvement. In the next section, we discuss how educational isolation affects teacher recruitment and retention by limiting the schools' access to a high-quality workforce.

The effect of educational isolation on teacher recruitment and retention

Teacher recruitment and retention for schools in England is a national challenge (NEU, 2019; DfE, 2019b; Foster, 2019), and there have been significant reductions in teacher trainee applications and acceptances reported since 2010 (Helm, Siddiqui, & Ratcliffe, 2017). Published data show that the proportion of teachers leaving the profession (teacher attrition) has increased every year since 2010 in primary schools (Worth & De Lazzari, 2017). The departure figures for early career teachers (ECTs) are arresting: 13 per cent of teachers leave teaching within one year of qualifying and 30 per cent leave within five years (House of Commons, 2017). Two school leaders commented in the EIP questionnaire about teacher attrition issues they faced.

> Historically, the school had a number of vacancies for staff year on year. There is a real coastal churn of staff – for example if someone is underperforming in one school, they just move on to the next school.

> We have to use Teach First as a recruitment stream and they tend to leave as soon as two-year contracts are complete – now extended to three years.

Teach First is a teacher training provider that places trainee teachers in schools with high levels of disadvantaged pupils. The teacher will work in the school from the start of their training and is contracted to remain with the school for a set time. As educationally isolated schools are located in socio-economically deprived areas, there is a strong chance that they will have Teach First trainee teachers. It has been demonstrated that more than 50 per cent of teachers trained by this route

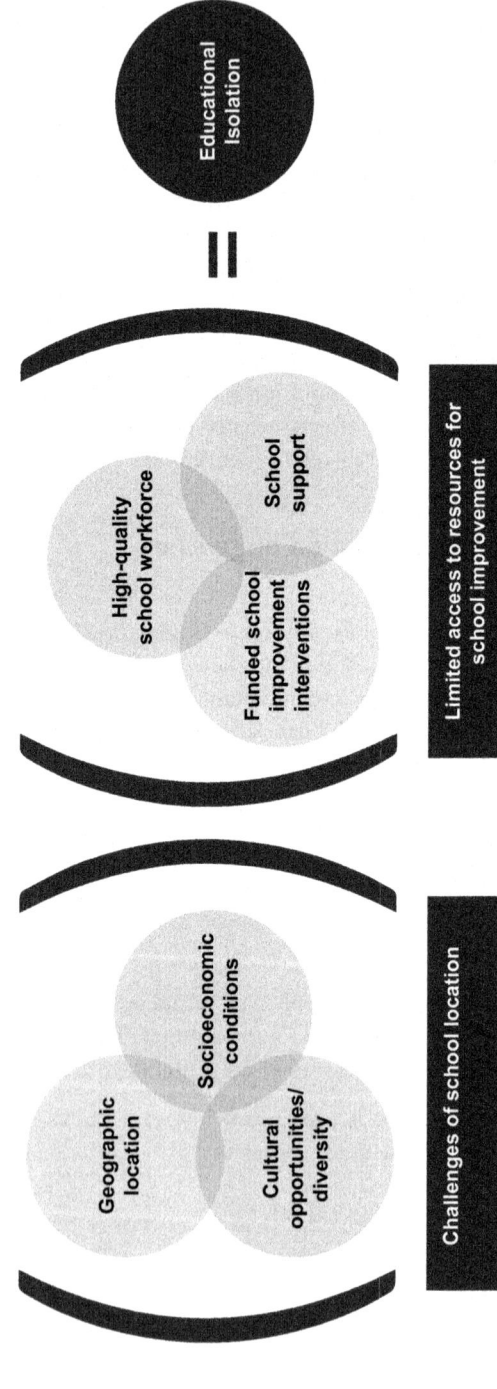

FIGURE 8.1 Visualising educational isolation

Source: Ovenden–Hope & Passy, 2019, p. 4.

have left teaching by year five (Allen, Parameshwaran, & Nye, 2016, p. 8). This teacher training route-based attrition issue, along with the other reasons articulated in the EIP for poor retention of teachers in educationally isolated schools (discussed later), make retention a concern for educationally isolated schools.

Recruitment is also proving to be difficult for schools, with the numbers of unfilled posts increasing at a time when overall pupil numbers are increasing (NEU, 2019). In the EIP questionnaire, all school leaders in both educationally isolated and non-educationally isolated schools reported that they found it difficult to recruit shortage subject teachers (maths, physics, design and technology), and that they had an easier time recruiting non-shortage subject teachers. Coastal and rural schools experiencing educational isolation found it more difficult to recruit senior leaders than school leaders in urban and coastal-urban schools, and they reported that it was much harder to recruit headteachers/principals. Small primary schools reported that they can face particular difficulties because of the anticipated heavy workload associated with a small number of staff (Ovenden-Hope & Passy, 2019). The whole presented a picture in which the challenges of location made recruitment difficult. The EIP also confirmed our earlier research findings (Ovenden-Hope & Passy, 2015) on coastal schools, which suggested that location was a factor that led to the long-term retention of teachers, which we refer to as a lack of teacher churn, leading to a different kind a retention problem, discussed later.

The effect of geographic remoteness

The first challenge of location, geographic remoteness, affected recruitment and retention in the first instance through resourcing work-related travel. Teachers were seen to be reluctant to spend large amounts of time when travelling to their workplace in areas where there was no reliable public transport:

> As an isolated school, our staff face challenges in travelling in and this has a knock-on effect on recruitment and retention. . . . Teachers in [town] probably travel for about half an hour whereas our staff that travel in from [city] are travelling an hour. When you say that in London you think it's not too bad, but actually that's a journey in a car on a single-track road. If you get delayed then it becomes problematic very quickly.
>
> *(school leader, case study school 4)*

School leaders reported in the EIP questionnaire that issues with travel increased during the summer months in areas that relied on tourism as 'the main arterial roads tend to be extremely busy with holiday traffic' (primary school leader). There was also the question of finance:

> I think we also struggle in terms of getting quality staff because we're . . . remote. . . . An awful lot of teachers that live and work in [local city] would

be going, Oh I don't want to . . . commit to that finance [for travelling] every day.

(principal, case study school 1)

The difficulties of negotiating the time and expense of travelling to schools in isolated locations was seen to lead to a disappointing response to job advertisements, with one primary headteacher commenting in the questionnaire that their location 'hampers our recruitment. We are lucky if we ever get more than six applications for a post.' This general difficulty could be avoided if the school had a strong reputation in a particular area – 'Recruitment is ok because of school-led CPD but the size of field is not always as big as one would hope' (primary school leader) – but could also be compounded by being in an Ofsted category, with another primary school leader reporting that recruitment was difficult because the school was

> just coming out of 'requirement to improve' [Ofsted] category in a small rural area [that is] very isolated and takes a long time to travel to.

An additional problem in popular tourist areas was the cost of housing, illustrated by a questionnaire response from a secondary headteacher:

> Trying to recruit young staff to coastal/rural areas is very difficult. . . . The high cost of housing does make a long-term commitment difficult for young staff, and rental properties are expensive due to the amount of holiday opportunities in the area.

While these challenges meant that recruitment and retention were often difficult, other respondents wrote or spoke of the problems of being in a location that staff settled into, perhaps had children and then did not want to move. One school leader responded in the EIP questionnaire that it was difficult to find staff with 'relevant qualifications' who were 'not parents of (or related to) children at the school' (primary headteacher); another that 'many long-serving teachers do not see themselves working anywhere else' (primary school leader). This latter comment represents the lack of teacher churn in some educationally isolated schools. Some teachers can remain in the school for the majority of their career, and this can mean that other staff have little or no chance of promotion and will leave as soon as the opportunity arises, illustrated in the following EIP questionnaire comment:

> Talented teachers and middle leaders often leave. We have a lot of staff who have been here a long time so internal promotion opportunities are low.

(secondary senior leader)

One of the interviewees gave another reason why a reluctance to leave the area could be a problem:

> There is a real coastal churn of staff [here] – for example if someone is underperforming in one school, they just move on to the next school.
>
> *(headteacher, case study 4)*

A static staff can result in school improvement tending to be inward-looking, with teachers resistant to new ideas and techniques (Ovenden-Hope & Passy, 2015). It can also mean that the leadership faces a destabilising change when a number of teachers reach retirement age at the same time:

> We have had a very stable staffing structure for a number of years. However, nearly 50 per cent of staff are approaching retirement from 2016–19, so this will be a particular challenge for us.
>
> *(secondary headteacher, school leader, EIP questionnaire)*

The effect of socio-economic deprivation

These challenges of geographical remoteness increase when the school is located in an area of socio-economic deprivation, the second locational factor of educational isolation. The case study headteacher just quoted spoke of the difficulty of recruiting staff to work in challenging circumstances, and this was particularly noticeable in areas of economic deprivation. In the questionnaire, we asked if participants considered their school to be isolated from employer engagement, economic opportunities (e.g., large employers willing to engage with schools) and social opportunities (e.g., accessing leisure facilities). Table 8.2 shows how school leaders in the different types of location responded and clearly identifies the additional challenges felt in this area by rural and coastal school leaders.

There are several implications for teacher recruitment and retention in schools that feel isolated from employer engagement and economic opportunities. These can be areas in which a diminishing number of young people – and therefore a smaller number on the school roll – contribute to staff reductions and low morale among the remaining teachers. In addition, in areas of low-wage, under- or unemployment, school leaders in the EIP found that pupils have little incentive to work hard at school, if their community offered few employment opportunities.

TABLE 8.2 Socio-economic elements of educational isolation

	Employer engagement	Economic opportunities	Social opportunities
Urban*	2 (9%)	10 (45%)	4 (18%)
Coastal–urban**	0	2 (33%)	0
Rural and coastal***	8 (24%)	28 (85%)	16 (48%)

*n = 22; **n = 6; ***n = 33. Percentages are calculated as the proportion of each of these three categories and are rounded to the nearest full number.

Source: Ovenden-Hope & Passy, 2019, p. 20.

These children displayed little expectation of leaving the area for work and did not relate school to future employment prospects. The result for schools in this situation was the development of a reputation as challenging and possibly a poor Ofsted grading. A case study interviewee commented that, when she started at such a school, her experience was that

> it had falling admission numbers due to a number of causes, including a bad Ofsted result. . . . In the years since, the school had garnered a bad reputation in the community, with parents taking children to schools they perceived as better. In an isolated coastal community with decreasing numbers of young people, I found the school with a community with no aspirations for their children. Morale amongst staff was low.
>
> *(headteacher, case study school 5)*

Finding high-quality staff to work in such schools is difficult, as another case study interviewee pointed out:

> In the past, when we have recruited new teachers we have not always managed to get the advert out to pick out the cream of the NQTs [newly qualified teachers] . . . we have to do a lot of work with them to get them up to the standard that we would need to work in these challenging circumstances with these challenging children.
>
> *(assistant principal, cast study school 1)*

At a time when teachers 'can pick and choose' where they work because of the 'difficult recruitment circumstances' for schools (EIP primary headteacher questionnaire response), it can be hard to make recruitment attractive to these schools:

> [We are a] small school, bottom of food chain, reluctance by teaching staff to teach in mixed year group classes, an awareness of workload in small school with so many responsibilities shared by so few despite having outstanding behaviour from children.
>
> *(primary headteacher, EIP questionnaire)*

In addition, experienced teachers often have families and, when they move to a new area, anticipate that their partner will be able to find work. Areas of socio-economic deprivation tend to offer limited employment opportunities for partners established in their careers; younger teachers, who are less likely to be in stable relationships and/or have children, often want to be in an area that offers a wide range of social opportunities (Ovenden-Hope & Passy, 2015, p. 13). As the EIP (Ovenden-Hope & Passy, 2019) and our previous research (Ovenden-Hope & Passy, 2015) shows, the combination of an isolated location and local socio-economic challenges can produce significant difficulties for teacher recruitment and retention, illustrated by one EIP secondary question-naire school leaders' comment:

> [We are located in a] coastal town with poor transport links and declining industry. This causes all of the above [difficulties with recruiting all types of school staff].

The effect of limited cultural opportunities and/or diversity

The third location or place-based factor of educational isolation, limited cultural opportunities and/or diversity, means that teachers have to work harder to offer children a cultural awareness that is part of the fabric of more multicultural areas:

> [There's] an awful amount of stuff we have to teach that you wouldn't teach in a school where you have that cultural diversity because children are just exposed to it. . . . It creates quite an insular feel. . . . We have to work quite hard just to make sure we are preparing children for modern global society and that they understand that global society doesn't look like [this town].
>
> *(assistant principal, EIP case study school 1)*

This school was a gender diversity champion for a national organisation but found that other local schools were reluctant to invest in training relating to gender diversity. The school leader reported that trips to offer children the chance to experience different environments and cultures were expensive, with the result that they tended to be rare. An EIP survey respondent described how this limited experience of cultural diversity can lead to local insularity:

> We are culturally very different to the rest of the country, with the indigenous Cornish identifying themselves as Celtic rather than English, and those attitudes towards 'outsiders' of any race, culture or colour of skin can be difficult. We are not culturally diverse in this part of the world, although that is beginning to change in some of the larger towns.
>
> *(primary headteacher)*

While we are not suggesting that this is the situation in all isolated areas, it adds to the factors mitigating against the recruitment and retention of teachers who are used to more cosmopolitan attitudes and find it hard to adjust.

The effect of limited externally funded educational interventions

The EIP found that school leaders from urban and coastal-urban schools were 'connected' to national funding streams more often than leaders in rural and coastal schools. Schools with less funding for new interventions and additional resources can be less attractive to potential recruits and can create difficulties with retention. In 2013, Ofsted stated explicitly that it was pupils from disadvantaged backgrounds in low-density populated coastal and rural communities (educationally isolated schools as we have defined them), rather than similarly disadvantaged pupils in urban schools, that were being let down by national education interventions:

> the focus has shifted to deprived coastal towns and rural, less populous regions of the country, particularly down the East and South-East of England. These are places that have felt little impact from national initiatives designed to drive up standards for the poorest children.
>
> (Ofsted, 2013: paragraph 6)

The DfE recognised the need to improve support for schools in areas with persistently disadvantaged pupils as a way to improve pupil attainment and progress. Opportunity Areas[1] were one Department for Education intervention that allocated funding to a range of different regions that included coastal, urban and rural communities, which met criteria that included multiple indices of deprivation. Geographic isolation was not considered as an area selection criterion. Coastal and rural areas selected for support appear to have geographical and cultural connectedness and with sizeable populations, the latter enabling the intervention to have larger reach. This may in some way explain why school leaders in educationally isolated rural and coastal schools are more isolated from funded interventions than their urban counterparts, as the principal in case study school 1 of the EIP stated:

> I think the starting point is statistical here. If you're looking at areas of deprivation, 97 per cent of those in the UK exist within cities or the urban network. Three per cent exist within rural communities. . . . So all of the funding has typically ended up in the big city. So you think London Challenge, you think Future Leaders.

The consequence of this is that educationally isolated schools appear a poor choice for teachers seeking employment when compared to a well-resourced and connected school.

The effect of limited school support/continuing professional development

The final area in which educational isolation affects teacher retention relates to the availability of school support. As Chapter 5 in this volume shows, high-quality CPD can make a difference to retaining teachers, but long distances and relatively few staff in smaller schools means that it can be difficult to find the time to release teachers for CPD:

In the rural school I worked in, the meetings that were held were very few and far between. . . . If your school is 20 miles from the nearest school that's similar to you, then that makes a huge difference, whereas we're 15 minutes down the road from one of our network schools . . . a lot of the rural schools are smaller, so if you have fewer staff you can't really have a member of staff who just disappears for a meeting for half the day.

(headteacher, EIP case study school 2)

Teacher absences of around a day from the classroom mean that primary children in particular lose the continuity of teaching, an important factor in supporting their learning. And the distances make networking more difficult, once again because of the time taken in travelling. Technology such as Skype can alleviate this problem, but, as one case study interviewee commented, 'Nothing replaces the whites of the eyes' – the sociability of networking is not easily replaced over the longer term. It is here that external funding, in this case for CPD programmes, can help to alleviate these issues and improve teacher retention and a high-quality workforce in educationally isolated schools.

Conclusion

The research discussed here brings into focus the challenges of educational isolation for teacher recruitment and retention, experienced at different levels and to different degrees by the responding schools. The tenor of our findings has been echoed by Ofsted (national inspection body), in which their 2020 evaluation report on 'stuck schools'[2] identifies geographical isolation and, less explicitly although clearly embedded in their findings, socio-economic deprivation and reduced cultural opportunities, as reasons for why schools, stuck and unstuck, struggle to recruit and retain high-quality teachers. This is a positive development; if the national regulatory body recognises the particular locational challenges of isolated schools, we can hope that policy measures might be taken to alleviate their position.

It is also encouraging that we have been consulted by charitable education organisations, such as Space Link[3] and The Talent Tap,[4] to support a new way of thinking about the criteria they can use to target schools for funding and interventions. Using the concept of educational isolation, these charities have refocused how they identify schools for support, ensuring that schools in less densely populated areas that are geographically, socio-economically and culturally isolated have a chance to receive externally funded interventions.

While this chapter has focused on the difficulties of teacher recruitment and retention, educationally isolated schools are working hard to achieve what they see as a 'fair deal' for students educated in areas of disadvantage, with high-quality teaching a priority (Passy & Ovenden-Hope, 2019). Our EIP research found that school leaders believe the most effective action for teacher recruitment was to work closely with or become an initial teacher education provider, followed by demonstrating a positive working environment within the school, which could include CPD programmes. This resonates with the findings both from our Coastal Schools Research, in which principals spoke of how changing perceptions about a previously underperforming school was the 'hardest nut to crack' (Ovenden-Hope & Passy, 2015, p. 37), and from the EIP, in which recruitment was found to be easier in schools that had positive local reputations. To support schools in this process, we close the chapter with a number of recommendations:

- *Supported collaboration opportunities for educationally isolated schools* – educationally isolated schools find it more difficult to engage with other schools for school support, and need direct support in this area. An example of how this might be realised comes from the Church of England, which is funding rural schools to develop networks for school improvement and effectiveness.[5]
- *Direct investment in high-quality contextualised continuing professional development and learning* – in-school professional development is the prevailing model offered to teachers in educationally isolated schools. Externally delivered or developed high-quality professional development would offer additional resource to these schools struggling with attracting and retaining high-quality staff. The Department for Education Early Career Teacher Framework (DfE, 2019c) will be available in all schools from 2021 and should be contextualised for educationally isolated schools.
- *Focused government reforms/initiatives/funding opportunities for school leaders* – educationally isolated schools have fewer opportunities to participate in funded national school improvement initiatives, such as the School Strategic Improvement Fund. The DfE and agencies providing funding to schools should support leaders in educationally isolated schools in applying for funds that enhance teacher retention and recruitment.
- *Targeted inclusion of educationally isolated schools in initial teacher education (ITE) provision* – this was considered by EIP school leaders to be the most effective action an educationally isolated school can take to improve teacher recruitment.

Notes

1 More information on Opportunity Area methodology can be accessed at: https:// assets.publishing.service.gov.uk/government/uploads/system/uploads/attachment_data/ file/650036/Opportunity_areas_selection_methodology.pdf
2 A stuck school is a school (including its predecessor if it has converted to become an academy) that has had consistently weak inspection outcomes throughout the last 13 years. This means that it has: been judged to be inadequate, satisfactory or to require improvement in every inspection it has had between 1 September 2006 and 31 August 2019; and had at least four full inspections in the period. Ofsted (2020, January). Fight or flight? How 'stuck' schools are overcoming isolation. No. 190042 6, pp. 5–6.
3 https://spacelink.org/
4 The Talent Tap: www.thetalenttap.com/

5 The Church of England Foundation for Educational Leadership, Rural Schools Network
   Project: www.cefel.org.uk/rural/

References

Allen, R., Parameshwaran, M., & Nye, P. (2016, July). *The careers of Teach First Ambassadors who remain in teaching: Job choices, promotion and school quality*. London: Education Datalab. Retrieved from FFT Education Datalab: https://ffteducationdatalab.org.uk/wp-content/uploads/2016/07/The-careers-of-Teach-First-Ambassadors-who-remain-in-teaching-FINAL.pdf

Department for Children, Schools and Families [DCSF]. (2008). *National challenge: A toolkit for schools and local authorities*. Nottingham: DCSF.

Department for Education [DfE]. (2019a). *Rural education and childcare*. Retrieved from gov.uk website: https://assets.publishing.service.gov.uk/government/uploads/system/uploads/attachment_data/file/828101/Education___childcare_-_August_2019.pdf

Department for Education [DfE]. (2019b). *Teacher retention and recruitment strategy*. London: DfE. Retrieved from gov.uk website: https://assets.publishing.service.gov.uk/government/uploads/system/uploads/attachment_data/file/786856/DFE_Teacher_Retention_Strategy_Report.pdf

Department for Education [DfE]. (2019c, January). *Early career framework*. London: DfE. Retrieved from https://assets.publishing.service.gov.uk/government/uploads/system/uploads/attachment_data/file/773705/Early-Career_Framework.pdf

Foster, D. (2019, December 16). *Teacher recruitment and retention in England*. House of Commons Briefing Paper, Number 7222. London: House of Commons.

Fowles, J., Butler, J. S., Cowen, J. M., Streams, M. E., & Toma, E. F. (2014). Public employee quality in geographic context: A study of rural teachers. *The American Review of Public Administration*, *44*(5), 503–521.

Future Leaders Trust. (2015a). *Isolated schools: Out on a limb*. London: Ambition Institute. Retrieved from Ambition Institute website: www.ambition.org.uk/research-and-insight/isolated-schools-out-limb/

Future Leaders Trust. (2015b). *Combatting isolation in coastal schools*. London: Ambition Institute. Retrieved from Ambition Institute website: www.ambition.org.uk/research-and-insight/combatting-isolation-coastal-schools/

Halsey, J., & Drummond, A. (2014). Reasons and motivations of school leaders who apply for rural, regional and remote locations in Australia. *Australian International Journal of Rural Education*, *41*(1), 69–77.

Hannay, T. (2020, March 3). Outliers: On geographically isolated schools [blog]. *SchoolDash*. Retrieved from SchoolDash website: www.schooldash.com/blog.html

Helm, T., Siddiqui, K., & Ratcliffe, R. (2017, September 2). Teachers £5,000 a year worse off under Tories. *The Guardian*. Retrieved from Guardian website: www.theguardian.com/education/2017/sep/02/teachers-5000-pounds-a-year-worse-off-under-tories-claims-labour

Higgins, S., Cordingley, P., Greany, T., & Coe, R. (2015). *Developing great teaching: Lessons from the international reviews into effective professional development* [report summary]. London: Teacher Development Trust. Retrieved from Teacher Development Trust website: http://tdtrust.org/about/dgt

House of Commons Education Committee. (2017). *Recruitment and retention of teachers: Fifth report of session 2016–2017*. (HC 199, 2016–17). London: House of Commons. Retrieved from gov.uk website: https://publications.parliament.uk/pa/cm201617/cmselect/cmeduc/199/19902.htm

The Key. (2018). *The challenges of leading a rural school.* London: The Key. Retrieved from The Key website: https://resources.thekeysupport.com/hubfs/Rural%20Schools%20Report/The%20Key_The%20Challenges%20of%20Leading%20a%20Rural%20School_Report%202018.pdf?hsCtaTracking=99b976aa-09d5-4a6a-af0d-1b340dd8877e%7Ca62f7ad1-4bbe-4832-8759-d9ddb9eaa246

National Education Union. (2019). *Teacher recruitment and retention.* Retrieved from https://neu.org.uk/policy/teacher-recruitment-and-retention

Odell, E. (2017). Lonely schools: The relationship between geographic isolation and academic attainment. *Educational Research, 59*(3), 257–272.

Ofsted. (2013, June 23). *Too many of England's poorest let down by education system* [press release]. Retrieved from gov.uk website: www.gov.uk/government/news/too-many-of-englands-poorest-let-down-by-education-system

Ofsted. (2020). *Fight or flight? How 'stuck' schools are overcoming isolation: An evaluation project.* Retrieved from gov.uk website: https://assets.publishing.service.gov.uk/government/uploads/system/uploads/attachment_data/file/856088/How__stuck__schools_are_overcoming_isolation_-_evaluation_report.pdf

Ovenden-Hope, T., & Passy, R. (2015). *Coastal academies: Changing school cultures in disadvantaged coastal regions in England.* Plymouth: University of Plymouth. Retrieved from University of Plymouth website: www.plymouth.ac.uk/uploads/production/document/path/11/11623/Coastal_Academies_Report_2015_final_2_Tanya_Ovenden-Hope_and_Rowena_Passy.pdf

Ovenden-Hope, T., & Passy, R. (2019). *Educational Isolation: A challenge for schools in England.* Plymouth: Plymouth Marjon University and University of Plymouth. Retrieved from Marjon University website: www.marjon.ac.uk/educational-isolation/Education-Isolation-Report.pdf

Passy, R., & Ovenden-Hope, T. (2017). *Class of 2010: A qualitative longitudinal study of an English secondary school that became an academy.* SAGE Research Methods Case Study in Education. Retrieved from SAGE website: http://methods.sagepub.com/case/qualitative-longitudinal-english-secondaryschool-became-academy

Passy, R., & Ovenden-Hope, T. (2019). Exploring school leadership in coastal schools: 'Getting a fair deal' for students in disadvantaged communities. *Journal of Education Policy, 35*(2), 222–236. https://doi.org/10.1080/02680939.2019.1573382

Social Mobility Commission. (2017). *State of the nation 2017: Social mobility in Great Britain.* London: Social Mobility Commission. Retrieved from gov.uk website: https://assets.publishing.service.gov.uk/government/uploads/system/uploads/attachment_data/file/662744/State_of_the_Nation_2017_-_Social_Mobility_in_Great_Britain.pdf

Woods, P., Woods, G., & Gunter, H. (2007). Academy schools and entrepreneurialism in education. *Journal of Education Policy, 22*(2), 237–259. https://doi.org/10.1080/02680930601158984.

Worth, J., & De Lazzari, G. (2017). *Teacher retention and turnover research: Research update 1: Teacher retention by subject.* Slough: National Foundation for Educational Research. Retrieved from NFER website: www.nfer.ac.uk/teacher-retention-and-turnover-research-research-update-1-teacher-retention-by-subject/

9

SENSE-MAKING OF EDUCATIONAL POLICY AND WORKFORCE SUPPLY FOR SMALL SCHOOLS IN ENGLAND

Tanya Ovenden-Hope and Ian Luke

Introduction

This chapter is situated within the authors' experience of working with leaders of small schools in England, Ofsted and the Department for Education (DfE). This experience has been gained through senior roles as Heads of Teacher Education, directors and members of multi-academy trusts (MATs) (that include small schools), and through board membership of a range of teacher education policy-influencing organisations, such as the Universities' Council for the Education of Teachers (UCET), and groups, such as the All Party Parliamentary Group for the Teaching Profession. Existing literature on small schools (typically rural schools) and contemporary education policy is used to explore the themes identified by the authors as important for 'sense-making' (Odden & Russ, 2019) the current position of small schools in England post-2010.

We consider that there is no nationally agreed definition of what constitutes a small school in England. Categorisation of small schools range from fewer than 210 pupils on roll (Church of England, 2018) to fewer than 101 (Carter, 2003), and as low as under 91 (Audit Commission, 1990) in the primary sector. For secondary, a small school has been identified as under 200 pupils (Coopers & Lybrand, 1995) in England, while internationally the threshold was under 400 for a secondary school (Harber, 1996). There is also little agreement among school leaders in England on what size a small school should be, as Craig and Blandford's (2004) study demonstrated, with primary headteachers identifying a range from 50 to 275 pupils as in this category.

The lack of consensus around what size a 'small school' is (or should be) means that it is difficult to make sense of the specific challenges, such as teacher recruitment and retention, as the range in size can have a considerable effect on the staff numbers employed and the range of activities within the school that they engage with. For the purposes of clarity, the authors will focus on small primary schools with 210 or fewer pupils.

In 2018, there were 5,406 small primary schools in England compared to 11,464 in 1980 (O'Brien, 2019, p. 0). This decline in small school numbers has been matched by an increase in large primary schools, categorised as having over 600 pupils; the number of these schools has grown from 49 in 1980 to 780 in 2018 (O'Brien, 2019, p. 0). The changes in small school numbers can be explained largely by education policy related to funding and school structures implemented since 2010 (see next section). However, this trend in the reduction in the number of small schools is located primarily in rural areas. Nearly a fifth of primary schools in England are located in a hamlet or a village and average just over a hundred pupils on roll (with an average of 400 pupils for primary schools in towns). They are twice as likely to close as the national average (O'Brien, 2019). This reduction in small rural school numbers has, in our experience, made them less attractive as a career choice for newly qualified teachers and more experienced teachers seeking promotion to leadership. The increased chance of small school closure, coupled with infrastructural challenges related to housing and transport in rural areas, create issues for recruitment (Ovenden-Hope and Passy, 2019; The Key, 2019).

We are aware that small schools in England are experiencing challenges in teacher recruitment and retention. The Department for Education (DfE) response to improve workforce supply and address teacher shortages in all schools is the teacher recruitment and retention strategy (DfE, 2019a). The impact of this strategy for small schools will emerge as the strategy is implemented from September 2021. However, the DfE measures of workforce supply in schools do not support an informed understanding of the situation for small school recruitment and retention. The DfE have identified different factors affecting workforce supply in schools; particularly pertinent to small schools is the school-structural factor (DfE, 2017). The school-structural factor includes the characteristics inherent in the school make up, such as pupil number on roll and number of staff. For a small school, the structure (size) limits the number of teachers in each school because of the small number of pupils. Schools with a small workforce (structural factor) are problematic for the DfE to include in workforce supply data due to the methodology used by the DfE to calculate workforce data in schools (DfE, 2017, pp. 15–29). This means that small schools are typically excluded from workforce supply data issued by the DfE, resulting in a paucity of accurate data specifically on small school workforces.

Educational policy changes and austerity for public service funding appear to make little sense for small schools and create tensions specific to the small school context for both the recruitment and retention of teachers and leaders, as the Church of England (who provide over 70 per cent of very small schools in rural communities [2018, p. 1]) identify:

> the situation [recruitment and retention] is exacerbated in this [small school] context. Small schools do not have sufficient funding to support

more than a skeleton staff, frequently no more than a teaching head, a part-time teacher and an administrator. . . . The situation also demands that staff are teaching across multiple age groups at all times and there is little opportunity to develop or access specialisms. . . . In the very situation where, arguably, we need the most talented and the most resilient staff, the odds are stacked against both their recruitment and retention.

(Church of England, 2018, p. 13)

These politically enhanced tensions, in our own experience and research, show small schools struggling to recruit new staff to replace long-serving teachers. The 'lack of teacher churn' can lead to challenges for school improvement (Ovenden-Hope & Passy, 2019, p. 7). Equally, small schools struggle to sustain (perhaps rather than retain) early career teachers as a result of fewer opportunities for release to develop networks and access professional learning opportunities due to low staff numbers in the school (Luke & Cade, 2017; Wildy, Sigurðardóttir, & Faulkner, 2014).

Educational policy relevant to small schools (2010 onwards)

England saw the election of a coalition government in 2010 (Conservative and Liberal Democrat) that declared in its Programme of Government (HM Government, 2010a, p. 28):

The Government believes that we need to reform our school system to tackle educational inequality, which has widened in recent years, and to give greater powers to parents and pupils to choose a good school. We want to ensure high standards of discipline in the classroom, robust standards and the highest quality teaching. We also believe that the state should help parents, community groups and others come together to improve the education system by starting new schools.

This statement signalled the start of a period of rapid and extensive educational policy reform. The then Secretary of State for Education, Michael Gove, was clear that the aim of policy would be to establish a school-led system underpinned by academisation (local authority schools to convert to academies directly funded by the government)[1] using the Academies Bill (HM Government, 2010b), which removed local authorities', parents' and teachers' power to stop or oppose a school becoming an academy and enabled schools categorised as 'outstanding' by Ofsted (national regulatory body for schools) to fast-track the process. The Academies Bill 2010 was challenged by the government opposition, with the Shadow Secretary of State for Education Ed Balls prophetically stating that creating academy schools with direct government grant funding and independent regulation alongside local authority grant maintained schools[2] would cause a dichotomy in the education system: 'the Bill will create unfair and two-tier education in this country. There will be gross unfairness in funding, standards will not rise but fall, and fairness and social cohesion will be undermined' (House of Commons, 2010, cols. 35–36).

The Academies Bill 2010 was, however, passed (becoming the Academies Act 2010) and laid the foundation for the current multi-type school system of education in England. For small schools, academisation brought both challenges and opportunities to the schools' workforce, as we discuss in the next section.

Michael Gove went on to develop further types of government-maintained schools in England: free schools (government-funded, independent community-run schools) and studio (small, vocationally focused government-funded schools) to develop alongside existing grant maintained local authority and faith schools. The new school types were given powers in 2012 to regulate their own teaching supply, including the appointment of unqualified teachers into teaching roles, and were able to call them teachers, effectively deregulating teaching. Our experience is that small schools were predominantly grant maintained in local authorities until relatively recently and therefore lacked the same options open to academies, free and studio schools to look at alternative workforce supply options. As small schools have been argued to have a long-serving workforce (Church of England, 2018), this can be more expensive, which in turn can limit the employment of more staff, such as teaching assistants or an early career teacher.

'The Importance of Teaching' (DfE, 2010) was the first White Paper for Michael Gove, and in it he stated that teachers needed to be freed from 'constraint and improve their professional status and authority' (DfE, 2010, p. 8) and extended academy status as desirable for all schools. Accepted variation in school funding between schools would be addressed by a 'national funding formula', under which money would go directly from the government to all schools, rather than through the local authorities (DfE, 2010, p. 82). As we shall discuss later in this chapter, funding for small schools continues to be an issue within a revised national funding formula that challenges their ability to provide sufficient resources to run their schools, including teachers.

Alongside Gove's proposed changes to the type and funding of schools, the coalition government made radical changes to the curriculum in primary and secondary schools. The 'English Baccalaureate' (EBacc) was announced in 2010 and would be awarded to students gaining GCSEs in English, maths, one science, one foreign language and one humanity, and would be used as a GCSE performance measure. The EBacc was introduced, alongside the return to examinations and testing for primary to secondary phases, with a move to an 'academic' knowledge-based curriculum. For small schools, the Standard Assessment Tests (SATs) offer little for a representative picture of pupil attainment, which the government measures in percentages against a national standard benchmark (floor) figure. In a small school where a class of 20 take the SATs, the percentages are skewed by the small number, making performance statistics an unreliable guide to the school's efficacy. This can result in significant concern for teachers and leaders in small schools, as Ofsted judgements on performance have been driven by data. In our experience, the additional pressures of potentially poor data can make it hard to sustain teachers in small schools and recruit leaders.

'Training Our Next Generation of Outstanding Teachers' (DfE, 2011) reformed initial teacher training (ITT) provision in England 'so that more ITT is led by schools' (DfE, 2011, p. 3), which sat comfortably within the government's thinking about a more autonomous school system being created through academisation. For small schools, leading ITT was not an option. Small staff numbers mean teachers/leaders are at capacity for their deployment (across a much broader range of tasks, including cross-phase teaching, compared to larger schools). Therefore, for the benefit of having trainee teachers, such as improved professional practice within the school (Hurd, Jones, McNamara, & Craig, 2007), small schools from 2010 have had to rely on other ITT providers, now other local schools, to provide them with trainees. As small schools are more likely to be educationally isolated (Ovenden-Hope & Passy, 2019) this has, in our experience, resulted in small schools having fewer trainee teacher opportunities.

Based on 'The Importance of Teaching' (DfE, 2010) discussed, the *Education Act* (HM Government, 2011) removed the education bodies/agencies that supported schools in the broadest sense, such as the General Teaching Council (Sections 10–12); the Training and Development Agency for Schools (Sections 14–17); and the School Support Staff Negotiating Body (Section 18), and it reformed broad areas of education, including academies (Sections 52–65), and the school workforce, such as the newly qualified teacher induction period (Sections 7–9). The new school-led system appeared very much to be under central government control and within an ideology based on an urban, metrocentric understanding of school size and performance.

In the Commons Education Select Committee's (CESC) report 'Great Teachers: Attracting, Training and Retaining the Best' (2012), the provision of school-based training was endorsed (CESC, 2012, p. 32), and the Committee recommended that the government introduce 'a formal and flexible career structure for teachers, with different pathways for those who wish to remain classroom teachers or become teaching specialists' (CESC, 2012, p. 44). These two areas in the report demonstrate a lack of awareness of the small school workforce and the specific context-based challenges they experience. We have already discussed the issue of school-led ITT for small schools, but small school teachers and leaders can experience more limited opportunities to engage with professional development than colleagues in larger urban schools (Ovenden-Hope & Passy, 2019) and thereby be restricted in developing specialisms within the curriculum.

School leadership in small schools has arguably received little attention in research (Wallin & Newton, 2014). Addressing this, Wallin and Newton (2014) suggest that leaders in small schools can be perceived as having greater credibility by colleagues (possibly due to the fact that they also teach) with a better understanding of government policies. However, the influence of small school leaders on educational policy can be seen to be minimal, even isolated (Wallin &

Newton, 2014, p. 711), with reforms focused on creating large, efficient, effective schools with leaders (MAT Chief Executive Officers in the later years of the decade) that work directly with the government. The precarious future for small schools imposed by policy change has created, in our experience, a challenge for the recruitment and retention of high-quality teachers and leaders.

The Blunkett Review in 2014, officially the 'Review of Education Structures, Functions and the Raising of Standards for All', by former Labour education secretary David Blunkett, challenged the efficacy of academies. The report stated that it was 'undemocratic' to have individual schools 'contractually bound to the Secretary of State and free-floating from the communities they serve' (Blunkett, 2014, p. 5). It called for all state schools to be co-ordinated under local control and proposed the appointment of local 'Directors of School Standards' to monitor schools (Blunkett, 2014, p. 6). The government's response was to introduce regional school commissioners (RSCs) to monitor the performance of academies.

The development of RSCs was an important step in reinforcing academies as the preferred school structure and paved the way for the White Paper 'Educational Excellence Everywhere' in 2016, which made it clear that groups of schools/academies working together (multi-academy trusts, or MATs) would be the future of school structures in England: 'The growth of multi-academy trusts (MATs) expands the reach and influence of the most successful leaders so more children can benefit from their expertise' (DfE, 2016, p. 14). Small schools in the evolving academised system in England appear to have little choice but to enter formal collaborations, preferably MATs, in order to survive (Church of England, 2018). After 2016, the policy focus changed from types of school to funding and a commitment to deliver a national funding formula (NFF) that would address what were seen as disparities in the system. These disparities saw a concentration of funds in cities and large schools, such as in London, and away from rural areas and small schools (Church of England, 2018). This refocus had the potential to bring opportunity for workforce development through additional funding to small schools, and the success of this is discussed later.

National funding formula

The national funding formula (NFF) was introduced for the school year 2018–19 (DfE, 2017) and updated for 2019–20 (DfE, 2018) and again for 2020–21 (DfE, 2019b). The NFF has not offered the anticipated significant increases in funding for small schools, despite government promises. Small schools appear under the NFF for 2020–21 to receive more funds per child than larger schools. However, this is because a school's 'lump sum' (a sum given in recognition of the school's fixed costs that is applied in the same way for all schools) is included in the per pupil calculation rather than separately, as had been the case before in the previous two iterations of the NFF.

Small schools will also not receive a per pupil funding increase because, with the lump sum included, their per pupil funding appears over the threshold of £4,000 that triggers additional funding. This means that a small school can only receive the minimum possible uplift in funding of 1.84 per cent. Larger schools will get an increase of between 6 to 8.5 per cent (Moore, 2019). In addition to this, the 'mobility factor', which is additional funding for small and rural schools, is also absorbed through the minimum funding guarantee (MFG) protection calculation undertaken for schools at the funding floor level, typically small schools. Therefore, any additional funds that the Department for Education believes small schools are gaining as a result of the NFF are, it appears, lost through complicated calculations and readjustments (Moore, 2019). In essence, the NFF will continue to distribute the majority of the funding to large schools in 2020/21.

The consequence of the NFF is to make small schools financially insecure, with resources reduced, including staff, to offset funding reductions, all of which creates a question mark over the long-term viability of the school and makes attracting new teachers challenging. As Corbett and Tinkham (2014) eloquently put it, the issues for small schools are a 'classic "wicked" policy problem' (p. 691), that is, they are complex to define and cannot be solved by data-driven processes.

Multi-academy trusts (MATs)

The political context in which small schools function in England has been one of rapid policy change and reform since 2010. Educational policy appears to have focused on, and been designed for, large urban schools that can run autonomously through direct funding from the government (academy) and more latterly as groups of academies run by a single organisation (MAT) (DfE, 2016). School/groups of school size are important for efficiencies of scale when considered within the framework of school funding cuts generally; as noted by an Ofsted report in 2019:

> The rationale for this growth [of MAT size] put forward by the government has been largely economic – for example, that larger MATs will secure economies of scale, more efficient use of resources, more effective management and clearer oversight of academies. . . . In 2017, Lord Agnew, the minister responsible for academies, said that small MATs should merge together in order to achieve financial viability.
>
> *(Ofsted, 2019b, p. 21)*

It therefore appears on first consideration that MATs work to the detriment of small schools and have elicited the increase in small school closures identified in the introduction (O'Brien, 2019). In our work with small schools, we have seen small school leaders struggle to maintain their schools financially outside of a MAT. It should be considered, therefore, whether small schools in a MAT have more opportunities to access a high-quality teacher supply, access to professional development and greater all-round resource than those that stand alone.

MATs have been championed as the purveyor of best practice by the government, as noted in 'Education Excellence Everywhere': 'Multi-academy trusts (MATs) and teaching school alliances have spread collaboration across the country, with the best school leaders providing challenge and support for underperforming schools' (DfE, 2016, p. 6). 'In 2017 almost three quarters of all academies were part of a MAT' (Ofsted, 2019b, p. 4), with academies being 35 per cent of all state-funded maintained schools in England in 2019. Primary schools make up 27 per cent of academies in England (Ofsted, 2019b) and is the phase in which the majority of small schools are operating.

Our experience of the way small schools are supported in MATs is variable. The initial challenge for the small schools is to be accepted by the MAT as a viable financial option. The continued underfunding of small schools (O'Brien, 2019) has created financial challenges that make them unattractive to MATs, particularly as MATs have to run on a zero budget (no financial deficits are allowed). 'Education Excellence Everywhere' (DfE, 2016) states that a MAT requires ten to 15 academies to develop centralised systems and functions to deliver benefits, such as to offer career opportunities. This sustainability of the MAT is associated with total pupil numbers, making the addition of a small school with financial challenges undesirable based on the increase in central administrative and capital costs in relation to per pupil funding.

There appears to be little reason for a MAT to take on a small school, yet many MATs in our experience have taken a more community-based view and absorbed the cost to support the value they perceive the small school brings to the community it serves. An example of a MAT working to support and develop small schools is Kernow Learning Trust, a 17-primary school MAT in Cornwall. Small schools have been welcomed into the MAT and are included in whole MAT professional development and school improvement practices, with specialist teachers and leaders being seen as a resource of the MAT to be shared with the schools that need them. This has worked especially well with the new Education Inspection Framework (EIF) focus on subject knowledge and leadership, allowing small schools to be supported by subject leads in the MAT.

In Kernow Learning Trust, staff appointments are made to the MAT, not individual schools. Opportunities for staff progression are made available within the schools of the MAT, which has supported an increase in both MAT teacher and leader recruitment and retention. The small schools have maintained their special features, and they have been provided with opportunities as part of the MAT to access additional resources, which was seen by the MAT Trustees as stabilising and sustaining for small schools' workforce. We have seen similar outcomes identified by the Trustees of The Learning Academy Partnership South West in Devon, a MAT also with small schools and MAT-based teaching contracts. Our experience suggests that a MAT that values small schools and has a

MAT-based teaching recruitment and professional development policy can create a positive professional experience for teachers and leaders in small schools, which by proxy supports recruitment and retention.

National standards

All schools in England are part of a performativity agenda and 'regulatory gaze' (Osgood, 2006, p. 7) that is focused on a national standard with target data. Small schools have been perceived as having 'an uncomfortable and sometimes adversarial relationship' with accountability and performativity measures (Strike, 2008, p. 169), due the inevitable unreliability of small pupil numbers on the statistics that are applied. National performance targets are skewed by small pupil number for per cent outcomes, for example, an attendance target of 95 per cent for all schools nationally.

It could be argued that the multiple responsibilities of a small teaching workforce and less funding (compared to larger schools) to implement regulatory body expectations, such as to have subject leads in primary schools (Ofsted, 2019a), results in huge challenges when held accountable in failing to meet performance targets. This performativity/accountability challenge should not be underestimated as an agent for discontent of the workforce in small schools, both for teachers and leaders.

Having a national standard of performance for all schools at the same per cent expectation does not take into account the school context and is set to create failure to achieve. The pressure in small schools to meet the expected standard for pupils in progress, attainment and attendance is huge and, as we have said before, easily lost through small pupil numbers skewing data. Added to this accountability for school performance is the Education Inspection Framework (EIF) (overseen by the Office for Standards in Education, Children's Services and Skills – Ofsted – as the regulatory and inspection body for school standards), which is again national and applied to all schools regardless of context.

In 2019, Ofsted introduced a new EIF (Ofsted, 2019a), having developed a greater understanding of contextual issues for schools in the preceding years of inspection and through research (such as Ovenden-Hope & Passy, 2019).[3] Ofsted had been criticised for its previous EIF focusing too heavily on pupil data to inform judgements on school performance. The new Ofsted framework will still look at pupil data, but to inform an understanding of the purpose and usefulness of those data and to inform judgements on 'intent, implementation and impact' (Ofsted, 2019a, pp. 9–10). For small schools, one of the biggest challenges of the new EIF, outside of data being reviewed against percentage national standards, is the requirement for subject leads to develop the curriculum. In small schools, teachers will teach a range of subjects, but having a specialist in each of the curriculum areas can be difficult, if not impossible to achieve, if not within a MAT.

An inspector noted on a government blog for Ofsted that small schools would be worried about this and attempted to offer reassurance:

> I know that some small schools are nervous about the new education inspection framework (EIF) and the demands that our 'deep dives' will place on staff. . . . Our inspectors understand the unique challenges you face as small schools.
>
> *(Sheridan, 2019)*

This reassurance and recognition of the context of small schools by Ofsted suggests progress, but the overview of policy affecting small schools' workforce we have offered in this chapter, and by proxy the effect on teacher recruitment and retention, does not create a sense of optimism for the fair treatment of small schools.

Sense-making for the small school workforce

So how can we 'sense-make' (Odden & Russ, 2019) education policy since 2010 in relation to small schools' teaching workforce in England? Using Odden and Russ' (2019) definition of sense-making, we must understand the 'dynamic process of building or revising an explanation in order to "figure something out"' (pp. 191–192). In this chapter, we have tried to 'figure out' the lack of consensus around small schools by exploring the relationship between government policy and small school workforce supply (and the survival of small schools in the future).

There has been a shift in Ofsted's consideration of small schools when making judgements under the new EIF, but this appears a minor change in the face of policy reform that is pushing through large schools in large MATs for an efficient education system. The NFF does nothing to rectify the disparity in funding that small schools have experienced, and the move of these schools to a MAT, if it will take them, appears inevitable.

A shift of government focus is required if the disadvantages experienced by small schools are to be addressed and the proposition of working in one is to become attractive to existing and new staff. Educational policymakers need to consider the specific contextual challenges (not only Ofsted), and adjust standards, targets and funding to reflect these. From a political perspective, it is important to note that 'small schools cannot flourish on the margins of the system: they need to be an integral part of it' (Raywid, 2002, p. 51). For small schools to sustain and recruit a high-quality workforce, the removal of policy-related challenges is essential.

Notes

1 Schools in England under Local Authority control receive a grant from the Local Authority the school resides in. The Local Authority receive school funding direct from the government for any schools within their control. Local Authority schools also have to

adhere to national regulations in relation to their policies and practices, including the curriculum, and achieve national benchmarks for performance. Academies receive their grant funding directly from the government and have independent regulations that allow them to develop their own policies and practices, including curriculum, but still have to achieve the national benchmarks for performance.

2 See note 1.

3 Professor Ovenden-Hope and Dr Passy were invited by Ofsted to deliver a seminar for Her Majesty's Inspectors in 2018 at Taunton on coastal, rural and small school challenges for school improvement and the ways school leaders were dealing with this to support their pupils' outcomes.

References

Audit Commission. (1990). *Rationalising primary school provision.* London: HMSO.

Blunkett, D. (2014). *Review of education structures, functions and the raising of standards for all: Putting students and parents first.* London: Labour Party. Retrieved from Education in England website: www.educationengland.org.uk/documents/pdfs/2014-blunkett-review.pdf

Carter, M. (2003). *What do we know about small schools? Review for National College of School leadership.* London: NCSL.

Church of England. (2018, March). *Embracing change: Rural and small schools.* London: Church of England Education Office. Retrieved from The Church of England website: www.churchofengland.org/sites/default/files/2018-03/Rural%20Schools%20-%20 Embracing%20Change%20WEB%20FINAL.pdf

Commons Education Select Committee [CESC]. (2012, May 1). *Great teachers: Attracting, training and retaining the best: Ninth Report of session 2010–12, vol. 1.* (HC 1515-I, 2010–12). London: TSO. Retrieved from parliament.uk website: https://publications. parliament.uk/pa/cm201012/cmselect/cmeduc/1515/1515.pdf

Coopers & Lybrand. (1995). *Safety in numbers: Small schools and collaborative arrangements.* Report commissioned by NASUWT, Birmingham.

Corbett, M., & Tinkham, J. (2014). Small schools in a big world: Thinking about a wicked problem. *Alberta Journal of Educational Research, 60*(4), 691–707.

Craig, I., & Blandford, S. (2004, September). *Building for the future: A study of small schools.* Paper presented at the British Education Research Association Annual Conference, University of Manchester. Retrieved from University of Leeds website: www.leeds. ac.uk/educol/documents/00003782.htm

Department for Education [DfE]. (2010). *The importance of teaching: The Schools White Paper 2010.* London: DfE. Retrieved from gov.uk website: https://assets.publishing. service.gov.uk/government/uploads/system/uploads/attachment_data/file/175429/ CM-7980.pdf

Department for Education [DfE]. (2011). *Training our next generation of outstanding teachers.* London: DfE. Retrieved from gov.uk website: www.gov.uk/government/publications/ training-our-next-generation-of-outstanding-teachers-an-improvement-strategy-for-discussion

Department for Education [DfE]. (2016, March). *Education excellence everywhere.* CM 9230. London: DfE. Retrieved from gov.uk website: https://assets.publishing.service. gov.uk/government/uploads/system/uploads/attachment_data/file/508447/Educa tional_Excellence_Everywhere.pdf

Department for Education [DfE]. (2017). *The national funding formula for schools and high needs* [policy document]. London: DfE. Retrieved from gov.uk website: https://assets. publishing.service.gov.uk/government/uploads/system/uploads/attachment_data/

file/648532/national_funding_formula_for_schools_and_high_needs-Policy_document.pdf

Department for Education [DfE]. (2018, July). *The national funding formulae for schools and high needs 2019 to 2020.* London: DfE. Retrieved from gov.uk website: https://assets. publishing.service.gov.uk/government/uploads/system/uploads/attachment_data/ file/728273/National_funding_formula_policy_document_-_2019_to_2020_-_ BRANDED.pdf

Department for Education [DfE]. (2019a). *Teacher retention and recruitment strategy.* London: DfE. Retrieved from gov.uk website: https://assets.publishing.service.gov.uk/ government/uploads/system/uploads/attachment_data/file/786856/DFE_Teacher_ Retention_Strategy_Report.pdf

Department for Education [DfE]. (2019b). *The national funding formulae for schools and high needs 2020–21.* London: DfE. Retrieved from gov.uk website: https://assets. publishing.service.gov.uk/government/uploads/system/uploads/attachment_data/ file/838394/National_funding_formula_policy_document_-_2020_to_2021.pdf

Harber, C. (1996). *Small schools and democratic practice.* Nottingham: Educational Heretics Press.

HM Government. (2010a, May 20). *The coalition: Our programme of government.* London: The Cabinet Office. Retrieved from gov.uk website: www.gov.uk/government/ publications/the-coalition-our-programme-for-government

HM Government. (2010b). *Academies Act.* London: HM Government. Retrieved from legis lation.gov website: www.legislation.gov.uk/ukpga/2010/32/pdfs/ukpga_20100032_ en.pdf

HM Government. (2011). *Education Act.* London: HM Government. Retrieved from legi slation.uk website: www.legislation.gov.uk/ukpga/2011/21/pdfs/ukpga_20110021_ en.pdf

House of Commons. (2010, July 19). *House of Commons debates.* Volume no. 514, part no. 34. Hansard. Retrieved from parliament.uk website: https://publications.parliament. uk/pa/cm201011/cmhansrd/cm100719/debindx/100719-x.htm

Hurd, S., Jones, M., McNamara, O., & Craig, B. (2007). Initial teacher education as a driver for professional learning and school improvement in the primary phase. *The Curriculum Journal, 18,* 307–326.

The Key. (2019). *The challenges of leading a rural school.* London: The Key. Retrieved from The Key website: https://resources.thekeysupport.com/rural-schools-report

Luke, I., & Cade, S. (2017). Big ideas about small schools. In GuildHE (Ed.), *World-class teachers, world-class education* (pp. 30–40). London: GuildHE.

Moore, T. (2019). Funding formula threatens small schools with extinction. *Schools Week.* Retrieved from Schools Week website: https://schoolsweek.co.uk/funding- formula-threatens-small-schools-with-extinction/

O'Brien, N. (2019, July). The decline of small schools and village schools [research note]. *Onward.* Retrieved from www.ukonward.com/wp-content/uploads/2019/07/ Primary-schools.pdf

Odden, T. O. B., & Russ, S. R. (2019). Defining sensemaking: Bringing clarity to a fragmented theoretical construct. *Science Education, 103,* 187–205.

Ofsted. (2019a, May). *Education inspection framework.* No. 190015. Retrieved from gov. uk website: https://assets.publishing.service.gov.uk/government/uploads/system/ uploads/attachment_data/file/801429/Education_inspection_framework.pdf

Ofsted. (2019b, July). *Multi-academy trusts: Benefits, challenges and functions.* No. 190032. Manchester: Ofsted. Retrieved from gov.uk website: https://assets.publishing.service. gov.uk/government/uploads/system/uploads/attachment_data/file/817085/Multi_ academy_trusts_benefits_challenges_and_functions.pdf

Osgood, J. (2006). Deconstructing professionalism in the early years: Resisting the regulatory gaze. *Contemporary Issues in Early Childhood*, 7(1), 5–14.

Ovenden-Hope, T., & Passy, R. (2019). *Educational Isolation: A challenge for schools in England*. Plymouth: Plymouth Marjon University and University of Plymouth. Retrieved from Marjon University website: www.marjon.ac.uk/educational-isolation

Raywid, M. A. (2002). The policy environments of small schools and schools-within-schools. *Educational Leadership*, February, 47–51.

Sheridan, M. (2019, October 8). 'Deep diving' in small schools [blog]. *Ofsted*. Retrieved from gov.uk website: https://educationinspection.blog.gov.uk/2019/10/08/deep-diving-in-small-schools/

Strike, K. A. (2008). Small schools: Size or community? *American Journal of Education*, May, 169–190.

Wallin, D. C., & Newton, P. (2014). Teaching principals in small rural schools: 'My cup overfloweth'. *Alberta Journal of Educational Research*, 60(4), 708–725.

Wildy, H., Sigurðardóttir, S. M., & Faulkner, R. (2014). Leading the small rural school in Iceland and Australia: Building leadership capacity. *Educational Management, Administration & Leadership*, 42(4S), 104–118.

PART II

Perspectives on teacher recruitment and retention internationally

10

PROFESSIONAL LEARNING AND RECRUITMENT AND RETENTION

What global regions can tell us

Philippa Cordingley and Bart Crisp

Introduction

System structures in education affect and model trust in teachers, individually and collectively. This trust can be either reinforced, or unintentionally undermined by decision-makers in schools and education systems, especially by those reacting to high-stakes accountability measures in short timescales. In the research discussed in this chapter (Cordingley et al., 2019), we explore how teachers' professional learning can be designed and deployed to address policy needs around recruitment and retention. Our findings suggest that teacher retention and recruitment are better achieved through ensuring teachers feel trusted, and this can be achieved through continuing professional development and learning (CPDL). We define CPDL as facilitator-led development and training for practitioners and leaders which is focused on providing an understanding of research evidence and how it can be applied to practice. The evidence indicates that, to have an impact, this CPDL needs to be structured in ways that enable teachers to feel accountable to their students and to each other. This is achieved through shared risk-taking and through pacing change, making space for teacher leadership and modelling and supporting its development.

Design of the underpinning research

The Centre for the Use of Research and Evidence in Education (CUREE) conducted a research study between 2015 and 2017 for Education International (Cordingley et al., 2019), a global union federation of teacher unions, which focused on seven research sites that all consisted of coherent and relatively autonomous education systems. The seven systems selected for analysis and comparison in the study were Berlin, Chile, Kenya, Ontario, Scotland, Singapore and

Sweden. These systems were mostly national ones, but also included two large-scale regional systems, operating within devolved national contexts. The study also aimed to ensure that it included a mix of systems from the developed and developing worlds, from the Anglosphere and non-Anglosphere, from the global North and global South, from high- and low-achieving systems as ranked by the Programme for International Student Assessment (PISA), and of industrialising and post-industrial contexts. For a summary of the jurisdictions researched and some of their key characteristics, see Table 10.1.

The mixed-method study spanned two major phases. In the first phase, the research team conducted a literature review of explorations of dimensions of educators' professional identities. This was closely followed by a series of high-level scans of each system, based on a combination of:

1   a sweep of policy documentation (identified in collaboration with key individuals in major teachers' unions in each system as well as policymakers and academic specialists from that system) aimed at understanding the core priorities, drivers and contextual elements at the core of each system's decision-making, and;
2   interviews with four to six key individuals (policymakers and teacher leaders) identified by the teachers' associations and government leads in each country, to understand the rationale and historical dimensions of policy which underpinned those priorities and drivers.

This high-level scan was then synthesised into a set of research posters, which provided a consistent analytical framework that both enabled us to check our data and interpretation with local actors, and to make systematic comparisons between systems. This framework split the high-level scan of the systems in question into areas such as: the public status of the teaching profession and degree of autonomy the system afforded individual teachers; approaches to training, employment and retention; focus on teachers' professional development and learning; and policy approaches to pedagogy, curriculum and classroom culture.

In the second phase of the project, the research team designed a series of data collection activities. These activities included a survey, which asked a total of 4,850 teachers questions about their reflections, experiences and perceptions of issues related to teachers' professional identities, and focus groups that explored similar questions. The activities were undertaken at international conferences of teachers and site visits in order to collect evidence for case studies through which key themes could be tested and explored in greater depth. The responses to these data collection activities allowed the research team to investigate how effectively the policies in each system translated into outcomes which matched their intent, to draw comparisons between different systems and different approaches to broader problems and to arrive at some conclusions about the ways in which policymakers can, intentionally and accidentally, shape the experiences of the teacher profession to which practitioners are subject.

TABLE 10.1 Research jurisdictions and some of their key characteristics

System	PISA Rank			Post-industrial or industrialising	Data Collection		Justification
	Science	Reading	Maths		Number and role of interviewees*	Number of survey respondents	
Ontario	–	–	–	Post-industrial	2 (Union contact, education ministry official)	1,674 (English), 399 (French)	Example of a system operating within a devolved national context. Two communities within one area: French and English.
Chile (Nb. this was a late addition because another country withdrew)	44	42	48	Post-industrial	2 (Union contact, education ministry official)	48	Example of a country which has average PISA performance. A relatively non-Anglosphere country with around 5 per cent of population speaking English.
Berlin	16	11	16	Post-industrial	2 (Union contact, education ministry official)	701	Operating within a devolved national context.
Kenya	–	–	–	Industrialising	2 (British Council Kenya, education ministry official)	109	Example of a developing, industrialising country. An example of a country within the African continent. Also provided an interesting case study on the impact of CPD on professional identities.
Singapore	1	1	1	Post-industrial	2 (Union contact, education ministry official)	207	Example of a high-performing system which is ranked at the top in PISA. Also provided an interesting case study around how teacher evaluation impacts on teachers' professional identities – particularly being a country where teaching is a high-valued profession.

(Continued)

TABLE 10.1 (Continued)

System	PISA Rank			Post-industrial or industrialising	Data Collection		Justification
	Science	Reading	Maths		Number and role of interviewees*	Number of survey respondents	
Sweden	28	17	24	Post-industrial	3 (Union contact, Policy adviser MoE, education ministry official)	351	Example of an Anglosphere country (one of the best English-speaking countries in the world). An interesting case study due to its high levels of migration.
Scotland	–	–	–	Post-industrial	3 (Union contact, Director of Learning for the Scottish Government, education ministry official)	1,361	Example of a country which is within the UK. Interesting system due to its recent curriculum reforms (Curriculum of Excellence) and its impact on the system – particularly in relation to teacher identity.

What emerged is a complex and dynamic interaction between a number of key drivers of teachers' professional identities which link with recruitment and retention, encompassing:

- Access to high-quality CPDL.
- Efforts by government to raise the status of the profession (through, for example, salaries that compare well with other professions and ensuring that government policies and communications include positive appreciation of teachers' contributions to society).
- Opportunities for career progression.
- Efforts to develop an increasingly teacher-led education system.

These all emerge as important, mutually reinforcing factors and, in the high-performing countries (Ontario and Singapore) where all these factors were firmly embedded in policies and day-to-day practices, the interactions between them worked to create a virtuous cycle of improvement.

While part of a broader whole, the nature of teachers' experiences of CPDL and its contribution to their professional identities proved to be an important and revealing avenue of exploration in their own right. The collection and cross-analysis of data focused on teachers' perceptions and the policy environments within which they were developed, and allowed us to draw some (tentative) conclusions about the impact of the CPDL teachers receive on their willingness to join and remain a member of the teaching profession. This chapter identifies and explores these conclusions, together with what they tell us about how teachers' professional learning can be designed and deployed to address policy needs around recruitment and retention.

Landscape of teacher recruitment and retention in case study countries

Participants in our study identified a number of links between teacher recruitment and retention and CPDL. Policymakers in high-performing countries saw investing in high-quality CPDL for all teachers as an important factor in recruiting and retaining a strong workforce. They also saw it as a way of building self-sustaining capacity. By creating career pathways that depend on CPDL for advancement, and which use the middle leaders to support the CPDL of less experienced teachers, high-performing systems established a virtuous circle. This linked CPDL with expanding specialist skills to support and inform the development of national policies in relation to the curriculum, pedagogy and/ or institutional leadership in Singapore, and pedagogic workforce development in Ontario.

This strategic investment also contributed to the national advancement of teachers' professional status as citizens more broadly began to recognise the strength not just of teachers' classroom contributions, but also their contributions to national economic, social and cultural successes through policy and/or work-force development. As we will see in our discussion of the nature and focus of CPDL across these jurisdictions, in countries where performance in PISA tests and against other measures is weak, the patterns of dynamic relationships between activities which promote teacher professionalism and the extent to which this process is visible to the wider public are more complex, and the links between CPDL, pupil progress and recruitment and retention are weaker. In particular, the links between policies which promote professionalism and the perceived status of the profession are dependent on the quality of the CPDL.

There are direct links to recruitment and retention, too. Within the seven case study systems, only the two high-performing education systems, Ontario and Singapore, are currently experiencing an oversupply of qualified teachers. For example, a 2015 survey (OECD, 2015) suggested that only one in five newly qualified teachers in Ontario was able to secure a permanent position within their first year of teaching, while in Singapore it is estimated that there are on average eight applicants for every teaching position which becomes available (OECD, 2015). By contrast the data collected for our study (Cordingley et al., 2019) show that in Scotland, Chile, Berlin, Sweden and Kenya the number of professionals entering the profession and the number that subsequently leave it are high, and both are major areas of policy concern. This churn has been associated with a range of factors, of which the attractiveness of the profession in relation to teachers' working conditions, the level of respect they are afforded and the quality of investment in CPDL emerged as significant, the latter a factor that was consistent across both the medium-performing countries (Berlin, Scotland and Sweden) and the low-performing countries (Chile and Kenya).

The education location within our research which can perhaps exemplify the recruitment and retention challenges that most education systems face is Sweden, where both issues were live challenges at the time of this research. According to the OECD (2015), teaching in Sweden in 2015 was considered a low-status and unattractive profession, and only 12 per cent of teachers who responded to the OECD's survey felt that teachers were respected in Sweden. The lack of enthusiasm for joining or remaining in the profession is, according to Swedish teachers participating in our research, due to the existence of a heavy workload for all Swedish teachers, salaries that are relatively uncompetitive with other professions, limited opportunities for feedback on quality of teaching practice, extremely low levels of CPDL and a lack of clarity around the working relationships between teachers and school leaders.

The wider evidence about CPDL and recruitment and retention

The wider research (described later) which appeared in the literature review for our study echoes features that emerge through our analysis of how governments seek to influence teachers' professional identities. There are, for example, a number of analyses of the trends underpinning the current, alarming reductions in teacher recruitment and increases in difficulties of retaining teachers in England that highlight the importance of increasing access to high-quality CPDL. This was emphasised, for example, in NFER's report on teacher supply (Worth, Lynch, Hillary, Rennie, & Andrade, 2018), in the Higher Education Policy Institute's report on the past, present and future of teacher training (Cater, 2017), in the House of Commons' Education Committee's report of its enquiry into the recruitment and retention of teachers (2017) and in the Sutton Trust's analysis of the shortfall in science teachers (Kirby & Cullinane, 2017).

Broader academic research echoes these findings. Sims (2018), for example, identifies a number of other researchers who found evidence that CPDL and teacher recruitment and retention were linked when analysed at the level of individual CPDL interventions, including Coldwell (2017), Taylor, Yates, Kinsella, and Meyer (2011) and Kraft, Marinell, and Shen-Wei Yee (2016). Although Sims (2018) notes that the picture emerging from these researchers does not support a simplistic relationship between the two, such as 'increasing CPDL increases teacher recruitment and retention', nevertheless, there is good evidence of a link of some kind, albeit one that is dependent in part on other factors such as quality of CPDL. Allen and Sims (2017) also found similar results for a National Science, Technology, Engineering and Maths (STEM) Learning Network CPDL course, leading in their research to an increase by 160 per cent in the odds of teachers who took part in the programme staying in the profession compared to those who had not taken part.

Key factors linking CPDL and teacher recruitment and retention

Our analysis of the survey data from the seven case study sites draws together policy data, survey data and contextual data from, for example, TALIS and PISA. It revealed the following linked factors as being strongly and positively associated with a relatively large number of professionals joining and remaining in the teaching profession:

- Teaching being regarded as a high-status profession and valued by society. As exemplification of this, in the survey for CUREE's research, 94 per cent (165 out of 176) of responding practitioners agreed that education is valued in Singapore (where recruitment and retention is high), in contrast to a TALIS survey where only 34 per cent of Chilean teachers and 22 per cent of Scottish teachers (where recruitment and retention are low) reported feeling valued by society.
- High levels of participation in CPDL. This was especially prevalent in Singapore, where, according to TALIS, 93 per cent of teachers reported participating in professional development workshops or courses, compared to the TALIS average of 71 per cent.

- Good opportunities for progression or promotion within the profession. For example, government and union officials cited recent policy reviews by the Kenyan Government, such as the internal review carried out by the government for the *Kenya Vision 2030* policy initiative as highlighting that limited opportunities for promotion and budgetary constraints have led to low morale among teachers and low levels of teacher recruitment and retention.

In addition, there was also an interesting trend across all seven jurisdictions involved in our study of responding to data from PISA about performance (whether high, medium or low) with an attempt to build an increasingly teacher-led profession. For instance, in Scotland there was an emphasis on teacher autonomy embedded within the Curriculum for Excellence and/or the development of middle leaders both as leaders of CPDL within their schools and as collaborative researchers.

The demands of prose require that each of these four factors be analysed in turn, and these analyses can be seen later. However, it is important to emphasise at the start that in the seven education systems studied there were dynamic interactions that meant that all were capable of setting up both virtuous and vicious cycles of development.

The status of the profession

Our research revealed a mixed picture with regard to the relative status of education as a profession. It also revealed an interesting interaction between the status of the profession and teacher supply. As Figure 10.1 shows, the relationship between teacher recruitment and retention and teacher status and working conditions is, more or less, a linear one.

By and large, systems that position teaching as a relatively low-level and undemanding profession and where CPDL is minimal in quantity or superficial in quality tend to struggle with teacher supply. Systems where teaching is considered a higher status and demanding profession and is accorded good working conditions, including high-quality CPDL that reflect those demands, are more likely to be experiencing oversupply of teachers than undersupply.

In Singapore, for example, 60 per cent (112 of the 176) of teachers who responded to our survey agreed with the statement that 'Education is valued in my country', as compared to a mere 4 per cent (7 out of 154) of teachers from Sweden, and 5 per cent (1 out of 8) of teachers from Chile (Cordingley et al., 2019). This also extended to the degree to which teachers felt they were respected as professionals – in Singapore 50 per cent (90 out of 176) respondents agreed, compared to only 9 per cent (1 out of 8) of teachers in Chile.

There is similar evidence of strong alignment between teachers' perceptions of their professional status and the performance of the system in which they are operating. As Figure 10.2 indicates, and even accounting for the degree to which esteem and status are culturally specific and relate to current and historical trends

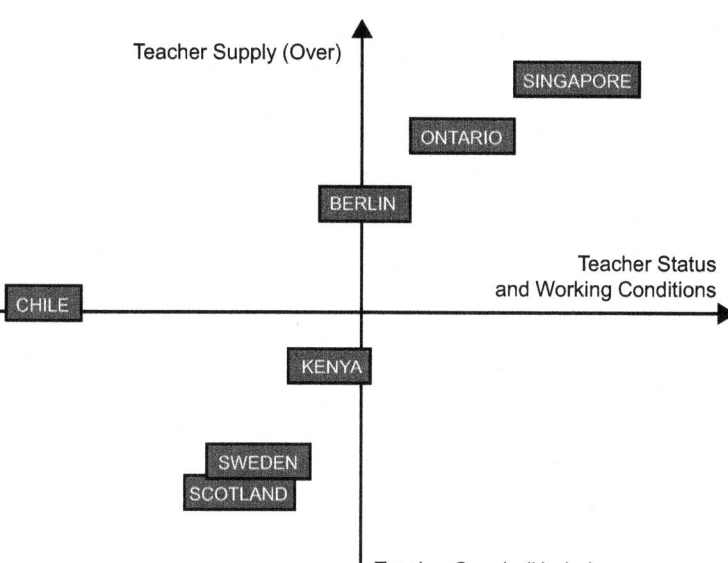

FIGURE 10.1   The relationship between teacher status and teacher recruitment and retention

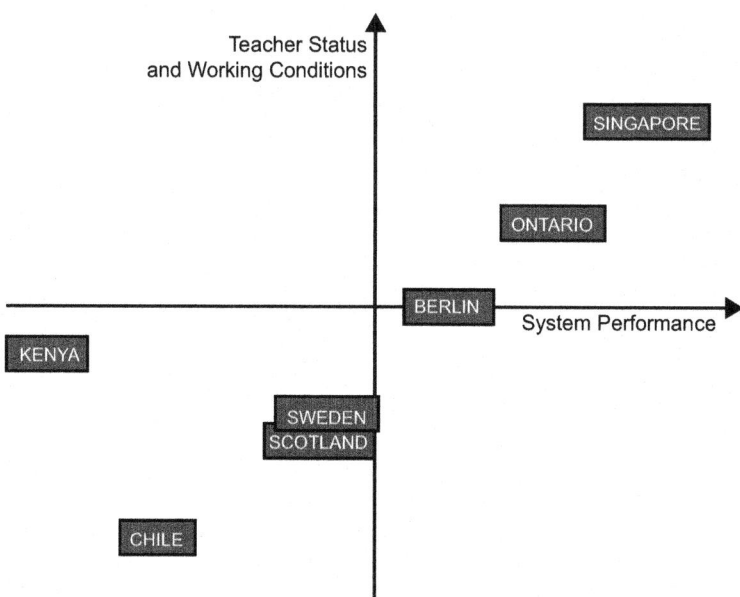

FIGURE 10.2   The relationship between teachers' perceptions of status and system performance

in the development of education provision, systems where teachers perceive their professional status to be high are also likely to be high performing.

The notable exception to this general trend is Kenya, where system performance was judged to be the lowest of the seven, but where a greater proportion of teachers felt themselves to be held in high esteem and working in good conditions than in Chile, Scotland or Sweden. Our contention, based on the information available about different policy contexts, is that this can be attributed to high levels of decentralisation and variance (such as between urban and rural schools) present in Kenya, as distinct from comparatively greater consistency between schools in different contexts in systems such as Scotland and Sweden. Further research in this area is needed to be able to draw firmer conclusions.

The fact that Figure 10.1 and Figure 10.2 illustrate a similar pattern suggests strongly that, perhaps unsurprisingly, the links between teacher supply and teachers' status, working conditions and system performance are strong and interconnected.

Participation in CPDL

There is also reason to believe from the evidence in our study that the amount of time teachers spend taking part in CPDL has an impact on teacher recruitment and retention in that system. The relationship, however, between these two variables is complex and non-linear.

The ways in which teachers experience and participate in centralised policy initiatives around CPDL vary greatly between the seven systems. It is possible to identify a relationship of some kind between a centralised, policy-driven focus on CPDL and the levels of teacher participation; the vast majority of Singaporean teacher respondents said that they did as much CPDL as they would like, while the corresponding figure for Swedish respondents was under a third.

In between these responses, however, this link becomes more complicated. For example, 74 per cent (28 out of 40) of surveyed teachers in Kenya reported that they were able to do as much CPDL as they would like to, compared to only 44 per cent (632 out of 1,389) of teachers in Ontario, despite Ontario having a much stronger policy commitment to CPDL. It is worth noting, however, that conceptions of CPDL in Kenya were much more strongly linked to specific formal qualifications and certification and that CPDL is a new policy initiative largely positioned as a driver of system reforms geared to correcting deficits. In Ontario, by contrast, CPDL is understood as a professional responsibility and is the result of a 15-year strategic commitment to investing in and strengthening the quality of CPDL. In addition, the commitment to formal qualifications in Kenya sits in contrast to approaches to CPDL in most or all of the other systems explored, meaning that comparing answers from Kenyan teachers to those in other systems is complex.

In Scotland, in spite of inconsistent and centralised resourcing for CPDL, nearly all responding teachers said that they actively sought to develop their teaching, and over three-quarters reported participating in development activities on an ongoing basis. It is also important to note that the strong commitment to CPDL in Singapore does not automatically equate to greater satisfaction from teachers and thus a stronger environment for teacher recruitment and retention. This is because, while Singapore has a significant system-level focus on providing teachers with a large amount of high-quality CPDL, from the perspective of some teachers this can and does give rise to 'professional development fatigue': a source of tension in terms of Singaporean teachers' (otherwise self-confident) professional identities.

As can be seen in Figure 10.3, it does not appear to be the case that merely increasing the concentration of CPDL that teachers experience leads to greater system performance.

Based on other evidence to emerge through the study, we believe that the key variable here is the quality and positioning (perceived and actual) of CPDL. In the case of Chile and Kenya, CPDL has largely been introduced via a deficit model in which CPDL's purpose is seen, more or less exclusively, as addressing weaknesses in the system, and thus is aimed at teachers' practice. In Sweden, Scotland, and to some extent Berlin, the issue appears to be more about the depth of CPDL. For example, in Berlin, according to our survey data, virtually all CPDL is perceived by teachers to be unsatisfactory in terms of depth and quality, and in particular to be too short term and lacking in opportunities for serious engagement from practitioners.

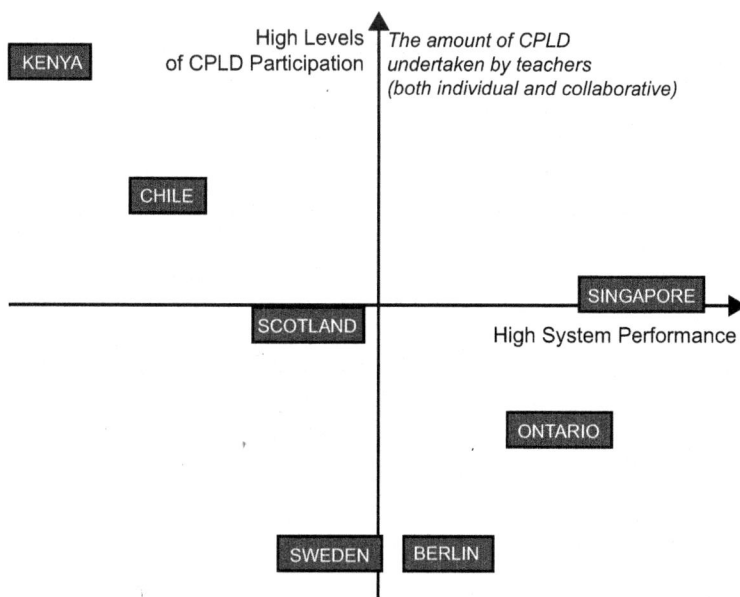

FIGURE 10.3 System performance and the quantity of CPDL undertaken by teachers

This speaks to a core part of our thesis about the links between CPDL and teacher recruitment and retention. The comparison between Singapore and Sweden demonstrates that while the simple volume of CPDL that teachers receive is important, more is not necessarily better. A deeper exploration of the data indicates that at least as important as *how much* CPDL teachers receive is *how good* the CPDL teachers receive is and how it is positioned. Superficial CPDL, or CPDL positioned as remedying deficits in teachers' practice (as opposed to CPDL designed to create and reinforce a mindset of lifelong teacher learning), seems to be at least as strongly linked with significant challenges in teacher recruitment and retention as an insufficient supply.

Links between CPDL, career pathways and opportunities for leadership, and teacher recruitment and retention

The extent to which performance appraisal, broadly conceived career pathways and progress are formally linked to CPDL opportunities, including coaching, varied across the seven systems. In Singapore and Ontario, the systems where CPDL is arguably the most centralised and prioritised by education policymakers, CPDL was linked to performance review through a process designed to identify ongoing support identified as advantageous as part of the review process. But this was not formally linked to career and/or pay progression. Rather the emphasis was on a process designed to foster teacher development and be specific about opportunities for additional support where required. By contrast in Berlin, another system with centralised CPDL resourcing, there is little to no evidence of performance-related appraisal structures linked to CPDL participation and/or certification. This may be linked to the relatively high number of teachers who believe they are not given sufficient incentives to pursue CPDL by their employers, and their view that the CPDL support available is short term, resembling briefings more than development opportunities.

Career progression and CPDL are each the product of complex factors, and link through to other elements of teacher recruitment and retention, often in dynamic ways. For example, the degree of decision-making authority that rests with teachers is a key factor in teachers' career progression, recruitment and retention, and the way in which CPDL provision is structured. Teacher decision-making, especially in relation to the CPDL teachers can access, is therefore a particularly interesting factor in recruitment and retention to explore. This is especially true given that the evidence appears to suggest that there are multiple ways in which teacher decision-making or autonomy, as well as leadership, can be used to establish a virtuous circle of strong career progression, linked to strong recruitment and retention regimes.

The evidence emerging from the illustrative case study from Ontario exemplifies the potential contribution of national investment in high-quality support for teacher leadership development, coupled with giving teachers responsibility for supporting colleagues early on in their careers. Here, a clearly articulated and supportive pathway for leadership development appears to have been both an outcome of and a contributing factor in developing a strong teacher recruitment and retention environment. In the case of Singapore, by contrast, the same outcome has been achieved via an alternative approach – specifically the creation of a series of diverse pathways of equal status (pedagogy, curriculum content and school organisation) for teacher career progression which enable practitioners to identify an area of specialism of practice which best suits their preferences and aptitudes.

This suggests two things: first, that providing teachers with clear and strong pathways for career progression probably has benefits from a teacher recruitment and retention standpoint, and second, that there is space for differentiation in how those pathways can be constructed to bring this about. But it also carries a third implication, that this is a two-way street; weak teacher recruitment and retention may well undermine the development of strong teacher career pathways and the effective development of teacher leadership and autonomy.

The picture, however, is not linear. For some factors, such as the initial qualifications required for entry into the profession, our research suggests a more complex relationship with teacher supply. For example, while setting the bar higher for entry into the profession can reduce the supply of new teachers, this also tended to be linked with the profession being seen as having a higher status. Commonly, the relationship between the requirements for initial qualifications and under- or oversupply of teachers is interconnected with other factors that play more of a role than the entry bar itself. For example, in Berlin, teaching is a master's-level profession, requiring the completion of a five-year course and a further 18 months' preparation. The number of students who complete the MA component is high, but close to half who pass do not go on to become newly qualified teachers, attributing their choice not to pursue a career in teaching to high stress levels and workload, thus resulting in teacher shortages.

The effects of government aspirations to develop teacher-led systems

The rise of the OECD's PISA test as a mechanism for supporting government decision-making in education policy has had a powerful impact on debates and policy-making in education around the world. In particular, the PISA tests have led to an intriguing convergence in approaches to policy-making from systems which are or can be otherwise highly distinctive from one another, and have led to a number of similarities across jurisdictions in relation to new directions of travel.

All seven jurisdictions in our research regarded an increasingly successful education system and, with that, an increasingly successful teaching workforce, as key to their nation's future prosperity. In this context, the influence of the trajectories revealed by OECD PISA data emerged as a common driver. Interestingly, different as they are historically, socially and culturally, representatives from each jurisdiction also explained that they were attempting to develop an increasingly 'teacher-led' education system, with the implication in all cases being that this included some form of teacher autonomy in terms of the professional learning they received. This meant different things in different settings and so was a fruitful avenue for teasing out differences in approaches to structuring and/or influencing the development of teachers' professional identities. Respondents to the CUREE country surveys in phase two of this project suggested that one key indicator that education systems are genuinely teacher-led could be that teachers felt they and their colleagues had a significant voice in national policy-making. Across the seven jurisdictions, relatively few teachers felt they could meaningfully affect national policy, despite often feeling high levels of autonomy in their own classrooms. For example, teachers in Chile did not seem to feel at all connected with educational policy in their jurisdiction, particularly regarding their pay and how they were assessed. The picture was similar in Kenya, with the recently introduced performance appraisal system having met with resistance from trade unions because it was seen as essentially a 'disciplinary' development. In Berlin, teachers' views of leadership were largely limited to their direct teaching, and teachers participating in the survey did not seem to want actively to pursue leadership roles at a local or national level. Many teachers reported feeling alienated about system-level decision-making in Ontario, too, believing themselves to have very little input into what happens in education and around the curriculum in particular, although they were much more confident about their contribution to decision-making about teacher development on the ground.

There were two key factors shaping the nature and effectiveness of the intentions to develop a teacher-led system. The first determining factor was the degree and type of decision-making available to teachers. We analysed this specifically in relation to the curriculum and pedagogy. In some countries, teachers had significant responsibilities regarding curriculum development, acting occasionally individually but rather more commonly collectively. More often, teachers had significant and increasing responsibility for shaping pedagogy. In Ontario and Singapore, two education systems which excel in PISA, both pedagogy and curriculum are specified to a significant degree at system level. But in Singapore, teachers collectively make a very strong contribution to those specifications through the creation and mobilisation of the three specialist development and leadership pathways open to teachers.

The second determining factor revolves around where pedagogical decisions are made. Interestingly, as Figure 10.4 suggests, the only really clear pattern to emerge from this analysis is that high-performing systems with strong teacher supply environments specify both curriculum and pedagogic practices in some detail. But, so does at least one somewhat less successful system. Equally, some systems focus central prescription on pedagogy and others on the curriculum.

Teachers in Sweden are reported to have a high degree of autonomy, the highest of any system explored in our study in relation to making decisions about the content of the curriculum. National education goals in Sweden are set and

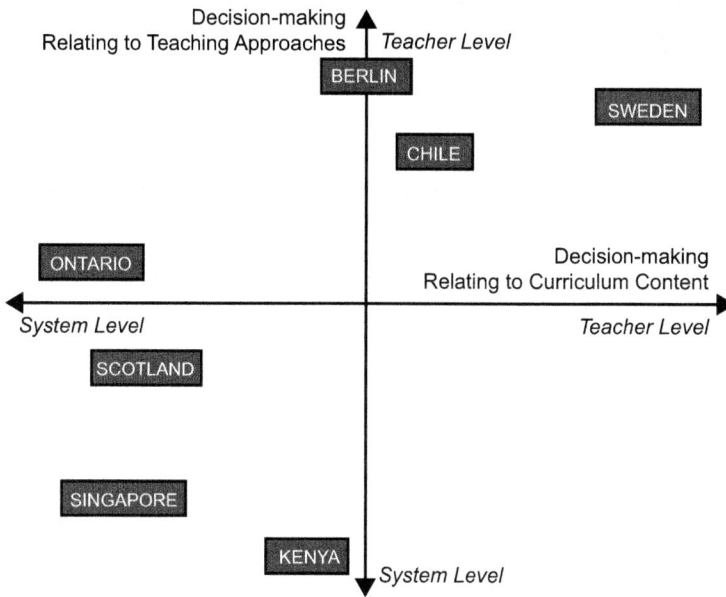

FIGURE 10.4 Decision-making relating to teaching approaches and curriculum content

evaluated by the Ministry of Education and Research, but decisions about how best to achieve these goals are made at the municipal and school levels. This is supported by an explicit commitment among policymakers to 'Trust in Teachers'. Teachers in Sweden who responded to our survey felt that they had the most control, relative to those in other systems, over how they teach, the schemes of learning they use in their class, the content of the subjects they teach and how their students are assessed. Teachers at the other end of the other spectrum in Ontario, Scotland and Singapore work in systems where a great deal is specified centrally (although in Singapore this is done using the expertise of teacher leaders).

An interesting outlier, though this is not necessarily immediately apparent from Figure 10.4, is Scotland, which provides a test case of the complexity of increasing teacher leadership in relation to recruitment, retention and school improvement policy. In Scotland, large-scale policy changes, especially those responding to OECD PISA data, have generated significant policy churn which makes the picture in relation to the locus of decision-making complex and transitional. As part of its response to concern about performance in PISA tests, the Scottish Government now aspires to create a 'genuinely school- and teacher-led system which is centred on the child' and is committed to shifting more responsibilities from local authorities to schools. But this newly powerful locus for decision-making is still set in the context of a national curriculum, a structure that gives teachers very significant curriculum design responsibilities and leadership opportunities. Unfortunately, in the eyes of the teachers, without the significant practical and CPDL support needed to carry out such responsibilities, such moves were not yet being experienced as opportunities for teacher-led system development.

More broadly, decisions about teachers are made increasingly in schools, generally by leaders with some kind of current or past teaching responsibility. This certainly creates greater opportunities for incorporating a degree of deference to teaching expertise into decision-making. But, as we have seen, school-led decision-making does not yet equate in teachers' minds to increased teacher autonomy or decision-making, and high-quality CPDL, or lack of it, plays a key role in creating such connections.

Conclusions

This research identifies four broad areas where there is scope for supporting the development of teachers' professional identities through a dynamic combination of CPDL and teacher leadership in ways that enhance teacher recruitment and retention:

- Investing in explicit, promotion and celebration of teachers and teaching to recognise and celebrate the status of the profession as a fundamental building block to national success.
- Increasing the focus on the quality of CPDL that teachers experience and using this to build a more sophisticated picture of the effectiveness of teacher CPDL and of the demands made upon the profession. This could include establishing and promoting CPDL standards, and embedding the quality of CPDL in professional standards; enhancing access to CPDL; and going significantly beyond a simple increase in quantity to the adoption of an evidence-based approach to CPDL processes. In particular, this should involve emphasising the role of CPDL as a component of developing teachers as lifelong learners, as opposed to a model in which it is used to 'fix' things which are wrong with them.
- Developing increasingly teacher-led education systems, and doing so in ways which, first, provide teachers with opportunities to learn and model leadership themselves and, second, provide clarity about how the system aims to give teachers greater control over their own progression, development and practice (and, where possible, to signpost successes and areas of learning related to this goal). An example of an effective teacher-led system is Ontario.
- Giving attention to how the system structures affect and model trust in teachers, individually and collectively. This can be either reinforced, or (at least as importantly) unintentionally undermined by decision-makers in schools and education systems, especially those reacting to high-stakes accountability measures to short timescales. Trust within CPDL and the context of retention and recruitment seems to be better achieved through ensuring

CPDL is structured in ways that enable teachers to feel accountable to their students and to each other through shared risk-taking and through pacing change, making space for teacher leadership and modelling and supporting its development.

References

Allen, R., & Sims, S. (2017). Improving science teacher retention: Do National STEM Learning Network professional development courses keep science teachers in the classroom? *Education Research in STEM Subjects: Main Collection*. Retrieved from STEM Learning website: www.stem.org.uk/resources/elibrary/resource/418071/improving-science-teacher-retention-do-national-stem-learning

Cater, J. (2017). *Whither teacher education and training?* Higher Education Policy Institute Report 95. Retrieved from HEPI website: www.hepi.ac.uk/wp-content/uploads/2017/04/Embargoed-until-00.01am-Thursday-27-April-2017-WHITHER-TEACHER-EDUCATION-AND-TRAINING-Report-95-19_04_17WEB.pdf

Coldwell, M. (2017). Exploring the influence of professional development on teacher careers: A path model approach. *Teaching and Teacher Education, 61,* 189–198.

Cordingley, P., Crisp, B., Johns, P., Perry, T., Campbell, C., & Bell, M. (2019, February). Constructing teachers' professional identities. *Education International*. Retrieved from https://ei-ie.org/en/detail/16177/teachers%E2%80%99-professional-development-andconditions-vital-signs-for-student-well-being-and-progres

House of Commons Education Committee. (2017). *Recruitment and retention of teachers: Fifth report of session 2016–17.* (HC 199, 2016–17). London: House of Commons. Retrieved from parliament.uk website: https://publications.parliament.uk/pa/cm201617/cmselect/cmeduc/199/199.pdf

Kirby, P., & Cullinane, C. (2017). Research brief: Science shortfall. *The Sutton Trust*. Retrieved from Sutton Trust website: www.suttontrust.com/wp-content/uploads/2017/01/Science-shortfall_FINAL.pdf

Kraft, M. A., Marinell, W. H., & Shen-Wei Yee, D. (2016). School organizational contexts, teacher turnover, and student achievement: Evidence from panel data. *American Educational Research Journal, 53*(5), 1411–1449.

OECD. (2015). *PISA 2015 results (volume 2): Policies and practices for successful schools.* Paris: OECD Publishing. http://doi.org/10.1787/9789264267510-en

Sims, S. (2018, July). *Essays on the recruitment and retention of teachers.* PhD thesis, University College London, London. Retrieved from UCL website: https://discovery.ucl.ac.uk/id/eprint/10053430/7/Sims_10053430_thesis__SamSims_PhDThesis_Final_NoPersonalInfo.pdf

Taylor, M., Yates, A., Kinsella, P., & Meyer, L. H. (2011). Teacher professional leadership in support of teacher professional development. *Teaching and Teacher Education, 27*(1), 85–94.

Worth, J., Lynch, S., Hillary, J., Rennie, C., & Andrade, J. (2018, October). *Teacher workforce dynamics in England*. Slough: NFER. Retrieved from NFER website: https://nfer.ac.uk/teacher-workforce-dynamics-in-england/

11

HOW TO RECRUIT AND RETAIN TEACHERS IN HARD-TO-STAFF AREAS

A systematic review of the empirical evidence

Beng Huat See, Stephen Gorard, Rebecca Morris and Nada El-Soufi

Introduction: common challenges in developed nations

Attracting and retaining suitably qualified teachers in some subjects and geographical areas is a challenge common to the school staffing policies of many developed countries. More than half of the countries in Europe and almost all school districts in the US report problems, and shortages and oversupply can coexist because of the uneven distribution of teachers across phases, subjects and regions. In Germany and England, for example, there is an oversupply in some subjects and a shortage in others (European Commission/EACEA/Eurydice, 2018). In Greece, there is a shortage on some remote and small islands while there is a general oversupply of teachers in the rest of the country. Teacher shortages related to the remoteness of some regions are mentioned in half of the countries that participated in the European Commission survey. In other countries, it was the high cost of living and high proportion of disadvantaged pupils in some large urban cities (such as Brussels and London) that reportedly made it difficult to attract and retain teachers.

In England, less affluent areas have had greater difficulties in attracting qualified teachers than many other parts of the country. The North East, West Midlands and East of England are less likely to have teachers with a relevant degree teaching shortage subjects compared to London. For example, only 17 per cent of physics teachers in poorer schools outside London have a relevant degree, compared with 52 per cent in affluent areas in the rest of the country (Sibieta, 2018). In coastal-rural areas, which can be highly deprived, seven per cent of secondary teachers are unqualified, compared with 4.6 per cent in more affluent inland rural areas. (Social Mobility Commission, 2017). In the House of Commons (2017) fifth report on teacher recruitment and retention, the government acknowledged that there were wide regional variations in teacher supply. While there have been plans to encourage more teachers to work in areas most in need, these have not been very successful. The pilot for a National Teaching Service, for example, which was set up to get teachers to teach in areas most struggling to recruit, had to be abandoned after managing to recruit only 54 of 1,500 intended teachers.

To tackle these challenges, many education systems have offered incentives and implemented a range of programmes to attract potential teachers to, and retain existing teachers in, difficult-to-staff regions and for some high-demand subjects. Some of these programmes have been evaluated and tested but there is, so far, no synthesis of the research findings, so the evidence of their effectiveness is still unclear. Many of these incentives and programmes are expensive, and it would be a waste of taxpayers' money and the country's resources to continue using them if there is no evidence that they work. There is also an opportunity cost, as the money used for these incentives could be otherwise channelled to more effective programmes. If they show promise it is important to know how they can best be implemented, and the extent to which they can be deployed in other countries facing similar challenges. It is therefore crucial that these strategies are robustly evaluated and tested before more money is spent on them worldwide.

As far as we know, there has been no large-scale, comprehensive single-study review of the evidence on teacher recruitment and retention policies with a view to addressing the recurring problems in teaching supply. Previous reviews have taken a narrower focus and have not taken into account the quality and design of research in each study (see, e.g., Wheeler & Glennie, 2007). This chapter presents the findings of a systematic review of international empirical research to identify the most promising approaches in attracting and retaining teachers in hard-to-staff schools and areas.

Methods for a systematic review of research into recruiting and retaining teachers

Identification of studies

Our review began with a broad search for studies that address teacher recruitment and retention issues in general, and from these the studies relevant to hard-to-staff areas were identified and analysed separately for this chapter. The list of search terms included substantive terms about teacher supply, teacher recruitment or retention, and any causal term (or a synonym) or any research design that would be appropriate for testing a causal model, such as experiment, quasi-experiment, regression discontinuity and difference-in-difference. These were applied to 13 educational, psychological and sociological electronic databases, plus Google and Google Scholar. The results were supplemented by further studies already known to us, or referenced in studies discovered. Programmes or strategies mentioned in this literature were also followed up via reference lists to see if they had been evaluated elsewhere. The search was limited to studies published in the English language. We intentionally did not set any date limiters to keep the search open. To avoid publication bias, the search included any material published or unpublished that mentions both substantive and causal terms. We included any empirical studies with at least some type of comparative design, many of which will have low ratings for trustworthiness in terms of causal claims. A total of 6,708 research reports were identified and exported to EndNote for screening.

Each identified study was screened to remove duplicates, and for relevance on the basis of title and abstract. Only studies that related specifically to recruitment and retention for hard-to-staff areas were retained. This process removed 6,161 studies, leaving 547 which were read in full. Of these, only 52 were retained further, deemed to be relevant to the research question and at least partly concerned with staffing in hard-to-staff schools and subjects.

Data extraction

Information from these papers was summarised, including details on research design, cases used, allocation to groups, outcome measures, missing data and the results. A further 17 studies were excluded when it became clear that they were not evaluations but narrative discussions of previous research or suggestions of strategies. Of the remainder, 13 studies were excluded because they merely involved asking respondents such as headteachers which strategies they thought worked, or were important to them. Three reports were of different approaches to evaluating the same intervention by the same set of authors, and are treated as being one report here. The remaining 20 reports were passed through a quality assessment 'sieve', judging the trustworthiness of each to address a causal question, ignoring its source, and allocating a score between 1* (the minimum standard to be given any weight, including some kind of comparison) and 4* (Gorard, See, & Siddiqui, 2017). The study outcomes are classified as relevant to recruitment and/or retention. Approaches with the most highly rated studies showing positive effects are considered the most promising.

Research results

We found 20 studies of interventions relevant to staffing in difficult areas, which had 26 outcomes relevant to either or both the recruitment and retention of teachers (Table 11.1). Perhaps the first thing to note is that none of these studies is of the highest quality of design and trustworthiness (4*). Most involved some kind of financial incentive to teach in hard-to-staff schools and, on balance, such approaches appear to work. Many are from the US, and very few are from England.

TABLE 11.1 Overall

Quality of study	Positive outcome	Unclear outcome	Negative or neutral outcome
4*	–	–	–
3*	2	–	1
2*	7	–	2
1*	8	4	2

Improving recruitment

There were nine studies in our review dealing with recruitment that met at least our minimum quality for a causal claim. Overall, their results are mixed. The highest quality study (3*) had positive outcomes for recruitment (Table 11.2), but not for retention. Hough and Loeb (2013) assessed the effect of awarding higher salaries/bonuses to teachers teaching shortage subjects in schools with a high proportion of poor and ethnic minority students, in the San Francisco Unified School District. Teachers were given a rise of $500 to $6,300 (depending on the salary scale), and a $2,000 bonus for teaching in hard-to-staff schools, a retention bonus of $2,500 if they stayed on after the fourth year, and $3,000 after the eighth year. Using a difference-in-difference approach, the authors compared the recruitment and retention of 1,611 applicants with teachers in different school districts before and after the introduction of the policy (a comparison made more difficult because of the economic downturn in 2008). There was an increase in the number (from 49 per cent to 54 per cent) and proportion (27 per cent to 37 per cent) of shortage subject teachers in hard-to-staff areas. However, there was no difference in the retention rates of targeted and non-targeted teachers. Over 90 per cent of teachers stayed on in the district and over 85 per cent stayed in their school, in both groups. The authors suggested that a policy aimed at retaining teachers in a competitive labour market when the economy is doing well may not be necessary when unemployment is higher.

The next two strongest pieces (2*) also have positive results for recruitment but not for retention. Steele, Murnane, & Willett (2010) evaluated the Governor's Teaching Fellowship (GTF) scheme, involving a $20,000 incentive to attract and retain new teachers to low-performing schools for four years after becoming licensed. The teachers had to repay $5,000 for each year that they did not meet the commitment, at a period when the average starting salary for California teachers was $33,121. An instrumental variable design was used, based on 718 GTF teachers, excluding those who could not be tracked, were missing data or not enrolled at recognised institutions. GTF recipients were not randomly selected, and so may have had a predisposition to teach in low-performing schools. More teachers were enrolled during GTF, around twice as many as in the years before and after, and 28 per cent more taught in low-performing

TABLE 11.2 Recruitment

Quality of study	Positive outcome	Unclear outcome	Negative or neutral outcome
4*	–	–	–
3*	Hough and Loeb (2013)	–	–
2*	Steele, Murnane, and Willett (2010) Glazerman et al. (2013)	–	–
1*	Clewell and Villegas (2001) Waters-Weller (2009)	Gordon and Vegas (2005) Goldhaber, Destler, and Player (2010) Fowler (2003)	Dwinal (2012)

schools. So it seemed that money was an attractor. However, there was no difference in retention rates (75 per cent over four years) between recipient and non-recipients, despite the penalty clause.

Glazerman et al. (2013) examined the impact of the Talent Transfer Initiative, which offered bonuses to the highest performing teachers (those ranked in the top 20 per cent in terms of raising student attainment from year to year using a value-added approach for each grade and subject) for agreeing to move to and stay in low-performing schools. The incentive was $20,000 paid in instalments over a two-year period. Some teachers were already teaching in low-performing schools, and they received a $10,000 retention stipend if they remained in the school over the two-year period. The participants included 85 teacher pairs matched on school characteristics and randomised to intervention or not, across 114 elementary and middle schools. Because the teacher pairs changed their personnel between randomisation and the start of the school year, the two groups were no longer equivalent at the beginning of the study. Of the vacancies assigned to the scheme, 88 per cent were filled, compared to 44 per cent the year before, and 71 per cent in the comparison group. Retention after one year was 93 per cent (70 per cent in the comparator group), and 60 per cent after two years (compared to 51 per cent). The results suggest, while the transfer incentive may have had a positive impact on teacher recruitment and then retention rates during the payout period, the effect did not last once the payment stopped.

The weaker studies (in terms of design for a causal question) are more mixed in results. Fowler (2003) examined the Massachusetts Signing Bonus Program for New Teachers, offering a $20,000 bonus for highly qualified people switching careers to teaching. Initially, recipients began teaching after seven weeks of training, although this was changed to a year-long programme in 2002, before being assigned to high-need schools, and provided with further training, support and mentoring. There was no explicit comparison group. The programme failed to recruit candidates from outside the area, and despite advertising across states only seven candidates outside Massachusetts were recruited over four years. This may be partly because other states were also experiencing severe teacher shortages, and some offered higher salaries. The programme also failed to place all teachers, mostly from Massachusetts, in high-need schools (only 71 per cent from the first cohort, 48 per cent and 35 per cent in following years). Dropout among bonus recipients was higher than the national average (46 per cent by the third year), and highest in the high-need districts (55 per cent). A survey of head teachers suggests that bonus recipients on the scheme were more attracted to the fast-track scheme and not the bonus incentive (Churchill et al., 2002). Evaluation of signing bonus incentives in general suggests that any effect tends to be short-lived (Choi, 2011).

Gordon and Vegas (2005) analysed the impact of the Fund for the Maintenance and Development of Basic Education and Teacher Appreciation – a funding reform in Brazil which stipulated that at least 60 per cent of additional funds be allocated to teacher wages. It has been linked to increased positive trends in student enrolment, and reduction in grade retention and dropout (World Bank, 2002; Castro, 1998). For this review, we considered only the impact of funding on teacher numbers and qualification. The study was a longitudinal retrospective cohort study. Because the intervention coincided with major education reform in Brazil, such as increased economic changes, educational resources for some municipalities and the legislation that all teachers must be qualified, it is difficult to attribute any causal effect. Many of the patterns reported were present before the intervention, which was linked to an increase in the number but not the qualification of teachers, and a reduction in student-teacher ratios in some areas, but not the poorest.

In America, Goldhaber et al. (2010) compared salaries in private and public schools using data from the 1999/2000 School and Staffing Survey, the 2000 Common Core of Data, and the 2000 census. The survey contains responses from 56,354 teachers in 5,465 public schools and 10,760 teachers in 3,558 private schools. Findings showed that private schools tended to pay slightly more for more qualified and experienced teachers than public schools, for teaching large classes, longer hours and in more disadvantaged schools with a high proportion of ethnic minority pupils. For example, private schools with a high proportion of poor students paid their teachers 17 per cent higher salaries than schools with an average number of poor students. This is more than in public schools, which often have similar schemes, and despite teachers working in public schools with a high proportion of ethnic minority students being paid a slightly higher salary. There are other differences between the two sectors, and teachers expressed concerns about working conditions, but one implication, as Goldhaber et al. concluded, could be that teachers will need to be paid more to get them to teach and stay in challenging schools.

Dwinal (2012) conducted a case study of Teach For America (similar to England's Teach First scheme) in the rural Mississippi-Arkansas Delta region, where there is a teacher shortage, geographical isolation and a heavily ethnically segregated school population. The programme recruited potential school leaders from university graduates and professionals, through an intensive selection process, and they committed to teach for at least two years in state schools. The low response rates (under 20 per cent) to interviews with principals, and a comparison between regions over time using the weaker measure of vacancy rates rather than number of teachers recruited, made it difficult to establish the impact of recruitment. There was no decrease in vacancy rates relative to other areas, partly because the programme imposed limits to the number of participants in each district (so directing them elsewhere). Other studies suggest that Teach For America teachers tend to leave teaching after a couple of years (e.g., Glazerman, Mayer, & Decker, 2006; Decker, Mayer, & Glazerman, 2004; Raymond, Fletcher, & Luque, 2001; Clark, Isenberg, Liu, Makowsky, & Zukiewicz, 2017; Henry et al., 2014).

Clewell and Villegas (2001) reported a six-year evaluation of the Pathways to Teaching Careers programme, including the paraprofessionals and non-certified teachers, and the Peace Corps Fellows strands. The paraprofessional and non-certified programmes involved identifying non-qualified staff already working in schools and offering them scholarships as well as other support services to help them obtain qualified teacher status, after which they are committed to continue teaching in the schools for a specified period. The Peace Corps Fellowship identifies and supports potential teachers from returning Peace Corps volunteers (similar to the Troops to Teachers programme in England). Fellows are placed in schools on a full-time contract and paid a salary where they work towards a teaching qualification. The study was largely based on self-report, with a high level of missing data. Only 44 per cent reported where they were teaching initially, and only 31 per cent after three years. Pathway teachers reported higher completion rates than traditionally certified teachers (75 per cent to 60 per cent). A high proportion (84 per cent) ended up teaching in hard-to-staff schools and had better retention rates over three years compared to the national average (81 per cent to 71 per cent). They were also perceived to be more effective than typically qualified teachers.

Waters-Weller (2009) explored the relationship between improvement in working conditions (which they defined as reduction in class size and teaching load, more planning time), retention bonuses, and teaching and staying in high-poverty schools. This was an exploratory cross-sectional study looking at the relationship between school intakes and attrition rates, the attitudes of teachers towards low socio-economic status schools and the kind of incentives likely to increase retention. The survey of 3,525 teachers in two urban districts only had a 29 per cent response rate. The majority of teachers indicated that they would stay in their current school for the next year, including those who were in high-poverty schools. They generally indicated that extra money for salaries and bonuses were not necessarily needed to keep them if the school had an excellent administrator, but money was an inducement to transfer to a poor school.

Improving retention

The strongest study (3*) by Hough and Loeb (2013) suggests no lasting benefit from financial incentives for retention of teachers in hard-to-staff schools. Other studies discussed in the section on recruitment also indicated no effects on retention (Steele et al., 2010; Glazerman et al., 2013; Fowler, 2003). There were a further 11 studies that dealt solely or mostly with retention of teachers in hard-to-staff schools (Table 11.3). Almost all of these reported positive effects, but these were largely very weak studies.

Although Clotfelter, Glennie, Ladd, and Vigdor (2008) in their 3* study indicated a positive effect of financial incentives on retention, it concurred with the other studies outlined that incentives work only as long as they are available and once removed, they have no lasting effect. Clotfelter et al. (2008) examined the impact of the North Carolina annual bonus scheme on the retention of qualified maths, science and special education teachers in high-poverty and challenging schools, using a difference-in-difference approach. Teachers received the bonus ($1,800 per year) for as long as they stayed in the eligible school. This was a reasonably well-conducted study, using administrative data for four years on public school teachers to estimate the likelihood of teachers leaving a particular school. The research compared hazard rates before and after the implementation of the bonus programme, eligible and ineligible teachers in the same schools, teachers in eligible schools and those in schools that narrowly missed out on being eligible. Teachers receiving the bonus were 15 per cent less likely to leave at the end of the school year compared to other teachers in the same schools.

TABLE 11.3 Retention

Quality of study	Positive outcome	Unclear outcome	Negative or neutral outcome
4*	–	–	–
3*	Clotfelter et al. (2008)	–	Hough and Loeb (2013)
2*	Fulbeck (2011), Fulbeck and Richards (2015), Fulbeck (2014) Fitzgerald (1986) Falch (2010) Feng and Sass (2018) Gold (1987)	–	Steele et al. (2010) Glazerman et al., (2013)
1*	Goldhaber et al. (2010) Lyons (2007) Anthony (2009) Helfeldt, Capraro, Caparo, Foster, and Carter (2009) Colson and Satterfield (2018) Fuller (2003)	Fowler (2003)	Waters-Weller (2009)

Five further studies in this section were rated 2*. Gold (1987) evaluated the New York City Retired-Teachers-as-Mentors Program by comparing mentees with a comparison group of non-mentored teachers. The programme recruited retired teachers as mentors for new in-service teachers. Mentors attended a four-day workshop conducted by staff at a training college, were paid for 66 hours a year for each of three mentees and assigned to schools with the highest attrition rate among new teachers. The study used Board of Education records and questionnaires completed by teachers, mentors and principals. Retention rates went up for all, but the rates were higher for the mentored teachers (85 per cent and 80 per cent in the second year). It is not clear that mentors were randomised to new teachers in eligible schools, and no account was taken of missing data.

Fitzgerald (1986) looked at offering an annual stipend (of between $500 and $2,000) to encourage teachers to teach in schools with a high proportion of pupils eligible for free or reduced lunches, in high priority areas in the US. The study used a difference-in-difference approach to compare the retention rates of teachers in 25 high priority schools with 25 high-poverty control schools not receiving the stipend. The groups were similar in terms of pupil and teacher characteristics. Vacancies dropped in treatment schools in the first year, and the drop in retention rates was lower than for control schools (ES = +0.39).

In Norway, Falch (2010) examined the impact on the retention of teachers in high-vacancy schools of paying teachers differential wages, using a difference-in-difference approach. In the period 1993/94 to 2002/03, Norway had a central wage system, but teachers in schools with high vacancies received a wage premium of between 7.5 per cent and 12 per cent. Over the nine years, schools were initially eligible if they had 20 per cent more 'shortages' than the previous year. This increased to 30 per cent for the 1996/97 and 1997/98, and then back to 20 per cent for the last four years. In total, 161 schools received the wage premium at least once, and in these schools the attrition rate of teachers was lower than comparison schools by 6 per cent. The reporting of this, however, was not clear, and the number of schools and teachers included varied considerably over time.

Feng and Sass (2018) considered the effects of the Florida Critical Teacher Shortage Program 1986 to 2011 on the retention of teachers in shortage subject areas (maths, science and special education). Loan forgiveness of up to $10,000 to pay off their student loan was offered to beginning qualified teachers, if they taught in a shortage subject for at least 90 days. There was a recruitment bonus for new teachers, of up to $1,200 (to cover removals or equipment), and a retention bonus of up to £1,200 if teachers continued to teach a shortage subject the following year and had favourable performance appraisals. These two were only available from 2000/01 to 2001/02. Since subjects designated as a shortage changed over time, the teachers eligible for these incentives also changed over time. These variations were used to compare bonus recipients with non-recipients, in terms of recruitment and attrition using a proportional hazard model, taking into account student demographics, pupil prior behaviour, prior achievement, class size, teacher gender, race/ethnicity, salary base and experience.

There is no report on attrition rates from the study. Loan forgiveness had a positive effect on the likelihood of teachers staying in teaching the following year, reducing attrition by 12 per cent, but not once funding was removed. The one-time retention bonus for shortage subject teachers also reduced the likelihood of teachers leaving by 25 per cent.

The next three studies have common authors and all examine the same intervention, and so they are treated as one complex study for this review. Fulbeck (2011) evaluated the impact of ProComp (Professional Compensation for Teachers) – a teacher-incentive programme in Denver – including ten financial incentives (seven individual, three school level). School-based incentives were awarded to teachers who teach at schools serving low-income students and high-performing schools and schools that make the most progress in maths and reading. Eligibility was restricted to those who were members of teacher unions not working in Charter schools. The total number of teachers included in the retention analyses was 4,145, representing 91 per cent of all Denver Public School District teachers. Retention figures exclude those who retired or whose service was terminated and those made redundant due to reduction in teaching posts. The study used interrupted time-series and difference-in-difference regression models. The average change in retention rate was −0.06 per cent before ProComp and +1.5 per cent afterwards, and participation in ProComp increased retention rates by 2.1 percentage points. It was more effective in hard-to-staff schools (ES 0.25) compared to others (ES 0.08). Retention was higher in high-poverty schools where teachers were eligible to receive a financial incentive to stay.

Fulbeck and Richards (2015) looked at all 7,333 public school teachers in Denver from 2006 to 2010 who were eligible for the ProComp incentive (regardless of whether they did receive it) and who made at least one voluntary move within the district (989). The incentive tended to attract teachers to high-growth and high-performing schools, and it was less successful for schools with high proportion of low-income pupils. A limitation of the study is its inability to take account of other factors that may over-estimate the effect of financial incentives, such as a principal's hiring preferences and the actual school vacancies advertised.

Fulbeck (2014) looked at participation in ProComp and teacher mobility in high-poverty areas, using longitudinal teacher-level data from 2001/02 to 2010/11, and comparing teachers who received ProComp with those who did not, and those who taught in high-poverty schools with those who did not. Teachers working in high-poverty schools were more likely to move but the odds of leaving the district (and so losing the incentive) were lower for ProComp teachers than for others. The study suggests that the incentive alone was not enough to compensate for poor working conditions, issues with school leadership and school climate.

A further five studies were rated 1*. Lyons (2007) considered a teacher preparation programme where participants were volunteers, selected for their commitment to the goals of the programme. Unfortunately, much of the reporting is unclear. Findings suggest that teachers exposed to all programme components were less likely than the national average to leave classroom teaching after a year in a high-poverty school.

Anthony (2009) considered the impact on teacher retention of a mentoring system for new teachers in a rural school district in North Carolina. All new teachers were given a two-week intensive session to help them adjust to the school, community and the teaching profession, and were assigned to a trained mentor for three years. The State Board of Education also required all new qualified teachers to complete a three-year induction period to obtain a continuing Standard Professional 2 licence. Both mentors and mentees were given training. Data on retention, measured as a proportion of teachers returning each year to the school system, was taken from the school system database. The proportion of teachers returning to the school system increased each year from 84 per cent in 2005/06 before the programme to 92 per cent in 2007/08. There was, however, no counterfactual as part of this study, and it is therefore a very weak study for a causal question.

Fuller (2003) examined the Texas Beginning Educator Support System on the retention of beginning teachers – a statewide comprehensive program offering instructional support and mentoring. Although this was a statewide programme, participation was selective, and it is unclear how selection was organised. Using the state personnel database, the study compared the retention rates of beginning teachers who participated in the scheme with those not participating, from 1999/2000 to 2002/03. The participants had higher retention, but this could be at least partly due to the prior selection process.

Helfeldt et al. (2009) described a four-year internship programme aimed at retaining new teachers in high-need urban schools. In this university-school partnership programme, interns were paid, with full teacher benefits, and worked as full-time regular teachers in the classroom. They were assigned an approved trained mentor, and $8,000 from the intern's salary was paid towards this mentoring scheme. The sample only included 38 interns and eight mentors, and the bulk of the analysis concerned participant perceptions of the programme. The programme was reported as effective in retaining teachers in high-need urban schools with 100 per cent of teachers staying on in teaching one year later, compared to state retention of 81 per cent.

Colson and Satterfield (2018) tested the effects of a teacher compensation plan, known as the Innovation Acceleration Fund, on the retention of SEN, maths, science and language teachers in a small rural district. This was a merit pay system, paying teachers deemed effective based on the contentious Tennessee Value-Added Assessment System. The total potential population was reported as 134. Of these, 93 volunteered for the compensation scheme. Teachers who did not want to have individual teacher effect results were excluded. Only 56 of these were deemed effective. Around 80 per cent of teachers who participated in the compensation scheme were retained compared to 70 per cent who did not participate. The report does not include effect sizes, and the design means that volunteers were compared with non-volunteers.

Conclusion

Most of the work here concerns financial incentives of some kind. In summary, financial incentives appear to work. Offering remission of student loans, higher salaries or premiums for teaching in hard-to-staff areas and schools is effective in attracting teachers. However, it is not clear that such external motivation is desirable, or attracts the best teachers, and it is quite clear that the attraction is not lasting.

While most studies considered retention as teachers staying within their current school, in others retention referred to teachers staying within the school district, the state, state-funded schools, or even within teaching as a profession. The same mix appears in claims about teacher wastage in England (See & Gorard, 2019).

The lasting impact of financial incentives on retention is less clear, even though some of the financial incentives used in the US involved a kind of a tie-in, where teachers are committed to staying on in the school or district for a specified period or else incur a penalty. To retain teachers in challenging schools or in difficult areas would require offering more than financial gain. Survey responses from teachers suggest that they are prepared to stay in less attractive schools or regions if they have supportive leadership and good working conditions (Waters-Weller, 2009; Goldhaber et al., 2010; Fulbeck, 2014).

There is little evidence that any approaches other than financial incentives work for recruitment, and no good evidence yet of anything else that works for retention, in high-need areas. Most of the research we found was very weak, and all of the higher-quality work involved easier-to-measure, more concrete strategies (such as financial incentives). More research with the kind of designs needed to address causal issues is urgently required to cover mentoring, support, training for teaching in difficult schools and a host of other alternative approaches that could be combined with financial interventions to recruit good teachers and then keep them where they are needed most. In the medium- to longer-term, a more comprehensive approach would be to change school allocation and economic policies so that there were no longer such clearly defined schools and areas with high levels of poverty (Gorard, 2018), meaning that these schools would not be as hard to staff, even though some would remain geographically isolated.

References

Anthony, J. (2009). *Teacher retention: Program evaluation of a beginning teacher and mentor program.* Ed. D. dissertation. Retrieved from Education theses, Dissertations and Projects. (Paper 100).

Castro, J. (1998, November). *O Fundo de Manutenção e Desenvolvimento do Ensino e Valorização do Magistério (FUNDEF) e seu Impacto no Financiamento do Ensino Fundamental* [*The fund for maintenance and development of teaching and appreciation of the Magisterium (FUNDEF) and its impact on financing of elementary school*]. Brasilia: Instituto de Pesquisa

Econômica Aplicada. Retrieved from Repositório do Conhecimento do IPEA website: http://repositorio.ipea.gov.br/handle/11058/2720

Choi, J. (2011). When are signing bonuses more than just 'pay to play'? An experimental investigation. *ProQuest Information and Learning, 72*, 3811.

Churchill, A., Berger, J., Brooks, C., Effrat, A., Grifin, L., Magouirk-Colbert, M., . . . Sheehan, A. (2002). *Revised interim report: The Massachusetts Institute for New Teachers and Master Teacher/NBPTS Programs*. Amherst, MA: Center for Education Policy, University of Massachusetts.

Clark, M. A., Isenberg, E., Liu, A. Y., Makowsky, L., & Zukiewicz, M. (2017). *Impacts of the Teach For America investing in innovation scale-up*. Princeton, NJ: Mathematica Policy Research.

Clewell, B., & Villegas, A. (2001). *Evaluating the Pathways to Teaching Careers program: Absence unexcused, ending teacher shortages in high-need areas*. Washington, DC: The Urban Institute.

Clotfelter, C., Glennie, E., Ladd, H., & Vigdor, J. (2008). Teacher bonuses and teacher retention in low-performing schools: Evidence from the North Carolina $1800 teacher bonus program. *Public Finance Review, 36*, 63–87.

Colson, T., & Satterfield, C. (2018). The effects of strategic compensation on teacher retention, *Power and Education, 10*(1), 92–104. Retrieved from SAGE journals website: https://journals.sagepub.com/doi/abs/10.1177/1757743818758782

Decker, P. T., Mayer, D. P., & Glazerman, S. (2004). *The effects of Teach For America on students: Findings from a national evaluation*. Madison: University of Wisconsin-Madison, Institute for Research on Poverty.

Dwinal, M. (2012). *Teach For America and rural southern teacher labour supply: An exploratory case study of Teach For America as a supplement to teacher labour policies in the Mississippi-Arkansas Delta, 2008–2010*. PhD thesis, University of Oxford. Retrieved from the University of Oxford website: https://ora.ox.ac.uk/objects/uuid:ec68169b-bf6c-4659-82a9-3fe8be3fa883

European Commission/EACEA/Eurydice. (2018). *Teaching careers in Europe: Access, progression and support. Eurydice report*. Luxembourg: Publications Office of the European Union.

Falch, T. (2010). *Teacher mobility responses to wage changes: Evidence from a quasi-natural experiment*. Working Paper Series 10910, Department of Economics, Norwegian University of Science and Technology. Retrieved from American Economic Association website: www.aeaweb.org/articles?id=10.1257/aer.101.3.460

Feng, L., & Sass, T. (2018). The impact of incentives to recruit and retain teachers in 'Hard-to-Staff' subjects. *Journal of Policy Analysis and Management, 37*(1), 112–135.

Fitzgerald, C. (1986). *Report on the high priority location stipend program*. Miami: Dade County Public Schools Office of Educational Accountability. Retrieved from ERIC website: https://eric.ed.gov/?id=ED283862

Fowler, R. (2003). The Massachusetts signing bonus program for new teachers: A model of teacher preparation worth? *Education Analysis Archives, 11*(13), 1–24.

Fulbeck, E. (2011). *Teacher retention: Estimating and understanding the effects of financial incentives in Denver*. PhD thesis, University of Colorado. ProQuest LLC. Retrieved from University of Colorado website: https://scholar.colorado.edu/educ_gradetds/100/

Fulbeck, E. (2014). Teacher mobility and financial incentives: A descriptive analysis of Denver's ProComp. *Educational Evaluation and Policy Analysis, 36*(1), 67–82. Retrieved from SAGE journals website: https://journals.sagepub.com/doi/abs/10.3102/0162373713503185

Fulbeck, E., & Richards, M. (2015). The impact of school-based financial incentives on teachers' strategic moves. *Teachers College Record, 117*, 9.

Fuller, E. (2003). *Beginning teacher retention rates for TxBESS and non-TXBESS teachers.* Unpublished. State Board for Education Certification, Texas.

Glazerman, S., Mayer, D., & Decker, P. (2006). Alternative routes to teaching: The impacts of Teach For America on student achievement and other outcomes. *Journal of Policy Analysis and Management, 25*(1), 75–96.

Glazerman, S., Protik, A., Teh, B., Bruch, J., Max, J, & Warner, E. (2013). *Transfer incentives for high-performing teachers: Final results from a multisite randomized experiment.* Executive Summary. NCEE 2014–4004. Washington, DC: National Center for Education Evaluation and Regional Assistance, Institute of Education Sciences, US Department of Education. (ED306928). Retrieved from ERIC website: eric. ed.gov/?id=ED306929

Gold, M. (1987). *Retired teachers as consultants to new teachers: A new inservice teacher training model.* Final report for American Association of State Colleges and Universities, Washington, DC; City University of New York; New York Institute for Research and Development in Occupation Education.

Goldhaber, D., Destler, K., & Player, D. (2010). Teacher labor markets and the perils of using hedonics to estimate compensating differentials in the public sector. *Economics of Education Review, 29*(1), 1–17.

Gorard, S. (2018). *Education policy: Evidence of equity and effectiveness.* Bristol: Policy Press.

Gorard, S., See, B. H., & Siddiqui, N. (2017). *The trials of evidence-based education: The promises, opportunities and problems of trials in education.* London: Routledge.

Gordon, N., & Vegas, E. (2005). Educational finance equalization, spending, teacher student outcomes: The case of Brazil's FUNDEF. In E. Vegas (Ed.), *Incentives to improve teaching: Lessons from Latin America.* Washington, DC: World Bank Press.

Helfeldt, J., Capraro, R., Caparo, M., Foster, E., & Carter, N. (2009). An urban schools' university partnership that prepares and retains high quality teachers for "high need schools". *The Teacher Educator, 44*(1), 1–20.

Henry, G. T., Purtell, K. M., Bastian, K. C., Fortner, K. C., Thompson, C. L., Campbell, S. L., & Patterson, K. M. (2014). The effects of teacher entry portals on student achievement. *Journal of Teacher Education, 65*(1), 7–23.

Hough, H., & Loeb. S. (2013, August). *Can a district-level teacher salary incentive policy improve teacher recruitment and retention?.* Policy Brief 13-4. Stanford: Policy Analysis for California Education [PACE]. Retrieved from Stanford CEPA website: https://cepa. stanford.edu/content/can-district-level-teacher-salary-incentive-policy-improve-teacher-recruitment-and-retention

House of Commons Education Committee. (2017). *Recruitment and retention of teachers: Fifth report of session 2016–17.* (HC 199, 2016–17). London: House of Commons. Retrieved from parliament.uk website: https://publications.parliament.uk/pa/cm201617/cmselect/cmeduc/199/199.pdf

Lyons, K. (2007). *Preparing to stay: A quantitative examination of the effects of pre-service preparation on the retention of urban educators.* Los Angeles, CA: University of California.

Raymond, M., Fletcher, S. H., & Luque, J. (2001). *Teach For America: An evaluation of teacher differences and student outcomes in Houston, Texas.* Palo Alto, CA: Stanford University.

See, B. H., & Gorard, S. (2019, January 18). Why don't we have enough teachers?: A reconsideration of the available evidence. *Research Papers in Education.* https://doi.org/10.1080/02671522.2019.1568535

Sibieta, L. (2018). *The teacher labour market in England: Shortages, subject expertise and incentives.* London: Education Policy Institute.

Social Mobility Commission. (2017, November). *State of the Nation 2017: Social mobility in Great Britain.* London: Social Mobility Commission. Retrieved from gov.uk website:

https://assets.publishing.service.gov.uk/government/uploads/system/uploads/attach ment_data/file/662744/State_of_the_Nation_2017_-_Social_Mobility_in_Great_ Britain.pdf

Steele, J., Murnane, R., & Willett, J. (2010). Do financial incentives help low-performing schools attract and keep academically talented teachers? Evidence from California. *Journal of Policy Analysis and Management, 29*(3), 451–478.

Waters-Weller, C. (2009). Attracting veteran teachers to low socioeconomic status schools: Initiatives and considerations, US. *ProQuest Information and Learning, 69,* 2979–2979.

Wheeler, J., & Glennie, E. (2007). *Can pay incentives improve the recruitment of teachers in America's hard-to-staff schools? A research summary: Policy matters.* Durham, NC: Center for Child and Family Policy, Duke University.

World Bank. (2002, December 20). *Brazil: Municipal education – Resources, incentives, and results (Vol. 2): Research report.* World Bank. Retrieved from The World Bank website: http://documents.worldbank.org/curated/en/969591468016270639/Research-report

12

TEACHER RECRUITMENT AND RETENTION IN CANADA

Programmes for teacher selection, support and success

Shirley Van Nuland, Catherine Whalen and Elizabeth Majocha

Introduction

In Canada, the responsibility to organise, deliver and assess education at the elementary, secondary and tertiary[1] (including university, college, technical and vocational) levels lies with provincial/territorial departments or ministries of education; no federal department of education and no integrated national system of education exist (Van Nuland, 2011). Each province or territory develops its legislation and curricula for elementary and secondary schools (Hamm, 2015). Canadian teacher education programmes are all university-based and available in different formats: teacher candidates enter with a three- or four-year bachelor's degree to complete a one- or two-year Bachelor of Education degree programme; others may complete a five-year concurrent Bachelor of Education programme together with a bachelor's degree; yet others may complete a four-year Bachelor of Education degree programme. As part of their programme, all teacher candidates generally complete their practica experience in school settings. Teacher education courses are determined by university faculty and/or may be influenced or directed by agencies or departments (e.g. regulatory agency, Ministry of Education). For example, through Regulation 347/02, the Ontario College of Teachers accredits all Ontario faculties of education; accreditation examines the programme to ascertain that it presents the current Ontario curriculum along with relevant legislation and government policy, which in turn greatly influence content and practica experiences.[2]

Researchers, writing on the Canadian contemporary research landscape, agree that educational change is an integral part (Crocker & Dibbon, 2008; Maynes & Hatt, 2015; Clandinin et al., 2015; Darling-Hammond, Burns, Campbell, Goodwin, & Low, 2018; Majocha et al, 2017). One change example includes novice teachers leaving the profession within the first five years of teaching. While Canadian school boards hire many highly qualified teachers, retaining these teachers for their full career is at times difficult, given the attrition rate for some jurisdictions. Karsenti and Collin (2013) determined that early Canadian teacher dropout rates occur due to excessive workload outside the workplace (at home, etc.), heavy workloads and lack of time as related to work conditions and expectations. Clandinin et al. (2015) concluded that 'approximately 40 per cent leaving teaching [are] within their first five years' (p. 1) of teaching in Alberta.

High attrition rates have profound consequences for school boards, teachers and, most importantly, students in Canada, as in the rest of the world. School boards invest financial expenditures (e.g. travel, accommodation, time away from the hiring personnel's other duties) and supervisors' time (e.g. principals, superintendents) in recruiting and mentoring new teachers. The high investment cost is impossible to recover when teachers leave the profession. While no cost analysis is available for Canada, the annual cost to school boards for teacher attrition in the United States is determined to be more than $2.2 billion dollars (Phillips, 2015; Haynes, 2014). The cost of leaving the profession early has an impact on teachers who have spent four or more years financing their university/ teacher education in preparation for a career that they no longer enjoy (Bonnet, 1996, as cited in Ng, Lim, Low, & Hui, 2018). Students taught by a struggling, unhappy teacher are not well-served, often to the detriment to their learning (Hong, 2012). Therefore, an emphasis on developing and hiring high-quality teachers is important to pre-service programme institutions, schools, school boards and students.

Recruitment of novice teachers

Public school[3] enrolment in Canada since the 1960s has followed an undulating curve of 'boom, bust and echo', with the last peak occurring in 1997 (Parent Advocacy Network for Public Education, n.d.). Teacher recruitment is affected by the concomitant rise and fall of elementary and secondary public school enrolment, that is, recruitment depends on student supply.

Few studies have examined to what extent recruitment strategies enhance teacher retention. Johnson et al. (2014) revealed how novice teachers are affected by educational policies and practices that influence recruitment and hiring processes and the working conditions once they are hired: these researchers linked the fact that 'personal and local challenges faced by graduate teachers [the personal] frequently have their genesis in broader political and social policies and practices [the political]' (p. 542). This statement referred to what a novice teacher experiences as a response to school board policies and practices to uphold along with the day-to-day functioning in a public school system. The hiring of teachers who are not able to navigate these factors while focusing on their personal and professional growth may require school districts to examine and amend the handling of the 'personal' and the 'political' steps that would lead more novice teachers to remain in the profession. Stotko, Ingram, and Beaty-O'Ferrall (2007) criticised the inefficiency and hyper-bureaucratisation of administrative processes and the lack of effective strategies to assess teacher candidates' dispositions toward students and teaching, which Ng et al. (2018) noted are strongly correlated with teacher retention. When school boards strengthen their selection procedures (e.g., training interview teams in performance-based interview techniques, developing well-constructed case studies and questions for interview) (Maynes & Hatt, 2015), their selected candidates will be well scrutinised before hiring occurs.

School boards engage interested and professionally qualified candidates in multiple interviews to examine their suitability for living and working in Canada. As an example, Northern Alberta found that using technological applications (e.g., videoconferencing) and face-to-face interviews coupled with extensive reference checking has made a positive difference (Brandon, 2015) in hiring its novice teachers. Teacher education programmes (e.g., *Aboriginal Teacher Education Program* and *Community-Based Teacher Education Program*) located in their home communities have employed '96 per cent of the graduates [teachers] in their home communities' (Brandon, 2015, p. 158). The early welcoming and supportive relationships in these communities provide new teachers with reasons to stay (Brandon, 2015).

Many school boards have changed their interview process from a formulaic structure that included a review of cover letters/résumés, short interviews and reference checks (Cranston, 2015) to a combination of these with a written exercise and oral interview. This is seen as a more wholesome process to gain a better sense of who they are interviewing to teach in their schools. Interviewees are often required to provide additional documentation that demonstrates their ability to teach and work with others in a collegial manner, such as reference letters generally written by someone who has observed them teach (faculty adviser or associate teacher); police reference check; successful coaching teacher and/or practica supervisor reports; and a portfolio demonstrating their learning as they progressed in their education programme. Successful candidates are offered a teaching position, subject to completion of their teacher education programme and certification. This in-depth process increases the likelihood of hiring strong candidates who have the potential of remaining in the profession due to the skills and attributes demonstrated throughout the hiring processes.

Ng et al. (2018) argue that teacher candidates must have extensive school experience as part of the teacher recruitment process; they believe, however, that this experience must occur before teacher candidates begin their pre-service programme in addition to their classroom teaching experience during their teacher education programme. Guarino, Santibañez, and Daley (2006) (cited by Ng et al., 2018) suggested that increasing 'clinical experiences could increase teacher recruitment and retention rates' (p. 633). While no Canadian teacher education programme has been found to mandate that teacher candidates have prior experience volunteering or working in schools before commencing pre-service teacher education, several programmes list prior work and volunteer experience with the K-12 school-aged population as desirable and place those with experience high on the applicant acceptance list. Our experience is that this prior work and volunteer experience is a positive indicator that the pre-service candidate may have the attributes we seek for teaching positions in our schools across the country. The one mechanism used to indicate the level of skills and attributes of developing teachers is presented in Canadian teacher education programmes through practica placements in classrooms that range from 80 to 120 days, with supervisors as mentors who have evaluative accountability.

Programmes to support retention of novice teachers

All Canadian provinces support policies and programmes for induction and/ or mentoring support (Kutsyuruba, Godden, Matheson, & Walker, 2016). The formal supports available to novice teachers are 'mentoring programmes, orientation/induction programmes, structured opportunity for reflection, reduction in breadth or quantity of teaching load, and follow up from the teacher education institute' (Kelly, Sim, & Ireland, 2018, p. 293). Two provinces address teacher induction and mentoring at a provincial level, while many provinces support 'these areas in a hybrid or collaborative manner' (Kutsyuruba et al., 2016, p. 66); furthermore, many provinces addressing 'teacher induction support and mentoring at a teacher federation or hybrid level, also had some form of decentralised support at the school district level' (p. 66). Kutsyuruba et al. (2016) found these supports at four levels: 'a) provincially mandated/ministry level support; b) provincial teacher association/federation/union level support; c) hybrid programmes (i.e., universities and teacher associations' collaboration) and d) decentralised programmes (school district level support)' (p. 8). Their study further identified the inconsistent role that school administrators played across all locations but where administrators were committed actively to teacher induction and mentorship; the result was teacher retention with improved morale and stronger self-concept for beginning teachers. As expected, variance exists within each province/territory concerning the school-level support, since Canadian education is provincially based rather than nationally based. This variance can be explained by the regional, social and cultural differences of each province and territory.

Programmes in Ontario

Ontario's Ministry of Education established and provided funding for its mandatory New Teacher Induction Program (NTIP) in 2006 to support new teachers in permanent and long-term occasional (LTO) positions (97 or more teaching days) in district school boards during their first two years of teaching. The programme includes 'orientation for new teachers to the school and school board; mentoring for new teachers by experienced teachers; and professional learning relevant to the individual needs of new teachers' (Ministry of Education, 2018, p. 4). Once the new teacher decides their learning needs, they collaborate with their mentors and principal to determine what elements (e.g., subject matter, strategies, release time) to include with timelines for completion. The principal approves and provides appropriate resources (Ministry of Education, 2018) to assist new teachers develop into effective and experienced educators.

The NTIP Review (2012–15), *Learning from the Ontario's New Teacher Induction Program*, found four factors that influenced the development of participating teachers: a mentoring web, differentiated professional learning, principal learning and school culture. Strachan (2016, n.p.) explained:

> [w]e know that learning is messy, recursive, iterative . . . there is no one right way . . . but these 4 factors working together can make a solid contribution to the success of our new teachers and ultimately their students. . . . Having a formally assigned mentor is not linked to growth . . . being mentored is.
>
> *(Factors that Influence Growth of NTIP Teachers)*

This review noted that significant growth occurred where new teachers accessed five to seven different mentorship supports (Frank, 2015). Frank found that the strongest predictor of growth occurs when the headteacher (or principal teacher of the school) shares ongoing feedback and encouragement from a collaborative school culture, which then builds a sense of confidence and efficacy in new teachers.

Mentoring and induction programmes

Effective mentorship is prevalent when an experienced teacher is paired deliberately with a new teacher with both working in a carefully structured programme. Working with a mentor has been found to be the most effective way to prevent attrition (Ingersoll & Strong, 2011, cited in Kelly et al., 2018). Booth and Coles (2017) described the most effective mentors as those experienced teachers who are able to observe and draw upon their mentees' strengths and attributes while working through the challenges in teaching. Ontario's mentors receive training and release time to coach, collaborate and consult with the new teacher to work through the approved plan, suggesting adjustments, and using available resources (Ministry of Education, 2018). The majority of the NTIP mentoring activities occur outside the classroom, with 85 per cent first-year NTIP participants meeting monthly with their mentor(s).

Similar to Alberta and Ontario, other jurisdictions in Canada provide temporary or short-term contract positions for novice teachers, with the result that these teachers receive insufficient attention and guidance from their administrators (i.e., principals, vice principals, head of school, etc.) who are 'reluctant to invest time, energy or resources in induction programmes or the like because they are considered as transient' (Farrell, 2016, p. 13). When novice teachers have little or no support, they are dissatisfied with professional relationships and career opportunities and over time may leave the profession (Kelly et al., 2018; Farrell, 2016; Johnson et al., 2014; OECD, 2011). Karsenti and Collin (2013) found that a 30 per cent dropout rate occurs in the first five years of service, with 50 per cent of those drop-outs in the first two years of service. Glassford and Salinitri (2007) cited W. D. Wilson (former registrar of the Ontario College of Teachers): the first two years of novice teacher service in the classroom is an extension of the learning experienced in the pre-service teacher education programme, which is then intensified as novice teachers learn on the job and progress in their careers. Glassford and Salinitri supported the importance of novice teacher induction and mentoring programmes for this exact reason.

In *Teacher Education in Canada*, Crocker and Dibbon (2008) reported on induction programmes that include formal school board-level orientation and individual school-level orientation to 'improve new teacher efficacy, job satisfaction and retention' (p. 55). Responding to school board or provincial department of education priority areas, novice teachers receive professional development in the 'use of technology, planning, assessment and evaluation, literacy, student success, and equity and diversity' (Ontario College of Teachers, 2018, p. 52). Some mentor teachers received either additional pay or release from classroom duties to perform their work as mentors (OECD, 2011), since mentoring activities most often occurred outside of the classroom. Geeraerts, Tynjälä, and Heikkinen (2018) determined that 'an intergenerational learning perspective is important with respect to demographic changes in school staff and in preventing knowledge loss and teacher dropout' (p. 479), where both older and younger teachers develop professional attitudes and identity in working with each other, a form of co-mentoring. In mentoring novice teachers, the mentor learns about the different methodologies (e.g., technology, literacy activities, student success) from the novice teacher while the novice teacher learns from the mentor teacher who supports the novice teacher as more professional learning occurs (Ontario College of Teachers, 2018). This support helps to develop confidence in the novice, who now believes that what may not have been possible in teaching can be done, thus encouraging continuation in the profession.

Crocker and Dibbon (2008) suggested implementing 'an extended paid internship before a teacher can assume full responsibilities' (p. 116) while the novice teacher transitions into full-time teaching. This gradual entry would lessen the stress and pressure that early career teachers experience. Currently, the expectations placed on novice teachers, identical to those placed on very experienced teachers, are 'unheard of in other professions' (p. 117). Canadian jurisdictions with standards of practice require the same standard of novice teachers as seasoned members, while others outside Canada (e.g., Scotland, Victoria Australia) have different standards of practice based on the experience level of the practitioner. An internship after certification would provide new teachers with more time and opportunity to develop these standards and may result in a higher retention of teachers after year five in the profession.

Programmes in other Canadian provinces

British Columbian school districts (e.g., Haida Gwaii, Kootenay Columbia, Kamloops Thompson) support novice teachers with programmes that address 'collegial sharing and support, collaborative planning, non-evaluative observation and feedback' (British Columbia Teachers Federation, 2015) and observation of colleagues in the classroom. A teacher self-initiated programme in the Maple Ridge – Pitt Meadows Schools (n.d.) in British Columbia aspires 'to increase teachers' ability to provide effective practice to students' (p. 5). The mentee identifies areas (e.g., 'information about policies and procedures, . . . working with students, managing time, and wellness') (p. 4) where growth is needed. Through mentorship, novice teachers receive personalised support to work on their goals and questions.

Canada's newest territory, Nunavut, recognises that new teachers require time to learn about the land and culture to help build connections with their students. The Nunavut Department of Education and Teachers' Association offered a three-day cultural awareness workshop addressing residential school awareness, Indigenous cultural competency and reconciliation to move knowledge into instructional practice (Government of Nunavut, 2017), with priority for new teachers to attend. To reduce the high teacher turnover rate and prepare potential teachers to teach in Nunavut and understand the culture, Mount St Vincent University (Nova Scotia) partnered with the Government of Nunavut to provide the MSVU Nunavut Teacher Practicum Program. As described by Newbery (2017):

> From the educational perspective, it provides them with the chance to see what life is like in a cross-cultural, English-as-a-Second-Language, often multi-grade northern classroom, one demanding initiative, flexibility and self-reliance. From the cultural perspective, the students get the opportunity to meet Inuit, get the feel of a Nunavut school, take part in community events and get out on the land so they then know exactly what they will face if they decide to apply for a Northern teaching position.
>
> *(para. 2)*

This programme is showing signs of success over its nine-year existence. Teachers from the 'south' have a better understanding of the culture and stay in teaching for a longer period than those without this experience.

'Teach for Canada' (2019, paragraph 2) supports novice teachers by providing 'three weeks of community-focused summer preparation and ongoing support during a teacher's minimum two-year teaching commitment in Canada's North . . . emphasizing a spirit of reciprocal learning in the classroom and community'. Even before teachers are hired, teacher-applicants gain an understanding about teaching in Northern Canada to determine if they want to pursue their idea. This orientation and ongoing support allow novice teachers to learn more about teaching in the north in an environment where they become more aware of expectations, and it will encourage their retention.

Ontario's NTIP participants are generally positive about the assistance they receive from mentors and other experienced teachers in their first year of teaching; this assistance included help with report card preparation (75 per cent), feedback from mentor on my teaching (74 per cent), curriculum planning with my mentor(s) (73 per cent), finding effective teaching resources (67 per cent), and advice on supporting individual students (67 per cent) (Ontario College of Teachers, 2018, p. 62). As an example of how a school board presents NTIP, the Thames Valley District School Board (2019) (Staff Development), similar to other Ontario school boards, provides each NTIP eligible teacher with four half-days of mentoring and five half-day NTIP professional development sessions. The principal matches the new teacher with a trained mentor. Professional learning sessions include Orientation Session, Classroom Planning, Organisation and Management, The Safe and Inclusive Classroom, Effective Teacher Strategies and Assessment and Evaluation. Mentoring options available are one-to-one mentoring, informal mentoring, classroom planning/observation, co-planning and mentoring network. These teachers participated in professional development beyond NTIP programmes by taking additional qualification courses, engaging in collaborative teaching, joining in collaborative learning in their schools, sharing in teacher enquiry with subject or specialist associations and making use of digital environments. These activities support the novice teachers who feel that they can become effective teachers who want to stay in teaching. NTIP is not available to all; daily occasional teachers (or supply teachers) experience a disadvantage with limited access to in-school orientations, principal evaluations and formal mentoring by experienced teachers (Ontario College of Teachers, 2018). These occasional teachers can become discouraged and leave teaching since the support that is offered in the NTIP program is not as available to them.

The Winnipeg School Division (2019) offers a two-year teacher induction programme that comprises recruitment and hiring of Early Service Teachers (EST), orientation to the workplace, mentorship opportunities (formal and informal) with orientation to the profession beyond the practicum or term teaching experience either individually or in groups (community of practice). Advanced Skills Teachers (AST) or teacher mentors, knowledgeable in key mentorship skills, engage and learn with ESTs. This programme is funded internally. Novice teachers benefit from 'training in action research that supports critical reflection and next steps; release time . . . to investigate student learning in various contexts, learning opportunities that support Indigenous education, community engagement, and social justice' (para. 10). The programme provides assistance to novice teachers to ensure success which, in turn, encourages them to remain in the profession.

The province of Saskatchewan does not regulate mandatory or formal teacher induction programmes. The mentorship programmes offered in the province are policy-driven at individual school districts or divisions; these programmes are accessible at the principal's discretion. A Saskatchewan study involving 12 novice teachers examined mentorship experiences from their first classroom teaching position following graduation from their teacher education programme (Hellsten, Prytula, Ebanks, & Lai, 2009). The researchers recommended that teacher mentorship be developed through an adaptation of the professional learning community model versus government-mandated mentorship programming. The authors reasoned that the principle of learning in community achieves learning outcomes and should be introduced in the pre-service teacher education programmes; this experience would naturally extend to their learning as they navigate their early career experiences. The professional learning community model has been shown to improve teacher retention (Bassi & Polifroni, 2005).

The Alberta Teachers' Association (2003) describes mentoring as a nurturing process, in which a more skilled person, serving as a role model, teaches, sponsors, encourages, counsels and befriends a less skilled or less experienced person for the purpose of promoting the latter's professional development to sustain an ongoing, caring relationship between the mentor and the novice. In northern Alberta, where it is more difficult to attract and retain teachers, their induction programme includes 'intense late-summer orientations, trained mentors and some opportunities to reflect and learn in beginning teacher cohorts' (Brandon, 2015, p. 160). Novice teachers' comments indicate the programmes support visits to other classrooms and schools, along with modest workload reductions to varying degrees (Brandon, 2015). Often 'instructional coaches' travel between schools to collaborate with new teachers and informally with in-school 'teacher buddy' and formally with school leaders dealing with practices identified as priority (Brandon, 2015). By providing these supports, novice teachers develop confidence and receive the help needed to succeed and remain in teaching. In Alberta's Clearview Public Schools (September 2016), new teachers complete two days' orientation in August and are assigned mentor teachers. They then partake in professional learning days: assessment (October), problem-based learning (November three days), inclusion (March), and literacy and differentiation (May). They are also encouraged to attend the new teacher conferences and have one additional day to work with their mentor.

These examples of teacher education, induction and mentoring activities demonstrate the commitment that institutions and teachers make to ensure that novice teachers have the support needed to make a successful transition to teaching. Successful transition provides novice teachers with an assurance that has a positive effect on their resilience and professional growth important to teacher retention.

Conclusions and recommendations

The activities that each jurisdiction in Canada provides to support novice teachers in their early years strengthen their teaching, but more should happen before a novice teacher enters the classroom.

Preparation for teaching has the potential to improve teacher recruitment and retention. Alcorn (2014) recommended improved standards for entry into teacher education programmes, with admission based on more than academic degrees. Several programmes require supplemental portfolios (Campbell, 2017) or applications to determine an applicant's reasoning to become a teacher. Recently, one Faculty of Education required potential candidates to complete a written assignment and be interviewed before admission was granted; due to the costs of hiring interviewers involved and the belief that this process was not seen as effective, these activities were discontinued. Hatt, Maynes, and Kmiec (2015) suggested that multi-staged hiring processes in school boards include:

> pre-screening applications; an initial phone interview; an observed teaching of a lesson; a short-term apprenticeship with a master teacher; a student-engagement problem-solving task addressed while on apprenticeship; a formal interview; a conflict-embedded problem-solving task; a student achievement data-action-planning task; and, a final screening interview.
>
> *(p. 178)*

These activities would be conducted over the applicant's first year of teaching without permanency attached to it. This multi-phased approach would provide more information about the teachers to be employed to determine the best candidate. This approach is designed to improve hiring practices and promote positive professional growth which will assist in reducing teacher attrition.

Alberta Education (2009) outlined four key elements of effective induction programmes: mentorship by trained master teachers; adjust the teacher's assignment consistent with training and experience; opportunity for reflection and follow-up planning with beginning colleagues; and scheduled time for beginning teachers to visit and team-teach with other professionals (Brandon, 2015). When early career teachers are involved in induction programmes as outlined, they have developed more confidence in their abilities as teachers, which in turn provides an environment where 'success breeds success'. As novice teachers move from an initial, early career orientation to an improved, professional practice stage, they become involved in the development of a learning community stage (Alberta Teacher Association, 2003).

Working with others in a learning community (Bassi & Polifroni, 2005), novice teachers learn from and with each other with a desire to stay in teaching, a profession that supports them. To ensure successful retention of teachers, 'reliable long-term funding, intergovernmental cooperation, innovation in teacher education, and greater local community engagement' (Brandon, 2015 p. 160) are needed. Governments must 'create equitable funding and partnership models' (p. 165) to further develop communities where teachers want to stay and teach. Where there is a strong school community culture in which novice teachers work with strong mentors, skills and confidence develop and effective teachers emerge with no desire to leave the profession. The best, most creative teachers become experienced teachers, finding new challenges and opportunities for growth by serving as mentors. They support an increased continuity of traditions and positive cultural norms behaviour. Through an establishment of professional norms of openness to learning from others and from new ideas, these novice teachers are aware of and attentive to instructional practices, continual improvement, collaboration, collegiality and experimentation which supports novice teacher retention.

Notes

1 Elementary school education generally begins in Kindergarten (age five) to the end of grade eight (age 13), at which time students enter secondary school (either a publicly funded or private institution) for a three- or four-year program. At the conclusion of their secondary education, students begin to work or enrol in college or university.
2 Teacher certification is granted by a regulatory board (e.g., Ontario College of Teachers) or by the provincial government on the recommendation of the university from which the novice teacher graduates after completing a period of initial teacher education. See www.ctf-fce.ca/en/Pages/TIC/CertificationRegulationsbyProvinceTerritory.aspx for each province's/territory's requirements.
3 'Public schools' refer to elementary and secondary schools that are funded by public dollars collected from the Canadian taxpayer. Each province sets its own taxation rate for education, as for all other public services.

References

Alberta Education. (2009). *A draft framework for provincial teacher induction programs*. Edmonton, AB: Alberta Government.

Alberta Teachers' Association. (2003). *Mentoring beginning teachers: Program handbook*. Retrieved from National Center on Education and the Economy website: http://ncee.org/wp-content/uploads/2017/01/Alb-non-AV-18-ATA-Mentoring-beginning-teachers.pdf

Alcorn, N. (2014). Teacher education in New Zealand 1974–2014. *Journal of Education for Teaching, 40*(5), 447–460.

Bassi, S., & Polifroni, E. C. (2005). Learning communities: The link to recruitment and retention. *Journal for Nurses in Staff Development, 21*(3), 103–109.

Bonnet, G. (1996). The reform of initial teacher training in France. *Journal of Education for Teaching, 22*(3), 249–270. doi:10.1080/02607479620232

Booth, D., & Coles, R. (2017). *What is a good teacher?* Markham, ON: Pembroke Publishers.

Brandon, J. (2015). Excellent teachers for northern and remote Alberta schools. In N. Maynes & B. E. Hatt (Eds.), *The complexity of hiring, supporting, and retaining new teachers across Canada* (pp. 150–68). Ontario: Canadian Association for Teacher Education (CATE). Retrieved from Canadian Society for the Study of Education website: https://csse-scee.ca/associations/cate-acfe/

British Columbia Teachers Federation. (2015). *Mentorship*. Retrieved from https://bctf.ca/mobile/NewTeachersHandbook/default.aspx?id=31859

Campbell, C. (2017). Developing teachers' professional learning: Canadian evidence and experiences in a world of educational improvement. *Canadian Journal of Education / Revue canadienne de l'éducation, 40*(2), 1–33. Retrieved from http://journals.sfu.ca/cje/index.php/cje-rce/issue/view/114

Clandinin, D. J., Long, J., Schaefer, L., Downey, C. A., Steeves, P., Pinnegar, S., . . . Wnuka, S. (2015). Early career teacher attrition: Intentions of teachers beginning. *Teaching Education, 26*(1), 1–16. http://doi.org/10.1080/10476210.2014.996746

Cranston, J. A. (2015). Navigating the Bermuda triangle of teacher hiring practices in Canada. In N. Maynes & B. E. Hatt (Eds.), *The complexity of hiring, supporting, and retaining new teachers across Canada* (pp. 128–49). Ontario: Canadian Association for Teacher Education (CATE). Retrieved from Canadian Society for the Study of Education website: https://csse-scee.ca/associations/cate-acfe/

Crocker, R., & Dibbon, D. (2008). *Teacher education in Canada.* Kelowna, BC: Society for the Advancement of Excellence in Education.

Darling-Hammond, L., Burns, D., Campbell, C., Goodwin, A. L., & Low, E. L. (2018). International lessons in teacher education. In M. Akiba & G. K. LeTendre (Eds.), *International handbook of teacher quality and policy* (Ch. 21). New York: Routledge.

Farrell, T. S. C. (2016). Surviving the transition shock in the first year of teaching through reflective practice. *System, 61,* 12–19. http://doi.org/10.1016/j.system.2016.07.005

Frank, C. (2015). *Longitudinal evaluation of Ontario's new teacher induction program.* Toronto: Government of Ontario. Retrieved from Teach Ontario website: www.teachontario. ca/docs/DOC-10789

Geeraerts, K., Tynjälä, P., & Heikkinen, H. (2018). Inter-generational learning of teachers: What and how do teachers learn from older and younger colleagues? *European Journal of Teacher Education, 41*(4), 479–495. https://doi.org/10.1080/02619768.2018. 1448781

Glassford, L., & Salinitri, G. (2007). Designing a successful new teacher induction program: An assessment of the Ontario experience, 2003–2006. *Canadian Journal of Educational Administration and Policy, 60,* 65–74.

Government of Nunavut. (2017). *Nunavut teacher induction program: Cultural awareness workshop.* Retrieved from https://www.gov.nu.ca/orientation-and-mentoring

Hamm, L. (2015). Hiring and retaining teachers in diverse schools and districts. In N. Maynes & B. E. Hatt (Eds.) *The complexity of hiring, supporting, and retaining new teachers across Canada.* Ontario: Canadian Association for Teacher Education (CATE). Retrieved from https://csse-scee.ca/associations/cate-acfe/

Hatt, B. E., Maynes, N., & Kmiec, J. (2015). What's wrong with getting teacher hiring right? In N. Maynes & B. E. Hatt (Eds.), *The complexity of hiring, supporting, and retaining new teachers across Canada* (pp. 169–183). Ontario: Canadian Association for Teacher Education (CATE). Retrieved from Canadian Society for the Study of Education website: https://csse-scee.ca/associations/cate-acfe/

Haynes, M. (2014). *On the path to equity: Improving the effectiveness of beginning teachers.* Washington, DC: Alliance for Excellent Education. Retrieved from https://all4ed. org/wp-content/uploads/2014/07/PathToEquity.pdf

Hellsten, L. M., Prytula, M. P., Ebanks, A., & Lai, H. (2009). Teacher induction: Exploring beginning teacher mentorship. *Canadian Journal of Education, 32*(4), 703–733.

Hong, J. Y. (2012). Why do some beginning teachers leave the school, and others stay? Understanding teacher resilience through psychological lenses. *Teachers and Teaching, 18*(4), 417–440. https://doi.org/10.1080/13540602.2012.696044.

Johnson, B., Down, B., Le Cornu, R., Peters, J., Sullivan, A., Pearce, J., & Hunter, J. (2014). Promoting early career teacher resilience: A framework for understanding and acting. *Teachers and Teaching: Theory and Practice, 20*(5), 530–546. http://doi.org/10.10 80/13540602.2014.937957

Karsenti, T., & Collin, S. (2013). Why are new teachers leaving the profession? Results of a Canada-wide survey. *Education, 3.* 141–9. https://doi.org/10.5923/j.edu.20130303.01.

Kelly, N., Sim, C., & Ireland, M. (2018). Slipping through the cracks: Teachers who miss out on early career support. *Asia-Pacific Journal of Teacher Education, 46*(3), 292–316. https://doi.org/10.1080/1359866X.2018.1441366

Kutsyuruba, B., Godden, L., Matheson, I., & Walker, K. (2016). *Pan-Canadian document analysis study: Understanding the role of teacher induction and mentorship programs in teacher attrition and retention final report*. Kingston, ON: Queen's University.

Majocha, E. F., Costa, M. A. M., Mpeta M., Ara N., Whalen C. A., & Fernandes T. A. (2017). Sustaining growth of novice teachers to leadership through mentorship process: A study of praxis in Brazil, Canada, Pakistan, and South Africa. In P. Miller (Ed), *Cultures of educational leadership: Intercultural studies in education*. London: Palgrave Macmillan. https://doi.org/10.1057/978-1-137-58567-7_9

Maple Ridge – Pitt Meadows Schools (n.d.). *Self-initiated mentorship for teachers*. Retrieved from www.sd42.ca/assets/media/2018-07-25-Mentorship-Brochure-Web.pdf

Maynes, N., & Hatt, B. E. (Eds.). (2015). *The complexity of hiring, supporting, and retaining new teachers across Canada*. Canadian Association for Teacher Education (CATE). Retrieved from Canadian Society for the Study of Education website: https://csse-scee.ca/associations/cate-acfe/

Ministry of Education. (2018). New teacher induction program induction elements manual. Retrieved from edu.gov.on.ca: http://www.edu.gov.on.ca/eng/teacher/induction.html

Newbery, N. (2017, August 31). *Preparing to teach in Nunavut*. Retrieved from A&B – Canada's Arctic Journal website: http://arcticjournal.ca/arts-culture-education/education/preparing-teach-nunavut/

Ng, P. T., Lim, K. M., Low, E. L., & Hui, C. (2018). Provision of early field experiences for teacher candidates in Singapore and how it can contribute to teacher resilience and retention. *Teacher Development*, 22(5), 632–650. https://doi.org/10.1080/136645 30.2018.1484388

Ontario College of Teachers. (2018). *Transitions to teaching 2018*. Retrieved from Ontario College of Teachers website: www.oct.ca/-/media/PDF/2018%20Transition%20 to%20Teaching%20Report/2018%20T2T%20Main%20Report%20EN_final.pdf

Organisation for Economic Cooperation and Development [OECD]. (2011). *Attracting, developing and retaining effective teachers – Final report: Teachers matter*. Retrieved from OECD website: www.oecd.org/education/school/attractingdevelopingandretaining effectiveteachers-finalreportteachersmatter.htm

Parent Advocacy Network for Public Education. (n.d.). *Declining enrollment and population distribution*. Retrieved from www.panvancouver.ca/declining-enrollment-population-distribution.html

Phillips, O. (2015, March 30). *Revolving door of teachers costs schools billions every year*. Retrieved from NPR website: www.npr.org/sections/ed/2015/03/30/395322012/ the-hidden-costs-of-teacher-turnover

Stotko, E., Ingram, R., & Beaty-O'Ferrall, M. (2007). Promising strategies for attracting and retaining successful urban teachers. *Urban Education*, 42, 30–51. https://doi. org/10.1177/0042085906293927

Strachan, J. (2016, September 22). *Learning from the Ontario's new teacher induction program (NTIP)*. Paper presented at Teacher and Induction Mentoring Forum, Ontario. Retrieved from https://spark.adobe.com/page/aeJmO/

Teach for Canada. (2019). *Why we exist*. Retrieved from Teach For Canada website: https://teachforcanada.ca/en/about/why-we-exist/

Thames Valley District School Board. (2019). *New teacher induction program*. Retrieved from http://sites.tvdsb.ca/StaffDev.cfm?subpage=88293

Van Nuland, S. (2011). Teacher education in Canada, *Journal of Education for Teaching*, 37(4), 409–421. https://doi.org/10.1080/02607476.2011.611222

Winnipeg School Division. (2019). *Professional learning and leadership centre*. Retrieved from www.winnipegsd.ca/PLLC/Pages/default.aspx

13

HIGH SCHOOL TEACHER RETENTION

Solutions in the Chinese context

Honggang Liu and Zongqiang Li

Introduction

Teachers play an important part in the growth of human beings (Hanushek, 1992), and how to retain them in teaching posts has been the focus of research around the globe since the 1980s (Hong, 2012; Ingersoll, 2001; Strong, 2005). Teacher attrition and retention are two sides of the same coin (Carmel & Badash, 2018); on the one hand, teacher attrition means that qualified teachers leave their jobs before the age of retirement (Kelchtermans, 2017), and on the other hand, teacher retention aims to combat teacher attrition or turnover to keep teachers in their positions. Retaining teachers is a systematic project involving multiple factors, from the macro-level of implementing positive education policies, to the micro-level of organising various programmes of teacher training.

In China, teacher attrition has been a focus of central government, and many policies have emerged to keep teachers in their posts. These include increasing the salaries and improving the social welfare of teachers by, for instance, providing a rental allowance for teachers who have no houses or offering them low-rent housing. In order to enlist more outstanding high school students to receive four-year teacher education in six selected top normal universities,[1] and to recruit them into the teaching profession, especially into teaching in rural areas after their graduation (Wang & Gao, 2013), the Ministry of Education (MoE) of China implemented the Free Teacher Education (FTE) policy in 2007 (MoE, 2007). In 2018, the FTE policy was renamed the Public-Funded Teacher Education (PFTE) policy (MoE, 2018); the different name foregrounds the features of this programme in which teacher education is free of tuition fees, accommodation is provided and students receive a stipend. PTFE also reduced the required period of service after graduation from ten years in FTE to at least six years.

In 2012, one year after the first group of FTE graduates had worked for a year, the MoE of China piloted The Implementation Measures of Master's Degree in Education (MAEd) Programme for FTE Graduates Implemented in Normal Universities under the Supervision of the Ministry of Education (Trial Version) (FTE-MAEd programme) (MoE, 2012). The FTE-MAEd programme offers in-service education to further advance teachers' professional development, and it is aimed at retaining more teachers in their posts. Different types of in-service teacher training, such as *Guo Pei* (National Teacher Training Programme) and online or offline school-based lectures on teacher development, have also been organised recently to strengthen teacher retention. In the following sections, I will firstly focus my attention on policies and then discuss the micro-level of retaining teachers through a university-based teacher training programme.

Free teacher education policy: explicit recruitment and implicit retention of teachers

The FTE policy was implemented from September 2007 in six top normal universities directly administered by the Ministry of Education. Beijing Normal University, East China Normal University, Northeast Normal University, Central China Normal University, Shaanxi Normal University and Southwest University were selected to run this programme.

Candidates become eligible for the programme by making the FTE their first choice in selecting their university study and achieving the required entrance marks. They are then admitted to one of these universities, where they follow a major of subject education, such as English or physical education. During their four-year learning, the central government of China provides them with a package of 'two-free, and one-support', which means free tuition, free accommodation and a monthly 600-yuan stipend. The stipend is dispensed for ten months of the year, and students can apply for other scholarships in addition to their stipend.

Students majoring in education under the policy of FTE can withdraw from this programme and change their majors into non-FTE within one year after they are enrolled the college. After graduation, the two versions of FTE require the FTE students to serve for a period of six to ten years in primary or secondary schools in their home provinces.[2] In some areas, such as Tianjin, they are asked to serve in rural schools for at least one year if they ultimately choose to work in urban schools.[3] Their employment (*bianzhi*) will be officially guaranteed by the government. *Bianzhi* is what graduates pursue, especially students graduating from education majors, because it is closely related to their social welfare, levels of salary and medical welfare, both when they are working and retired.

The Chinese Government implemented this policy for the purpose of channelling outstanding pre-service teachers into underdeveloped or rural areas (Wang & Gao, 2013). Although the FTE/PFTE policy explicitly functions as a teacher recruitment instrument at the macro-political level, it also has a potential or implicit impact on retaining teachers. For example, FTE/PFTE policy requires the graduates to work as teachers for a period of six to ten years because their contracts stipulate that if they leave the profession they must refund the monthly stipend, tuition and accommodation fees, pay a penalty, and they will be black-listed in National Credit Record Archives (MoE, 2007, 2018). According to Zhou (2010), the most attractive incentive of this programme is that it offers financial support for outstanding students from families in poverty; this suggests that most of the FTE graduates will not break their contracts because they are not able to pay back the required amounts. *Bianzhi* and the reputation of the normal universities involved in the FTE programme are another two attractions for FTE graduates when they choose this programme (Wang & Gao, 2013), and can play a role in retaining teachers in their profession. *Bianzhi* is a key issue related to salary and other welfare benefits, such as healthcare insurance, which is provided during FTE graduates' working lifetime and after their retirement. The universities' reputation and ranking support the FTE graduates once they are employed; their training gives them the symbolic capital of being a talented teacher who has graduated from a top university, and they will be treated as future leaders in their schools.

Shang & Yu (2018) investigated the FTE graduates of different disciplines ten years after the FTE programme was implemented and found that over 97 per cent of graduates who worked for one to six years still stayed in their posts as teachers in urban primary schools and high schools. Over 90 per cent of students have been officially guaranteed their employment *bianzhi*. There has been no official data to show the retention and attrition of FTE graduates, but Shang and Yu's study suggests that FTE was an important factor in retaining most of the graduates as teachers in urban areas.[4]

Foreign Teacher Education-Master's Degree of Education (FTE-MAEd) programme: a way to retain teachers

In 2012, a year after the first group of FTE graduates had worked for one year, the FTE-MAEd programme was piloted by the MoE. The aim was to encourage these novice teachers to participate in continuing professional development as part-time MAEd students. The six normal universities involved in the FTE programme were selected to recruit the in-service teachers whose BA degrees were obtained from FTE/PFTE, thereby waiving the entry examinations. If they obtain enough credits within three to five years, and pass the candidature confirmation viva and final viva, they are awarded their MAEd degree.

The courses offered by this programme have compulsory and optional modules. All the courses are delivered by a combination of distance learning and face-to-face teaching in the winter and summer vacations. Let me provide an example of the MAEd Programme of English Education designed by the School of Foreign Languages, Northeast Normal University (NENU). The compulsory modules are, for example, courses on Politics; General Teacher Education; The History of Schools of Modern Foreign Language Teaching; English Curriculum

Development and Textbook Analysis; English Teaching Design; and English Learning Theory. Optional modules include Applied Linguistics and Second Language Acquisition, and Cross-language Cultural Research. These courses become the major channels for the students to gain knowledge, explore effective solutions to their teaching problems, and motivate themselves to work harder to become excellent teachers.

The FTE-MAEd programme, as a continuing policy of FTE, gives the FTE graduates access to furthering their education in their first five working years. This period is critical for both their development and for preventing their attrition from their posts (Ingersoll, 2001) because burnout, job dissatisfaction, lack of recognition from other colleagues and school leaders (Kelchtermans, 2017) are all factors that are likely to affect novice teachers' motivation to continue. This policy offers an opportunity for them to refresh their knowledge, and to give them the strength to continue with teaching.

This policy stipulates that local governments must pay due attention to providing necessary working and living conditions for FTE graduates in rural areas, such as office space and dormitories, and to giving these teachers the required allowances (MoE, 2012, Article 17). Improving the living and working conditions, and increasing the salary and other welfare benefits, such as providing low-rent housing, have been evidenced as effective ways to retain teachers (Shang & Yu, 2018). These measures are aimed at meeting teachers' basic safety and physiological needs (Maslow, 1957), removing any worries relating to their living and working conditions. This policy also emphasises the importance of in-service teacher training and requires the local Bureau of Education and school to support FTE graduates' professional development by organising training (MoE, 2012, Article 16). Between 69 and 76 per cent of the schools and local governments fulfilled their promises of supplying graduates with houses or other extra benefits as contracts required (Shang & Yu, 2018), suggesting that action needs to be taken to ensure that all graduates receive the welfare to which they are entitled.

In the following section, a case of training of English teachers will be reported to illustrate the impact of further training on teacher retention at a micro-level.

Teacher retention: evidence from a university-based, in-service training of English teachers in NENU, China

Whether university should play a role in initial teacher education or teacher professional development has been a hot topic since the last century. Until now, enough evidence has shown that universities effectively prepare teachers and carry out in-service training to sustain teachers' motivation, and refresh and expand their professional knowledge to retain them in their profession (Moon, 2016). Various forms of university-based training and education have emerged in the process of teacher professionalism in different nations and various contexts. In China, there are three major types of in-service training, namely, the programmes initiated by the MoE of China, such as the FTE-MAEd programme and the National Training Programme (*Guopei*); local training organised by local education bureaux; and university-based collaboration with high/primary schools or other education institutions.

In this section, I will report on interviews with a male teacher, Thomas, who participated in a university-based training programme in 2015 to illustrate the effect this training can have. This project was initiated by my university (NENU), and the School of Foreign Languages (SFL), my working unit, was assigned to carry out this English teacher training. This project was designed as a five-day intensive in-service teacher training for the supervisors of undergraduates' teaching practicum who worked in local high schools in rural or underdeveloped areas. Sixty English teachers involved in this training were selected on the basis of their contribution to teaching quality in their own schools (seen, for instance, in the number of students successful in entry examinations to universities), and the quality of their support for undergraduates undertaking teaching practice in the school. The first aim of this training was to augment the participants' professional knowledge with the introduction of theories of linguistics, applied linguistics, English education and related theories by the professors of English education in my school. The second was to implement these theories in English classes under the guidance of expert teachers in the top high schools in Changchun, the city in which NENU is located.

At the end of this training, participants were invited to fill in a questionnaire to give feedback on this programme. Based on the contact information given voluntarily by the respondents of the questionnaire, ten teachers came to the follow-up interview. All of them reported that they were happy to learn about why and how to teach, and expressed strong motivation to put what they had learned into practice. However, I selected only one respondent, Thomas, as the example for this chapter, because he was the only one who participated in two interviews with an interval of three years (the first interview was at the end of the course in 2015, and the second was in October, 2018). Thomas' longitudinal view can offer me more insights into the effects of the training.

Thomas works in a rural senior high school where I have supervised the teaching practicum for the FTE candidates since 2012. He is the team leader of English teaching in his school and is also the local supervisor for this teaching practicum every year. This made it possible for me to carry out two interviews with a long interval between them. However, the most important thing is that when I came to this school in 2018 and talked about the training in 2015, he described how he missed it and what he learned from it. The training seemed to have left a deep impression on him, so I invited him to take part in a second interview. Before both interviews I explained the ethical processes of the research in terms of aims, confidentiality, data security and the contact information for the academic committee and myself; he voluntarily signed the consent form in which he agreed to participate in the research under the terms we discussed.

Thomas was a novice English teacher who, in 2015, had been working in a senior rural high school for three years. During the training, he involved himself in all the lectures on different topics such as Dialogue Structure and High School English Classroom Teaching; Lesson Design: A Perspective of Scaffolding; and

Group Collaborative Learning in English Classroom Teaching. He actively participated in group discussions, submitted his reflective journals on time every day, and completed two observations of the demonstration lessons in a top senior high school. He was awarded a certificate for completing the training at the end of the course. In what follows, I quote verbatim from his interview to illustrate his immediate response to the course:

Excerpt 1 (2015):

LIU: Would you mind talking about your achievements in this training?

THOMAS: At the first sight of my name of the training list, I couldn't believe my eyes, since I haven't received systematic training since I entered this current high school in 2012. The lectures during this week were very impressive to me, because I knew little about the themes of what the professors delivered. Professor A introduced the concept of classroom discourse, a relatively new term to me, and I think I will pay more attention to adjusting my discourse during my classroom teaching in order to facilitate students' learning. Miss B [the expert teacher from a key high school in Changchun] described her strategies of organising group work in her class, which were very beneficial for me. I plan to try it. I also went to the key high school to observe how the expert teacher carried out their teaching. During training breaks, I wrote my reflective journals. From the training, my dried pool of knowledge was irrigated. You may not believe it but my university didn't offer such excellent lectures or courses to us during my learning many years ago. It's the first time for me to learn so much. In fact, I had burnout, academically speaking, when I finished my first year of teaching, for I was burdened with a huge workload of more than 15 hours (four classes, 1 lesson/45 minutes) per week, and countless hours of supervision. This burnout became more severe day by day, and I even doubted whether I was suitable for this profession. I also wanted to do other jobs, for example, to run my own business of selling fashionable clothes. During this week of training, I actively involved myself in every activity, and group or individual reflection. It seemed that I found a key to solve the above difficulties.

LIU: Will you stay in your school when going back?

THOMAS: Yes, of course. I think I may stay in school for a period to see whether I can change my teaching style, and use more effective teaching strategies by reviewing what I learned in this training and reading the books recommended by the teachers in their lectures.

During this interview, over-work caused Thomas to be 'burnt out' and even intending to leave this job; his lack of professional in-service training worsened his feelings of burnout. As the literature on teacher attrition has indicated, school characteristics (such as location, school size, pupil characteristics and opportunities for professional development) and other factors can influence teacher retention. A lack of professional development means that practicing teachers risk losing confidence and can contribute to them seeking to change job, especially novice teachers in their first five years of teaching. However, high-quality training will be of help in retaining teachers to some extent. The training Thomas received supported his development as a teacher and re-motivated him, possibly building up his confidence to be a teacher for a longer period. In the autumn of 2018, when I met Thomas in his school, I asked him about effects of the training in 2015 and the connections between the training and his teaching in the past three years. These are described in Excerpt 2.

Excerpt 2 (2018):

THOMAS: After my return to school, I tried to change my teaching. The strategies of carrying out effective group work, of regulating discourses in praising students and correcting them, and ways of managing the classroom that I observed in the demonstration classes assisted me in regulating my teaching and improving my teaching efficiency. I once told you I was highly burnt out and wanted to give up teaching, because I was bored with teaching ineffectively; the average marks of the whole classes I taught were always lower than the others. After that training, I tried the methods I learned and had some achievements in terms of improved marks of the whole classes I taught. I came out of the burnout step by step, since the teaching became less burdensome. I felt happier in teaching. I think effective classroom teaching helped me out of my unhappiness and I naturally didn't have feelings of burnout, since I found a balance in my working life.

LIU: Will you run your own business of selling some clothes, for example, which you mentioned in 2015?

THOMAS: Well, I said it in our interview in 2015. But now, I think I will stay in my post for at least ten years, even when my contract runs out, because I can distribute my time and energy to my current work in a balanced way, and gain enjoyment through my work.

LIU: Is there any relationship between your plan to stay in your post and the training in 2015?

THOMAS: Yes, I think there must be some relationship, not completely but at least to a large extent. As I once mentioned, that was my first in-service training from the time I entered my school. What I learned in my first teacher training university didn't help me to run my class effectively, and I was not able to enjoy and feel confident in my work. The training in 2015 was like a charger to empower me, an out-of-power battery, by inputting new knowledge, demonstrating effective teaching, and introducing me to reflective teaching. Thanks to this training, I came back to school with energy, made some changes in my teaching and I am now enjoying being an English teacher.

This dialogue suggests that the in-service training can play a part in retaining teachers, as it 'was like a charger to empower' this research participant. Thomas could utilise what he learned to enhance his teaching quality, found effective ways to balance his workload and finally enjoyed his work. As he suggested, the training cannot be a 100 per cent useful tool to keep him in his post, but it functioned greatly as a re-motivator 'to a large extent' for his planning to stay in his post 'for at least ten years', even when the restrictions under his contract run out. Thomas' experiences shows that university-based training for in-service teachers can genuinely help to provide them with weapons to fight against teaching burnout, and most importantly, to co-function with policy and other measures as a tool to retain teachers in their profession.

Conclusion

In this chapter, the roles of policies and in-service teacher training programmes have been carefully examined. For the retention of teachers in China, the FTE/PFTE programmes help to retain teachers for a certain period of at least six to ten years through their contracts and other measures, such as improving social welfare by guaranteeing basic working and living conditions. The sister FTE-MAEd programme gives teachers from the FTE programme the opportunity to receive postgraduate education, the major aim of which is to empower them in terms of their professional knowledge, reflective skills and capacity to undertake research to improve their teaching. The coherence of these policies enriches the FTE teachers' bank of knowledge and increases their education level. The accrued cultural capital (Bourdieu, 1986) can implicitly raise the teachers' social prestige of being teachers and help teachers to win more admiration, helping teachers to be more motivated to work in their posts for a longer time.

University-based training is a highly recommended model for retaining teachers. The in-service training offered by universities can be organised in a flexible way in terms of frequency, time, place, course modules and structure. Designing further effective training programmes and tracing their effects in retaining teachers is another task for us in the future.

Notes

1 Normal university in China refers to the university whose major role is to train school teachers. The six normal universities are Beijing Normal University, East China Normal University, Northeast Normal University, Central China Normal University, Southwest University and Shaanxi Normal University.

2 The first version of FTE (MoE, 2007) requires a 10-year compulsory service and the second requires a six-year service (MoE, 2018).

3 The FTE programme requires the candidates to return to their home province and sign a working contract either directly with a local school or with the local Bureau of Education, which offers students the possibility of working in rural or urban schools.

4 A certain quota is dispatched to rural areas, but the policy of 'where you come, where you return' does not restrict the candidates to going back to the schools of their childhood. They can go back to the city or the county in their home province to work after graduation, although they may come from villages. So the students have some rights to choose

whether they work in rural or urban areas. That is a possible reason why Shang and Yu (2018) did not tell us about the retention of FTE candidates in rural areas.

References

Bourdieu, P. (1986). The forms of capital. In J. Richardson (Ed.), *Handbook of theory and research for the sociology of education* (pp. 241–58). Westport, CT: Greenwood.

Carmel, R., & Badash, M. (2018). Views on attrition and retention among beginning English as a foreign language (EFL) teachers in Israel and implications for teacher education. *Teaching and Teacher Education, 70*, 142–152.

Hanushek, E. A. (1992). The trade-off between child quantity and quality. *Journal of Political Economy, 100*, 84–117.

Hong, J. Y. (2012). Why do some beginning teachers leave the school, and others stay? Understanding teacher resilience through psychological lenses. *Teachers and Teaching, 18*, 417–440.

Ingersoll, R. M. (2001). Teacher turnover and teacher shortages: An organizational analysis. *American Educational Research Journal, 38*, 499–534.

Kelchtermans, G. (2017). 'Should I stay or should I go?': Unpacking teacher attrition / retention as an educational issue. *Teachers and Teaching, 23*, 961–977.

Maslow, A. H. (1957). *Motivation and personality*. New York: Harper & Row.

Moon, B. (Ed.). (2016). *Do universities have a role in the education and training of teachers?: An international analysis of policy and practice*. Cambridge: Cambridge University Press.

Ministry of Education [MoE]. (2007). *Implementation measures of Free Teacher Education Policy enforced in normal universities under supervision of the Ministry of Education* [in Chinese]. Retrieved from http://news.xinhuanet.com/edu/2007-05/14/content_6098291.htm

Ministry of Education [MoE]. (2012). *The Implementation measures of Master's Degree in Education (MAEd) Program for FTE Graduates enforced in Normal Universities under Supervision of the Ministry of Education (Trial Version)*. Retrieved from www.moe.gov.cn/srcsite/A10/s7011/201005/t20100526_145913.html

Ministry of Education [MoE]. (2018). *Implementation measures of Public-Fund Free Teacher Education Policy enforced in normal universities under supervision of the Ministry of Education* [in Chinese]. Retrieved from www.moe.gov.cn/jyb_xxgk/moe_1777/moe_1778/201808/t20180810_345023.html

Shang, Y., & Yu, S. (2018). A follow-up study on the implementation of free normal students employment policy: Situations, achievements, and measures: Taking the Five-year Free Normal graduates from Northeast Normal University as an example. *Journal of Northeast Normal University, 5*, 195–199.

Strong, M. (2005). Teacher induction, mentoring, and retention: A summary of the research. *The New Educator, 1*(3), 181–198.

Wang, D., & Gao, M. (2013). Educational equality or social mobility: The value conflict between pre-service teachers and the Free Teacher Education Program in China. *Teaching and Teacher Education, 32*, 66–74.

Zhou, H. (2010). Analysis and policy adjustment on the contradiction of free of charge in normation education in practice. *Educational Research, 8*, 58–61. (in Chinese).

Funding

This paper was supported by The Key Project Research on the Construction and Development of Excellent High School English Teachers' Professional Capacities in Rural Areas: A Bronfenbrenner Perspective, funded by the Academy for Research in Teacher Education, Northeast Normal University (JSJY20180105).

14

TEACHER SHORTAGE AND TEACHER SURPLUS

Jewish vs. Arab educational sectors in Israel

Smadar Donitsa-Schmidt and Ruth Zuzovsky

Introduction

In the past few years, Israel, like many other countries, has been confronted with a severe teacher shortage, especially in core school subjects such as mathematics, science and English as a Foreign Language (EFL) (Donitsa-Schmidt & Zuzovsky, 2014). This teacher shortage demonstrates an interesting social disparity because it only exists within the Jewish educational sector, while the Arab education sector is experiencing a substantial teacher surplus (Hasaisi, 2013; Worgan & Fidelman, 2008).

In terms of the labour market, a shortage occurs when demand exceeds supply, which can be caused by an increase in demand, a decrease in supply or the simultaneous occurrence of both (Guarino, Santibañez, & Daley, 2006). A shortage of qualified teachers can also be caused by a 'revolving door', wherein a large number of qualified teachers depart their jobs for reasons other than retirement (Ingersoll, 2001) (such as teacher job dissatisfaction, working conditions and the pursuit of other jobs). Regardless of the cause, teacher shortages and school staffing problems lead to inadequate school performance (Darling-Hammond, 2003).

Teacher surpluses, which occur when teacher supply exceeds demand, are much less prevalent internationally than are teacher shortages. A large oversupply of qualified teachers raises its own policy challenges, as too great a supply is not necessarily a blessing (OECD, 2005). Although oversupply might enhance teacher quality (Hendrick, 2011), it is also associated with increasing teacher unemployment rates and ineffective public funding expenditure (Hsiao-Jung, 2013).

This chapter examines the current teaching workforce situation in the Israeli context by focusing on the teacher shortage in the Jewish sector and the teacher surplus in the Arab one. The chapter concentrates on the magnitudes and causes of these phenomena, as well as on several national policy initiatives that were enacted in the past decade to remedy the situation in the hope of creating appropriate teacher supplies in both communities.

The chapter is divided into four main parts. The first part provides a general introduction to the State of Israel, its population, its school education system and its teacher education structure. The second part presents facts and figures from multiple sources related to the teacher shortage and surplus in Israel. The third part elaborates on the reasons why Israel is currently experiencing both a teacher shortage and surplus. The fourth part presents the main policy actions that were implemented in recent years to remedy the situation and the challenges that accompany them.

The Israeli education context

The State of Israel has a population of approximately 9,000,000 inhabitants, with 74 per cent Jews (whose first language is Hebrew) and 21 per cent Israeli Arabs (whose first language is Arabic). The remaining 5 per cent are various non-Israeli groups (Central Bureau of Statistics [CBS], 2019). This division directly impacts the education system, which is nearly completely segregated. Jewish pupils study in Jewish schools, are taught by Jewish teachers and their language of instruction is Hebrew, while Arab pupils study in Arab schools, are taught by Arab teachers and their language of instruction is Arabic. As of 2019, there are approximately 1,800,000 pupils in the Israeli education system, with 80 per cent in the Jewish sector and 20 per cent in the Arab one (CBS, 2019). Further, there are 157,610 teachers in total, with 115,738 (73 per cent) teaching in the Jewish sector and 42,872 (27 per cent) in the Arab sector. The pupil/teacher class ratios are similar in the two sectors (CBS, 2019).

Despite the two separate systems, nearly all the schools in Israel are state schools, publicly funded and governed by the Israeli Ministry of Education (MoE). The schools in each sector are also appropriately adjusted to fit each population's language, culture and religion.

The division between the Jewish and Arab education systems directly impacts initial teacher education, which mostly occurs in academic colleges of education. Of the existing 21 academic teacher education colleges, 18 are Hebrew-speaking teacher colleges and three are Arabic-speaking teacher colleges. Approximately ten per cent of the teachers are studying at the nine research universities (which serve both populations). Additionally, there are 30 small, non-academic ultraorthodox teacher seminaries, whose graduates only teach in an independent ultraorthodox stream. This chapter does not discuss this latter stream.

Regardless of the higher education institution type, initial teacher education is mostly a four-year academic programme that awards a teaching diploma and either a Bachelor of Education (BEd) or a Bachelor of Arts (BA). Following their studies, new teachers in both sectors complete a one-year induction programme that consists of several support mechanisms to ease their entry into the profession. A teaching licensure is granted after new teachers have successfully completed their induction year, and teachers are entitled to tenure following two additional years of work.

In the academic year 2018/19, of the 28,495 students studying in the teacher education colleges, 75 per cent were Jews and 25 per cent were Arabs (CBS, 2019).

Teacher shortage and teacher surplus in Israel

Over the past decade, national statistics have consistently predicted there to be a huge teacher shortage in the Jewish sector (CBS, 2007, 2010, 2013). The 2013 projections expected there to be a shortage of approximately 8,000 teachers in the year 2018, comprising about 7 per cent of the Jewish sector teachers (Hasaisi, 2013, p. 5). However, MoE reports do not corroborate these shortage projections, supporting their claims with the fact that there are no vacant teaching positions at the beginning of every school year (Worgan, 2007, p. 6). Despite the MoE claims that there is no teacher shortage in Jewish schools, studies reveal the exact opposite (Donitsa-Schmidt & Zuzovsky, 2014, 2016). These studies have shown that, to solve the qualified teacher shortage problem, principals utilise a variety of strategies. One of the main strategies is the hiring of unqualified and uncertified personnel to fill in the needed teaching positions. A State Comptroller report (2019) corroborated these findings, criticising the situation and claiming that a large percentage of elementary and secondary school teachers do not have the necessary qualifications. In some cases, more than half of the teachers are unqualified, as often occurs with science and mathematics teachers (State Comptroller, 2019, p. 938).

In the Arab sector, the opposite situation exists, as national statistics document that there is a massive surplus of teachers, which leads to extensive and cumulative lists of unemployed qualified teachers. For example, the data indicate that less than half of the Arab pre-service teacher graduates were able to find teaching positions after graduation in the years 2012/14 (Wininger, 2018). The MoE does acknowledge the superfluous situation in the Arab teaching force (Parliamentary Inquiry Committee, 2008).

The authors undertook to compare the teacher supply and demand in the two sectors to provide an estimation of the teacher shortage (Jewish sector) and surplus size (Arab sector). We received the teacher supply data by request from the Israeli MoE (CBS published figures 2018), and this included the number of student teachers who began their induction year between 2008 and 2018. We then measured the teacher demand data against the number of new teachers who joined the workforce to teach all subjects in all school levels during the years 2008/18. The following figures display the supply and demand of new teachers in the Jewish sector (Figure 14.1) and in the Arab sector (Figure 14.2) for the years 2008/18.

Figure 14.1 indicates that, although more student teachers have been trained every year over the past decade to teach in Jewish schools, these numbers do

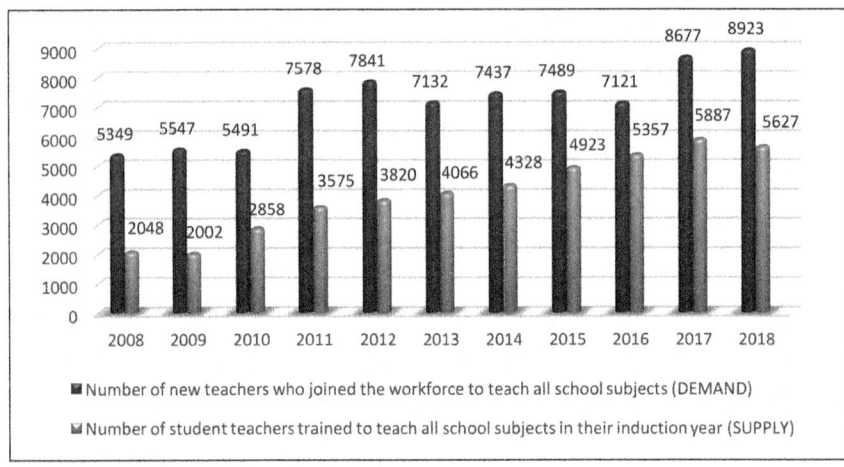

FIGURE 14.1 Teacher supply and demand in the Jewish sector in 2008/18

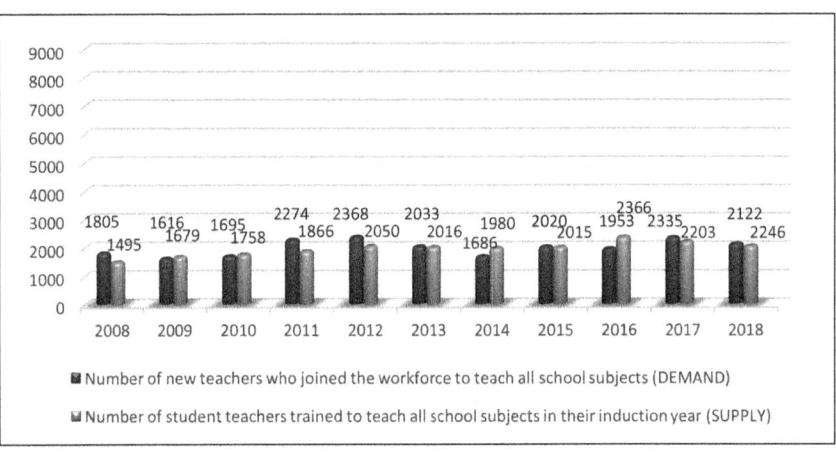

FIGURE 14.2 Teacher supply and demand in the Arab sector in 2008/18

not meet the growing demand for teachers in the Jewish education system. Demand has exceeded supply over the years, leading to a severe teacher shortage of approximately 4,000 teachers in 2009, 2011, 2012 and 2018. The shortage decreased between 2013 and 2016, but it again increased in 2017 and 2018 to a similar magnitude as the previous decade's (2008) shortage.

Figure 14.2 depicts that the Arab sector situation is entirely different than the Jewish sector one. Throughout the years, there has been a very small notable difference between the number of student teachers completing their induction each year (supply) and the total number of new teachers joining the teaching force (demand). Over the years, it appears that supply and demand are balanced, as demand has not exceeded supply (and vice versa). Yet, this is not entirely true because there are many student teachers who could not find teaching positions for their induction year.

Figure 14.3 presents a graphical display of the gaps between supply and demand in the two sectors, that is, subtracting the number of new teachers who joined the teaching force (demand) from the number who were in their induction year (supply). The zero line presents a balanced state between supply and demand. Values below zero indicate a shortage while values above zero indicate a surplus.

As demonstrated in Figure 14.3, all of the Jewish sector values fall below the zero line, indicating a teacher shortage. The gaps range from a shortage of 3,301 teachers in 2008 to 3,296 teachers in 2018. Although the gaps appear to decrease from 2013 to 2016 (reaching 1,764 teachers in 2016), the gap increases again in 2017 and 2018 to a magnitude similar to the 2008 shortage. In sharp contrast with the Jewish sector, the Arab sector gap values fall around the zero line (i.e., a supply/demand balance). Yet, the actual reality in schools is that the new teachers cannot outnumber the recruited ones. These findings suggest that a surplus still exists.

The shortage and surplus also become evident upon examining the differences between the two sectors in relation to the percentage of teachers leaving the profession. Table 14.1 presents the percentage of teachers leaving teaching

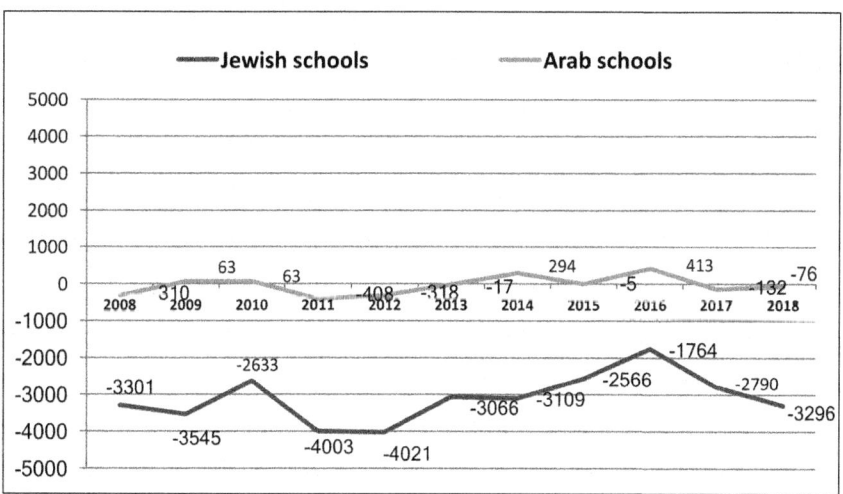

FIGURE 14.3   Gaps between teacher supply and demand in the Jewish and Arab sectors

TABLE 14.1 Percentage of all teachers leaving the education system during the years 2009/16

Jews	4.8	4.2	4.6	4.2	4.3	4.3	4.3	4.8
Arabs	2.5	2.4	2.4	2.6	2.5	2.5	2.7	3.6
Year	2009	2010	2011	2012	2013	2014	2015	2016

Source: CBS, 2019, p. 12.

TABLE 14.2 Percentage of pre-service graduates entering the education system within two years of graduating during the years 2005/15

Jews	52	50	54	55	59	59	58	62	64	65	66
Arabs	67	67	67	62	65	59	62	55	47	51	53
Year	**2005**	**2006**	**2007**	**2008**	**2009**	**2010**	**2011**	**2012**	**2013**	**2014**	**2015**

Source: Wininger, 2018, p. 8.

from 2009 to 2016 (CBS, 2019), and the table illustrates that these percentages are much higher in the Jewish sector than in the Arab sector. This indicates that there is a higher attrition rate in the Jewish sector, which leads to more open teaching positions. The exact opposite is true in the Arab sector, where a lower attrition rate is noticeable. In addition to the total percentage of teachers leaving the profession every year, the statistics also indicate that there is a significantly higher teacher attrition in the first three years of work for the Jewish sector teachers in comparison with the Arab ones – 22 versus 16 per cent (CBS, 2015, p. 3).

Table 14.2 presents the percentages of pre-service teachers who graduated between 2005/15 and who entered the education system within two years after graduation (Wininger, 2018). The table shows that only 50 to 60 per cent of the graduates in both sectors enter the teaching profession. These percentages are seemingly similar, but the underlying reasons for these occurrences differ by sector. The low percentages in the Jewish sector, despite the recent increases, reflect the existing teacher shortage as graduates choose not to enter the teaching profession. The low percentages in the Arab sector, which have even decreased over the years, reflect the inability of graduates to find teaching positions as there are fewer open positions. The next section elaborates on the reasons why these situations have arisen (Wininger, 2018).

Reasons for the teacher shortage and surplus

The unattractiveness of Israel's teaching profession can explain the teacher shortage in Jewish schools (Weisblay, 2013). Israeli teachers at all levels of education are civil servants who perform their duties under fixed-term contracts, which are set by the Israeli Government and agreed upon by the teacher unions. In comparison with other OECD countries, Israeli teachers' average gross salaries are ranked as one of the lowest at all school levels (OECD, 2018). When compared to other professions' salaries, teachers (most of whom are women) still earn below average salaries and even earn less than those in similar professions, such as nursing and social work (CBS, 2017). Furthermore, salaries of new teachers are particularly low during their first years of teaching (Ritov & Karil, 2017). After ten years in the profession, teachers' salaries are still slightly below the average wage for all workers in Israel. Their salaries only equal the total workers' average after teaching for 11 years (Ministry of Finance, 2019).

The Israeli teachers' working conditions are also unappealing. In terms of teachers' workloads, compared to other OECD countries, class size is one of the largest at all school levels and the average number of weekly working hours is slightly above the OECD average at all school levels (OECD, 2018). The physical conditions provided to teachers in the schools are also not satisfactory, as they do not have any private workspace (State Comptroller, 2015).

Not surprisingly, the professional status of teaching in Israel is considered to be relatively low. In a carefully designed international survey of 21 countries that compared the global status of teachers using the Teacher Status Index scale, Israel was ranked at the bottom (Dolton & Marcenaro-Gutierrez, 2013) in comparison to Brazil, China, Czech Republic, Egypt, Finland, France, Germany, Greece, Italy, Japan, the Netherlands, New Zealand, Portugal, Turkey, Singapore, South Korea, Spain, Switzerland, the UK and the US. The survey also found that Israelis do not trust teachers to deliver quality education to pupils, and that Israeli teachers ranked lowest in terms of how respected they are. Finally, fewer than ten per cent of the respondents stated that they would encourage their child to become a teacher.

The low professional status, low salaries, heavy workloads and lack of appropriate physical conditions have led to the current teacher shortage in the Jewish sector. These conditions have made it challenging to recruit suitable teacher education college candidates and to retain them as teachers, which ultimately leads to a shortage.

Given the low salaries and poor professional status of teaching in Israel, it seems rather surprising that there is a teacher surplus in the Arab sector. As minorities living in a conflictual situation, Arab academics encounter numerous social, cultural and linguistic difficulties that hinder their integration into the labour market (Al-Haj, 2012). The majority of Arabs prefer holding stable public-sector positions, as it is difficult for them to find employment in private Jewish companies (whether due to linguistic or social barriers) (Agbaria & Pinson, 2013; Arar & Massry-Herzllah, 2016). The public-sector positions that are open to Arabs are mostly in healthcare and teaching, and these positions provide occupational security, allow them to work in close proximity to their homes and enable them to use their first language (Al-Haj, 2012). The combination of high numbers of pre-service Arab teachers and the low teacher attrition rates in Arabic-speaking schools has led to a teacher surplus in the Arab sector.

Policy actions that aim to balance teacher supply and demand in Israel

Several national policy actions have been implemented to address the gaps between teacher supply and demand in the two sectors. The policy actions aimed at addressing the Jewish sector shortage focus on recruiting and retaining teachers. The policies endorsed to cope with the Arab sector surplus largely concentrate on both limiting the number of student teachers in initial education and on expanding existing teachers' employment opportunities.

The most comprehensive policy actions resulted from a 'National Task Force' (the Dovrat Committee), which the MoE appointed in 2003 to promote the teaching profession. Subsequently, two major reforms were launched at the primary school level in 2008 (the 'New Horizon' reform) and at the secondary school level in 2012 ('Courage to Change' reform). In both these reforms, the two teacher unions were actively involved in defining the collective agreements which included a raise in teacher salaries and improvements in teacher working conditions. They were accompanied by massive media campaigns, encouraging candidates to opt for teaching as their career choice. Yet, although teachers' salaries were raised, they remained low in comparison to other academics in the labour market. Moreover, the hourly wages did not change much, since teachers were expected to work longer hours to perform additional administrative tasks and/or to meet with their pupils. In addition, some aspects of the reforms were not implemented, such as providing teachers with private work spaces to accommodate their heavier workloads (State Comptroller, 2015). The policies did not improve the teaching profession, as the teachers' workloads increased and their salaries and working conditions did not improve.

Another policy action to increase teacher recruitment followed international trends and opened alternative routes for initial teacher education for the first time in 2008. These include shortened and fully funded teacher education programmes aimed to recruit university graduates, particularly in core-subject areas such as mathematics, science and EFL. These programmes are largely directed at the Jewish populations that traditionally have not turned to teaching (e.g., high-tech professionals) (Weinberger & Donitsa-Schmidt, 2016). Although several alternative initial teacher education programmes have opened since 2008, there are not enough of these programmes and they have only been opened in moments of crisis. In addition, Weinberger and Donitsa-Schmidt (2016) found that many of the teachers who were trained in these programmes dropped out of the system within their first five years of teaching.

An additional national policy that aims to increase teacher recruitment in the Jewish sector focuses on lowering the admission criteria for initial teacher education programmes. This policy is executed by accepting applicants based only on their high school diploma results and disregarding the required psychometric entrance test that measures academic competencies. While 84 per cent of all first-year student teachers had psychometric scores in 2010, these numbers dropped to 55 per cent in 2017 (CBS, 2011, Table 8.49; CBS, 2017, Table 8.55). In addition, the high school grade point average required for admission was also lowered. Lowering the entrance requirements did attract more students; yet, claims have been made that these policies lower the quality of soon-to-be teachers (Ritov & Karil, 2017).

An additional strategy to attract teacher candidates is the MoE's tuition incentive offer, which is extended to pre-service teachers to study school subjects that have specific teacher shortages (MoE, 2019). Yet, these monetary incentives are not attractive, as they are limited to a small number of school subjects, cover only half of the tuition costs and require candidates to commit to teaching for several years. In addition, these incentives are offered only to applicants who have taken the psychometric test. Yet, since the psychometric test was no longer a requirement, only a few student teachers benefited from these incentives.

Finally, to lower teacher attrition rates, and based on international studies (e.g., Ingersoll & Strong, 2011), Israel has been focusing on the professional support processes provided to beginning teachers. As of 2015, the induction year can only be completed in approved schools and under the MoE's direct supervision. Furthermore, during their induction year, student teachers are required to only teach the school subjects that they were trained in. In 2018/19, a new type of induction workshop was launched. These workshops are less generic and more tailormade to the needs of teachers in a specific local authority or educational institution. They are aimed at generating more responsibility and direct involvement of school principals and other community officials to support new teachers' needs (MoE, 2019). It is too early to assess the induction workshops' effectiveness, as they are still in their pilot stages.

The first policy action that was implemented to reduce the Arab sector's teacher surplus, which was designed by the MoE in 2011, focuses on limiting the number of student teachers in the three Arab colleges by setting quotas. In 2017, a new regulation scheme was added in which the Arab colleges would receive less funding for each recruited student even with the quota regulation in place (Wininger, 2018). These policies for the Arab sector failed, as the colleges did not comply with the regulations. It is too early to determine whether or not the 2017 economic sanctions for exceeding the quotas have been useful in reducing the surplus. It should be noted that the Arab colleges appealed to the Supreme Court of Israel to annul this decision and the case is still under consideration (Wininger, 2018).

The second policy action that was implemented in the Arab sector is a five-year plan to integrate 500 Arab teachers in Jewish schools. The Israeli MoE and the *Merhavim* Association (a non-profit organisation aimed at promoting Israeli democratic culture through multicultural education) launched this plan in 2014. It was decided that 100 new Arab teachers would join the programme every year and that funds be allocated for such integration (MoE & Merhavim, 2014). Ostensibly, there is nothing more logical than directing Arab teachers to Jewish schools and thus solving both sectors' problems. Yet, logic and reality cannot always coexist, particularly in a conflict-ridden state. This five-year integration plan has been partially implemented at best. The main obstacle has been the refusal of Jewish school principals to employ Arab teachers due to their fears of tension in the classrooms and parent/student objections. In a special audit devoted to this topic, the MoE was severely criticised for not proactively reducing the stereotypes held by the Jewish school principals and teachers to change their attitudes toward their Arab counterparts (State Comptroller, 2016).

Another obstacle to this integration is overcoming the language challenges, as Hebrew is the Arab teachers' second language. There is no evidence in regard to whether the integration plan's inherent deficiencies have been rectified.

Finally, another strategy to solve the surplus is to offer the unemployed, qualified Arab sector teachers other work opportunities in informal education. This strategy was part of a five-year plan endorsed by the Ministry for Social Equality in 2016 and was expected to create more teaching posts in community centres, extracurricular recreational activities and summer camps (Ministry for Social Equality, 2017). As this is a recent plan, there is no data in regard to whether the strategy has been successful.

Conclusion

The state of affairs portrayed in the current chapter reveals that, despite the enactment of several national policy actions, there has been no change in the past decade in relation to the teacher shortage in the Jewish sector and the teacher surplus in the Arab one. It appears that the various national policies designed to solve the dual problem have been either partially implemented or ineffective. In addition, some policies are recent and have not yet had a substantial impact on the problem.

The Jewish sector's teacher shortage has led to school principals employing large numbers of unqualified teachers, thus jeopardising the Hebrew-speaking schools' educational quality (Donitsa-Schmidt & Zuzovsky, 2016). The Arab sector's teacher surplus has led to significant unemployment and to the trend of hiring part-time teachers, which contributes to job insecurity, burnout and lower job satisfaction (Agbaria & Pinson, 2013). It is considered that this situation jeopardises the level of instruction provided in Arabic-speaking schools (Parliamentary Inquiry Committee, 2008).

Given the severe ramifications of the teacher shortage and surplus on education in Israel, it is puzzling that the MoE is not taking more extreme measures to amend the situation. This is particularly perplexing, as the surplus of Arab teachers was acknowledged more than a decade ago. In addition to continuing to implement the existing policies (aside from lowering the bar for acceptance in the Jewish sector), other avenues should be explored in order to engender real change. Continuous emphasis and persistent efforts should be placed on increasing the share of Arab teachers employed in the Jewish sector. Besides solving both educational sectors' problems, this strategy is likely to strengthen the coexistence between Jews and Arabs in Israel.

References

Agbaria, A. K., & Pinson, H. (2013). When shortage coexists with surplus of teachers: The case of Arab teachers in Israel. *Diaspora, Indigenous, and Minority Education*, 7(2), 69–83.

Al-Haj, M. (2012). *Education, empowerment, and control: The case of the Arabs in Israel.* New York: SUNY Press.

Arar, K., & Massry-Herzllah, A. (2016). Motivation to teach: The case of Arab teachers in Israel. *Educational Studies, 42*(1), 19–35.

Central Bureau of Statistics [CBS]. (2007). *Statistical almanac for Israel, no. 58* [in Hebrew]. Jerusalem: CBS.

Central Bureau of Statistics [CBS]. (2010). *Statistical almanac for Israel, no. 61* [in Hebrew]. Jerusalem: CBS.

Central Bureau of Statistics [CBS]. (2011). *Statistical almanac for Israel, no. 62* [in Hebrew]. Jerusalem: CBS.

Central Bureau of Statistics [CBS]. (2013). *Statistical almanac for Israel, no. 64* [in Hebrew]. Jerusalem: CBS.

Central Bureau of Statistics [CBS]. (2015). *New teachers dropping out of the education system 2000–2014* [in Hebrew]. Jerusalem: CBS.

Central Bureau of Statistics [CBS]. (2017). *Statistical almanac for Israel, no. 68* [in Hebrew]. Jerusalem: CBS.

Central Bureau of Statistics [CBS]. (2018). *Statistical almanac for Israel, no. 69* [in Hebrew]. Jerusalem: CBS.

Central Bureau of Statistics [CBS]. (2019). *Media release: Teaching staff 2018/19* [in Hebrew]. Retrieved from www.cbs.gov.il/he/mediarelease/DocLib/2019/093/06_19_093b.pdf

Central Bureau of Statistics [CBS]. (2019). *Statistical almanac for Israel, no. 70* [in Hebrew]. Jerusalem: CBS.

Darling-Hammond, L. (2003). Keeping good teachers: Why it matters, what leaders can do. *Educational leadership, 60*(8), 6–13.

Dolton, P., & Marcenaro-Gutierrez, O. (2013). *2013 global teacher status index.* London: Varkey Gems Foundations.

Donitsa-Schmidt, S., & Zuzovsky, R. (2014). Teacher supply and demand: The school level perspective. *American Journal of Educational Research, 2*(6), 420–9.

Donitsa-Schmidt, S., & Zuzovsky, R. (2016). Quantitative and qualitative teacher shortage and the turnover phenomenon. *International Journal of Educational Research, 77,* 83–91.

Guarino, C., Santibañez, L., & Daley, G. (2006). Teacher recruitment and retention. *Review of Educational Research, 72*(2), 173–208.

Hasaisi, R. (2013). *Teacher shortage* [in Hebrew]. Jerusalem: Government Research Center.

Hendrick, I. G. (2011). California's first 100 years: Establishing state responsibility for quality of teachers (1850–1950). In E. G. Brown, Jr. (Ed.), *A history of policies and forces shaping California teacher credentialing* (pp. 17–31). Sacramento, CA: Commission on Teacher Credentialing.

Hsiao-Jung, L. I. (2013). The oversupply of teachers in Taiwan: Causes and consequences. *Education Journal, 41*(1–2), 107–133.

Ingersoll, R. M. (2001). Teacher turnover and teacher shortages: An organizational analysis. *American Educational Research Journal, 38*(3), 499–534.

Ingersoll, R. M., & Strong, M. (2011). The impact of induction and mentoring programs for beginning teachers: A critical review of the research. *Review of Educational Research, 81*(2), 201–233.

Ministry for Social Equality. (2017). *Governmental Act 922: Economic development in minority populations 2016–2020, implementation guide* [in Hebrew]. Jerusalem: Ministry for Social Equality.

Ministry of Education [MoE]. (2019). *'Greenhouse' induction workshops for new teachers* [in Hebrew]. Jerusalem: Ministry of Education.

Ministry of Education [MoE], & Merhavim. (2014). *Integrating and being integrated: The integration of Arab teachers in Jewish school. A guide for teachers and principals* [in Hebrew]. Lod: Merhavim.

Ministry of Finance. (2019). *Yearly report of the Supervisor of wages and labour agreements for the year 2017* [in Hebrew]. Jerusalem: Ministry of Finance.

Organisation for Economic Cooperation and Development [OECD]. (2005). *Teachers matter: Attracting, developing and retaining effective teachers.* Paris: OECD Publishing.

Organisation for Economic Cooperation and Development [OECD]. (2018). *Education at a glance: OECD indicators.* Paris: OECD Publishing.

Parliamentary Inquiry Committee (Tibi Committee) (2008, September 8). *The integration of Arab employees in the public sector* [in Hebrew]. Minutes No. 7. Jerusalem: Retrieved from the Knesset website: https://oknesset.org/meetings/3/0/307878.html

Ritov, M., & Karil, Z. (2017). *The qualification of teaches in the Israeli educational system* [in Hebrew]. Jerusalem: Ministry of Finance.

State Comptroller. (2015). *Yearly Report 65c: Implementing the 'Courage to Change' in secondary schools* [in Hebrew]. Jerusalem: State Comptroller's Office.

State Comptroller. (2016). *Special audit report: Education for a shared society and prevention of racism* [in Hebrew]. Jerusalem: State Comptroller's Office.

State Comptroller. (2019). *Yearly Report 69b: Aspects in the management of teaching personnel in the education system* [in Hebrew]. Jerusalem: State Comptroller's Office.

Weinberger, Y., & Donitsa-Schmidt, S. (2016). A longitudinal comparative study of alternative and traditional teacher education programs in Israel: Initial training, induction period, school placement, and retention rates. *Educational Studies, 52*(6), 552–572.

Weisblay, E. (2013). *Teacher status in Israel and OECD countries – training, certification, wages and working conditions* [in Hebrew]. Jerusalem: Government Research Center.

Wininger, A. (2018). *The academic colleges of education – A general survey* [in Hebrew]. Jerusalem: Government Research Center.

Worgan, Y. (2007). *Claims regarding teacher shortage in the education system* [in Hebrew]. Jerusalem: Government Research Center.

Worgan, Y., & Fidelman, I. (2008). *Teacher shortage in the education system* [in Hebrew]. Jerusalem: Government Research Center.

15

STEMMING THE TIDE

A critical examination of issues, challenges and solutions to Jamaican teacher migration

Carol Hordatt Gentles

Introduction

Over the last 30 years, Jamaica has been grappling with the loss of large numbers of its teachers through recruitment to overseas jobs. This has created a shortage of teachers across all of Jamaica's 833 schools, particularly in subject areas such as mathematics, science and foreign languages. The responses of successive governments over this period indicate concern about the migration of its teaching workforce. However, as I suggest in this chapter, these responses have been ineffective in managing the problem. They have focused on finding ways to mitigate the fallout from teacher migration, replacing these teachers instead of focusing on retaining teachers already in classroom. This suggests a devaluing of Jamaican teachers' work because it implies that the professional knowledge and experience they enact in classrooms can be easily replaced. It also suggests Jamaican policymakers are ignoring the factors that are driving Jamaican teachers out of Jamaican classrooms to take up teaching positions abroad. They are failing to consider how poor remuneration, heavy workloads, poor working conditions, feelings of disempowerment, low professional autonomy, lack of meaningful professional preparation, low status and disrespect affect the capacity of teachers to be effective and influence their decisions to leave.

As a Jamaican teacher educator, whose job entails professional capacity-building for teachers at the graduate level, I am committed to the view that provision of quality education by quality teachers is critical for the continued social and cultural development of Jamaica. The loss of trained and experienced teachers has serious negative implications for our capacity to provide effective education.

The extent of the problem

Although statistical data on the loss of teachers from Jamaican classrooms has been poorly documented, various reports from the Ministry of Education (MoE), the Jamaica Teachers' Association (JTA) and press releases (identified later) provide a picture of the scope of the problem. These suggest Jamaica has been losing between 350 and 1,000 of its 25,000 teachers a year since 2000. This is a direct consequence of recruitment drives by overseas agencies from the US and the UK. In 2002, a meeting of the CARICOM (Caribbean Community) Ministers of Education was convened to discuss the recruitment of Caribbean teachers to the UK, the US and Canada. There the Jamaican Government reported that in 2001, 350 teachers had migrated to New York and 100 to the UK (Rudder, 2011). The trend has continued. In 2016, the Minister of Education reported that between 2014 and 2015 more than 500 mathematics and science teachers at the secondary level left the classroom to go overseas (Wilson, 2016). Later that year he explained the impact of this, pointing out that migration was severely eroding the population of fully qualified mathematics teachers. Consequently, of the 207 mathematics teachers available in 2015, 111 had left, leaving only 96 in the system (Saunders, 2016). In March 2019, there were reports of the loss of another 100 mathematics and science teachers who left to take up jobs overseas (Saunders, 2019). Shortages of geography, history and religious education teachers due to migration have also been reported (Virtue, 2018).

Until recently, recruitment agencies came predominantly from the UK and the US. Now, recruiters and job advertisements are coming from China, Japan, Kuwait, Qatar, UAE and Saudi Arabia. Jamaican teachers have also historically migrated to other Caribbean countries, such as the Bahamas, the Cayman Islands, Trinidad and Tobago and Barbados. More recently, there have been reports of young tertiary graduates without teaching certification (who might normally consider training to teach and work in Jamaica), finding jobs as English as a Second Language (ESL) teachers in Asian countries.[1] Anecdotal evidence suggests that foreign language, English language, geography, religious education, early childhood and primary teachers are also leaving to teach in the Middle East.

The fallout from this exodus is particularly problematic at the secondary level, where it is crucial to have specialist mathematics and science teachers in place. For example, in August 2018, the principal of a prominent secondary school reported to the local press that his mathematics department had lost four of its eight mathematics teachers over the summer (Gilpin, 2018). The principal of another top-performing school in science reported it had lost its only physics teacher (Davis, 2018). In 2016, the president of the Jamaican Association of Principals and Vice Principals reported that more than a dozen experienced mathematics teachers had left his secondary school during the last academic year (RJR News, 2016). The fact that similar stories are echoed across Jamaica year after year suggests teacher attrition due to migration is a growing crisis for the education sector and the country.

The vacancies created by teacher migration affect both the quality of teaching and thus student achievement. As early as 2005, Sives, Morgan, Appleton, and Bremmer reported: 'the migration of experienced teachers has undoubtedly had an impact on the quality of education that some schools have been able to provide Jamaican children' (p. 98). At the time, the principals they interviewed were able to hire newly qualified teachers to fill vacancies left by teachers who had migrated overseas, but they complained these new teachers lacked competence and experience. Some 14 years later, principals are still distressed that teachers they hire to fill vacancies are inexperienced and even poorly qualified. However, given the current mass exodus of teachers, it is increasingly difficult to find replacements to hire. Thus, principals have little choice but to work with the teachers they can find. In cases where no replacements can be found, schools have to implement extraordinary and unsatisfactory measures to offset the loss of teachers. For example, in schools where geography, history or science teachers have left, schools simply either stop offering these subjects or assign unqualified teachers to teach them.

The fallout from such measures is detrimental to students, teachers and parents alike. When students take weekend and evening classes, they miss opportunities to participate in sports and other extracurricular activities. When teachers and administrative staff step in to do the work of teachers who have migrated, they become overburdened with the increased workload. The sudden departure of teachers, often without notice, places tremendous pressure on principals to find new staff from a shrinking pool of subject specialists. Parents are stressed when their children sit in classrooms without a teacher (Davis, 2018). Teacher shortages also affect student achievement. In 2016, the education minister blamed teacher shortages due to migration for a 6.2 per cent decline (from 53.9 to 47.7 per cent) in Jamaica's overall pass rate in CSEC (Caribbean Secondary Education Certificate) mathematics (*Jamaica Gleaner*, 2016a). More recently, the president of the Jamaica Teachers Association stated publicly that 'the constant migration of Jamaican teachers to greener pastures is having a crippling effect on the quality of education being offered to the nation's children'; he noted that that critical subjects have had to be dropped because there were no teachers to teach them and warned of the negative implications of this for the production of functional graduates from the education sector in the future (Jackson, 2019).

Attempting to stem the tide of teacher migration

Before considering how to address the problem of teacher migration, it is important to note it is a subset of the larger problem. Jamaicans have always had a 'high propensity for migration that has persisted [from the 1850s] to the present time' (Thomas-Hope, 2018, p. 3). The number of Jamaicans living abroad is estimated at 1.3 million. Together with 'the foreign-born second and third generations who associate their identity with Jamaica', they represent a Jamaican diaspora 'equivalent in size to that of the population of 2.8 million in Jamaica itself' (Thomas-Hope, 2018, p. vii). This diaspora contributes heavily to the Jamaican economy through remittances sent back to Jamaica. The most recent Migration Report for Jamaica (Thomas-Hope, 2018, p. 82) states that 'remittances contributed some 14 per cent to the national GDP each year over the ten years 2006/15 and was 16.1 and 16.3 per cent in 2015 and 2016, respectively'.

The propensity to migrate is influenced by push factors in Jamaica, such as lack of economic and social opportunities, and high rates of unemployment and underemployment, as well as high levels of crime, violence, lawlessness and general societal indiscipline (Parkins, 2010; Thomas-Hope, 2018; Glennie & Chappell, 2010). This is offset by the promise of what is possible abroad: higher levels of income and increased purchasing power, along with the more attractive lifestyle of developed countries. For many Jamaican migrants, the family networks of the diaspora are a strong pull factor. For teachers and other professionals, the lure of what is offered by recruiters from abroad is also very persuasive. Media reports suggest Jamaican teachers who take up jobs in the UK are paid five times more salary than they earn in Jamaica (Neufville, 2016). Through conversations with former students who have migrated, I have learned that many teachers who have recently migrated to the US enjoy high levels of support from recruitment agencies. Recruiters process work visas for them, pay their airfare abroad and provide financial support for initial settlement such as accommodation and a car. Migrating teachers also report they are given strong professional support through structured orientation and mentoring, along with ongoing professional development opportunities. Additionally, their immediate families can join them in the US after a probationary period.

A critical examination of government responses to the issue of teacher migration suggests that what is happening *is* recognised as a problem. However, it seems more value is placed on the prospect of securing income through remittances from the teachers who migrate than on attempting to stem the tide of teacher attrition from Jamaican classrooms. In practice, government policies seem to focus on *replacing* rather than *retaining* teachers to serve the education sector. According to Jamaica's Migration Report (Thomas-Hope, Knight, & Noel, 2012, p. 57), policy responses to address 'the problem of the outflow of high-level skills ("brain drain") . . . have included bonding, increased training output and recruitment of workers from overseas'. Thus, for example, in 2016 reports of heavy losses of teachers spurred a debate about giving substantial salary increases to mathematics and science teachers to encourage them to stay. In response to protest from the teachers union (which objected to offering a raise to only mathematics and science teachers), the government backed down, opting instead to extend a previous initiative to fill existing shortages by offering scholarships to suitable persons in the field (*Jamaica Gleaner*, 2016b). This was done through a recruitment drive for mathematics and science teachers under a $13 million USD programme to provide 1,200 scholarships to pre- and in-service teachers by 2021. In 2017, 440 of these scholarships were awarded. Successful candidates were to be bonded for service as teachers for five years (Buckley, 2016). As a stopgap, in 2017, the Ministry of Education trained and deployed 70 mathematics coaches and tutors to serve 4,000 students in 118 secondary schools until the newly trained teachers were ready for the classroom (Linton, 2017).

Other strategies to replace teachers have included recruitment of retired teachers and teachers from overseas. Thus, since 1997, 72 teachers have been recruited from Cuba to teach the sciences, Spanish and other subjects at primary, secondary and tertiary level. In 2016, the then Minister of Education even suggested a 'quick fix' of using technology, with strategies like flipped classrooms as possibilities for filling the gap left by migrating teachers (Wilson, 2016).

Teacher replacement rather than retention

Policies that focus on replacing teachers who have migrated instead of trying to retain them suggests failure to sufficiently value and respect the work that teachers do. It shows poor understanding of what it takes to produce a quality teacher and the value an experienced teacher adds to the teaching and learning environment. Research shows that teachers continue learning to teach over the entire course of their career (Feiman-Nemser, 2001). Professional learning and development, if done well, contributes to teacher effectiveness (OECD, 2005; Hargreaves & Fullan, 2012). Thus, replacing an experienced teacher with one who is less experienced is likely to decrease the quality of teaching that is provided. As shown, 'there is . . . growing evidence that teacher turnover is detrimental to students . . . because teachers' effectiveness increases with experience, at least during the first few years' (Rinke, 2014, p. 6).

Replacing rather than retaining teachers in the Jamaican context is proving to be an inefficient and wasteful strategy. Government initiatives to incentivise the recruitment and retention of teachers through scholarships for training and bonding appear ineffectual because the Ministry of Education is not enforcing its contractual bonding arrangements (Thomas-Hope, 2018) overseas. There are reports in the press that many students in receipt of scholarships ignore their contracts and migrate as soon as they graduate. In some cases, recruitment agencies are buying out their bonds so they can recruit them more quickly. Those who do stay teach for only a short time and then leave as soon as they are able (Dunkley, 2011). Thus, the government's intention to replace teachers is not working the way it was intended. Teacher shortages persist and a return on investment of public funding is not realised.

What is needed instead are policies and strategies that are informed by *teachers'* understanding and ideas around the issue of migration. This approach may reveal possibilities for structuring more effective retention protocols that are better aligned to the professional needs of teachers. Research on teacher migration and teacher shortages globally suggests there are many factors that motivate teachers to leave their jobs. For example, Manik, Maharaj, and Sookrajh (2006) found that among South African teachers, job dissatisfaction due to displeasure with new educational policies, increased workload, reductions in leave days, poor remuneration and lack of confidence in their competence to teach new curricula, was a key factor motivating teachers to migrate. In the US, job dissatisfaction for reasons other than salary has also been identified as a key predictor of teacher attrition (Buckley, Schneider, & Shang, 2004).

Research into teacher attrition

I am currently conducting research into these issues at the School of Education, University of the West Indies, Mona, Jamaica. Approval to conduct the survey was obtained from the Director of the School of Education, UWI. Mona. The study was conducted anonymously and was not an intervention. Participation was voluntary in that respondents who consented were assured they were under no obligation to complete the survey and they were informed the survey would protect their anonymity. At the time of the study, formal ethical approval was administered at the department level as a study with non-vulnerable groups for the purpose of teaching. Therefore, the researcher was allowed to conduct the study as a minimal risk activity. The findings suggest that remuneration is not the only factor influencing teachers' decisions to migrate.

I asked 58 part-time graduate students, teachers who are pursuing master's in education degrees, to complete a self-administered questionnaire. They were asked whether they want to leave teaching, whether they plan to leave the classroom, whether they plan to migrate and, if so, how soon. They were also asked to share their reasons (in response to open-ended questions) for wanting to leave teaching and for wanting to migrate. Respondents were from a cross-section of programmes in Teacher Education and Teacher Development, Curriculum Studies, Science Education, Leadership in Early Childhood Education and Educational Psychology. The results are shown in Table 15.1:

TABLE 15.1 Responses to questions about leaving teaching and migration (n = 58)

I want to leave teaching	Strongly agree	Agree	Disagree	Strongly disagree
	20 (34%)	22 (38%)	13 (22%)	3 (5%)
	42 (72%)		16 (28%)	
I plan to leave the classroom	Very soon	In the future	Never	
	25 (43%)	26 (45%)	7 (12%)	
	51 (88%)		7 (12%)	
I am planning to migrate	In the future	In the near future	Never	
	25 (43%)	25 (43%)	10 (17%)	
	48 (83%)		10 (17%)	

Table 15.1 shows respondents' answers to questions about leaving teaching and about migration. The results suggest that 72 per cent (n = 44) of responding teachers surveyed want to leave teaching; 88 per cent (n = 51) of them plan to leave teaching very soon; and 83 per cent (n = 48) are planning to migrate. Factors identified as influencing these intentions centre on dissatisfaction, with

issues such as poor remuneration, student indiscipline, working conditions, lack of resources, poor professional support, low professional status of teachers and poor administrative support. Table 15.2 and Table 15.3 list these in detail and indicate the number of students / teachers who identified each reason.

It is instructive that, when asked if they would be encouraged to stay if these factors were improved, 38 per cent said yes, 36 per cent said maybe, 6 per cent said no, while 17 per cent declined to answer.

Table 15.4 shows that better salary and more benefits were listed most often as incentives for retention. However, improvements such as better working conditions, more support from administration and parents, greater respect, appreciation and inclusion in policy-making were also identified as factors that would encourage them to stay.

TABLE 15.2 Respondents' reasons for wanting to migrate (n = 58)

Better working conditions in teaching abroad	28
fewer students per class	7
more administrative support	2
more resources	8
more appreciation and respect	4
professional development opportunities	3
efforts will be rewarded	1
Salary is better	26
Better opportunities	14
Seeking new experiences	11
Personal goals	4
Family live overseas	7
Crime and violence in Jamaica	2
Gain international teaching experience	1

TABLE 15.3 Respondents' reasons for wanting to leave teaching (n = 58)

Poor salary/remuneration	32
Workload is heavy and stressful	17
Student indiscipline	16
Poor resources	10
Government policies unsupportive	10
No respect for profession	9
Student disinterest	8
Poor administrative support	7
Lack of professional support/development	7
Poor working conditions	7
Demotivated	6
Poor parental involvement	5
Teachers have no rights	3
Student-Teacher ratio	3
Nepotism	3

TABLE 15.4 Improvements that would encourage respondents to stay in teaching in Jamaica (n = 58)

Better salaries	36
Benefits and incentives, such as increased pension benefits, access to housing and car	17
More resources	19
Fewer students in class	16
Better working conditions	10
More administrative support	10
More accountability by parents and students	10
More appreciations and respect	6
Inclusion in policy-making	4
Teaching assistants in class	3

These results suggest respondents were experiencing strong job dissatisfaction. They felt unsupported, undervalued and voiceless. While they acknowledged poor remuneration as a key factor for their discontent, they were also unhappy with many aspects of their work contexts, such as student ill-discipline and disinterest, poor resources and poor working conditions. They saw these as having a negative impact on their capacity to teach effectively and were therefore a push factor for migration.

The findings of this survey counter the notion that teacher migration from Jamaica is inevitable. The government's response to this problem has typically pointed to its inability to pay better salaries and the belief that Jamaicans have a traditionally high propensity for migration (Thomas-Hope, 2018). This argument is used to support the view that nothing can be done to prevent teachers from leaving, so replacing them is the next best option. What the findings of this survey suggest is that there are other factors that government should consider when exploring strategies to manage teacher migration.

Contrary to the impression that teachers in Jamaica just get up and leave in response to recruiters' calls, the decision to migrate is not in fact an easy one to make. Many Jamaican teachers report they love the job of teaching and what Lortie (2002) called its 'psychic rewards'. Many of them see themselves as caring agents of change with the professional knowledge and skills to help Jamaican children overcome the burden of poverty (Collins-Figueroa, Down, Hordatt Gentles, Newman, & Davis-Morrison, 2011), but the stresses of teaching in Jamaica often become overwhelming. As one respondent wrote on her survey form: 'I love my country and do not want to leave, but they make it too bad for us.' Bond (2017) reports an interview with a Jamaican teacher in which she explained:

> salary is not the only problem . . . parents and administrators alike are of the view that teachers are 'miracle workers'. Parents fail to make meaningful contributions to the lives of their children, yet they blame teachers for students' failures. Administrators on the other hand are nothing but task

masters. One teacher is burdened with the responsibility of teaching 12 classes with an average of 40 students in each class. Furthermore, lesson plans must be ready every Monday morning; grades must be entered on the system, just to name a few of our responsibilities. 'We can't make blood out of stone' and we 'can't squeeze milk from coffee.'

(online)

The last sentence suggests that it is impossible for teachers to accomplish what is expected with insufficient resources.

Policies that tip the scales in favour of the teachers staying are needed to stem the tide of teacher attrition. Studies on the status and role of teachers in countries with high-performing education systems suggest provision of support to teachers is key for promoting job satisfaction and quality teaching. Provision of adequate resources, good student-teacher ratios, supportive principal leadership, opportunities for professional collaboration and leadership are all associated with job satisfaction and teacher retention (Darling-Hammond, 2012; Johnson, Kraft, & Papay, 2012; Podolsky, Kini, Bishop, & Darling-Hammond, 2017; Borman & Dowling, 2008). These countries treat and compensate their teachers in ways that convey recognition and high social regard for the work they do (Darling-Hammond et al., 2017). Strong professional support has implications for teachers' motivation, sense of self-efficacy, job satisfaction and ultimately student learning (OECD, 2005, 2014; World Bank, 2018). If Jamaica's policies recognised what such research suggests and invested in improving their working conditions, providing better professional support, uplifting teachers' professional status, Jamaican teachers may reconsider their decision to leave Jamaican classrooms.

Conclusion and recommendations

Although much of the discussion concerning the issue of teacher attrition in Jamaica has focused on replacing rather than retaining teachers, there are some stakeholders who advocate for a different approach. For example, the JTA has spoken of incentivising teacher retention through 'specific scholarships, access to government lands and houses, reduced mortgages and duty concessions to improve the economic wellbeing of the teacher' (*Jamaica Observer*, 2016). This may be a welcome idea, because it will help address not only economic reasons for teacher migration but may also offer teachers some sense of being valued. Indeed, the survey just presented indicates that such incentives are seen by teachers as factors that would encourage them to stay.

It is critical that the government invests in improving the job and work context of teaching in Jamaica. Helping teachers to feel valued, autonomous and respected must be a priority. This can be accomplished through policies that facilitate more professional autonomy and empower teachers to engage in professional collaboration about issues affecting student learning. This will acknowledge the capacity of Jamaican teachers to produce viable strategies to address issues that affect them, such as student ill-discipline, poor parental involvement and student disinterest. Government must also do its part to address those concerns over which it has control, such as training school leadership to provide better administrative support and to take a hard look at the workload assigned to teachers.

On paper, these suggestions for improving teacher retention in Jamaica may seem simplistic, because they suggest a level of common sense that somehow often appears to elude policymakers. In practice, of course, they will be less simple to implement, particularly in a country like Jamaica where bureaucracy can be burdensome and restrictive. It will also be challenging to support teachers to have power over their own affairs, as this requires a huge cultural shift. However, given the crisis of teacher attrition that has loomed over the sector for over three decades, the Jamaican Government must reconsider how to keep its teachers. If we continue to fail to manage teacher migration, the outlook for education in Jamaica will be very grim.

Glossary

CARICOM   Caribbean Community.
Jamaica Gleaner   Major Jamaican newspaper.
Pre-service teachers   Teachers who are not certified to teach in the classroom. The term is used to describe teachers who are enrolled in initial teacher training programmes.
Inservice teachers   Teachers who are certified and employed as teachers.

Note

1 In Jamaica, all teachers entering the classroom are required to have professional certification to teach. This is acquired through completion of a Bachelor's in Education degree. This can be earned from a variety of government subsidised teacher training programmes offered by tertiary-level institutions. These include eight designated Teachers Colleges – members of a consortium called the Teachers Colleges of Jamaica (TCJ), one specialist college (Edna Manley College of the Performing Arts), a vocational institution (The Vocational Training and Development Institute – VDTI), one University College (The Mico University College), three universities – the University of the West Indies (UWI, Mona), the University of Technology (Utech) and Northern Caribbean University (NCU). B.Ed. degrees are also offered through private religious institutions such as the Mandeville Catholic College, International University of the Caribbean (IUC). All these programmes must be accredited by the University Council of Jamaica (UCJ) which provides benchmarking through standards for B.Ed. programmes. These standards specify required numbers of credit hours for various elements of training required, including internship (called the practicum). The standards espouse the academic model of teacher training, which views theory and practice as discrete yet related to one another.

At the secondary level, teacher shortages in some subject areas can be offset by hiring persons who hold a first degree in a subject. They do not require professional certification and are hired as Graduate Trained teachers.

Currently all teachers are required to register with the Jamaican Teaching Council (JTC). This government-funded body is responsible for regulating and professionalising the teaching profession in Jamaica, to be accomplished through licensing. The JTC has not yet, however, starting its licensing regime.

References

Bond, L. (2017, March 8). *Rapid migration of our best teachers from Jamaica*. Retrieved from Trends and Issues in HE website: https://trendsandissuesinhe.wordpress.com/2017/03/08/rapid-migration-of-our-best-teachers-from-jamaica/

Borman, G. D., & Dowling, N. M. (2008). Teacher attrition and retention: A meta-analytic and narrative review of the research. *Review of Educational Research, 78*(3), 367–409.

Buckley, B. (2016, February 3). Initiative to increase and retain the number of fully qualified mathematics and science teachers. *Jamaica Information Service*. Retrieved from Jamaica Information Service website: https://jis.gov.jm/initiative-to-increase-and-retain-the-number-of-fully-qualified-mathematics-and-science-teachers/

Buckley, J., Schneider, M., & Shang, Y. (2004). *The effects of school facility quality on teacher retention in urban school districts*. Washington, DC: National.

Collins-Figueroa, M., Down, L., Hordatt Gentles, C., Newman, M., & Davis-Morrison, V. (2011). Concepts of professionalism among prospective teachers in Jamaica. *Caribbean Journal of Education, 33*(2), 176–201.

Darling-Hammond, L. (2012). *Creating a comprehensive system for evaluating and supporting effective teaching*. Stanford, CA: Stanford Centre for Opportunity Policy in Education.

Darling-Hammond, L., Burns, D., Campbell, C., Lin Goodwin, A., Hammerness, K., Low, E-L., . . . Zeichner, K. (2017). *Empowered educators: How high-performing systems shape teaching around the world*. San Francisco, CA: Josey-Bass.

Davis, C. (2018, October 14). Teacher shortage hits Titchfield – Portland-based school with part-time physics teachers. *The Gleaner*. Retrieved from Gleaner website: jamaica-gleaner.com/article/news/20181014/teacher-shortage-hits-titchfield-portland-based-school-part-time-physics

Dunkley, A. (2011, November 6). Teachers flee bond obligations. *Jamaica Observer*. Retrieved from Jamaica Observer website: www.jamaicaobserver.com/news/Teachers-flee-bond-obligations_100974

Feiman-Nemser, S. (2001). From preparation to practice: Designing a continuum to strengthen and sustain teaching, *Teachers College Record, 103*(6), 1013–1055. Retrieved from Teachers College Records website: www.tcrecord.org

Gilpin, J. (2018, August 28). Teacher shortage! Schools lament lack of seasoned educators for the classrooms. *The Gleaner*. Retrieved from Gleaner website: http://jamaica-gleaner.com/article/lead-stories/20180828/teacher-shortage-schools-lament-lack-seasoned-educators-classrooms

Glennie, A., & Chappell, L. (2010, June 16). Jamaica: From diverse beginning to diaspora in the developed world. *Migration Policy Institute*. Retrieved from Migration Information Source website: www.migrationpolicy.org/article/jamaica-diverse-beginning-diaspora-developed-world

Hargreaves, A., & Fullan, M. (2012). *Professional capital: Transforming teaching in every school*. Columbia University, NY: Teachers College Press.

Jackson, L. (2019, November 14). Migration of teachers impacting schools severely – Speid. *The Gleaner*. Retrieved from Gleaner website: http://jamaica-gleaner.com/article/news/20191114/migration-teachers-impacting-schools-severely-speid

Jamaica Gleaner. (2016a, August 19). *Teacher migration reason for low CSEC math performance – Ministry*. Retrieved from Gleaner website: jamaica-gleaner.com/article/news/20160819/teacher-migration-reason-low-csec-math-performance-ministry

Jamaica Gleaner. (2016b, January 14). *No differentiated pay for math and science teachers, gov't backs down from proposal*. Retrieved from Gleaner website: http://jamaica-gleaner.com/

article/news/20160114/no-differentiated-pay-math-and-science-teachers-govt-backs-down-proposal

Jamaica Observer. (2016, April 7). *JTA calls for Gov't incentives to keep teachers from migrating*. Retrieved from Jamaica Observer website: www.jamaicaobserver.com/news/JTA-calls-for-Gov-t-incentives-to-keep-teachers-from-migrating

Johnson, S. M., Kraft, M. A., & Papay, J. P. (2012). How context matters in high-need schools: The effects of teachers' working conditions on their professional satisfaction and their students' achievement. *Teachers College Record, 114*(10), 1–39.

Linton, L. (2017, March 7). Ministry intensifies measures to improve CSEC Maths passes. *Jamaica Information Service*. Retrieved from Jamaica Information Service Website: https://jis.gov.jm/ministry-intensifies-measures-improve-csec-maths-passes/

Lortie, D. (2002). *School teacher: A sociological study* (2nd ed.). Chicago, IL: University of Chicago Press.

Manik, S., Maharaj, B., & Sookrajh, R. (2006). Globalisation and transnational teachers: South African teacher migration to the UK. *Migration and Ethnic Themes, 22*(1–2), 15–33.

Neufville, Z. (2016, March 11). UK recruiters exacerbate Jamaica's education brain drain. *Equal Times*. Retrieved from Equal Times website: www.equaltimes.org/uk-recruiters-exacerbate-jamaica-s?lang=en#.XL-0K_ZFyUk

Organisation for Economic Cooperation and Development [OECD]. (2005). *Teachers matter: Attracting, developing and retaining effective teachers*. Paris: OECD Publishing. Retrieved from OECD website: www.oecd.org/education/school/34990905.pdf

Organisation for Economic Cooperation and Development [OECD]. (2014). *TALIS 2013 results: An international perspective on teaching and learning*. TALIS. Paris: OECD Publishing. doi:http://doi.org/10.1787/9789264196261-en

Parkins, N. C. (2010). Push and pull factors of migration. *American Review of Political Economy, 8*(2), 6–24.

Podolsky, A., Kini, T., Bishop, J., & Darling-Hammond, D. (2017). Sticky schools: How to find and keep teachers in the classroom. *Phi Delta Kappan, 98*(8), 19–25.

Rinke, C. R. (2014). *Why half of teachers leave the classroom: Understanding recruitment and retention in today's schools*. Lanham, MD & Plymouth, UK: Rowman & Littlefield Education.

RJR News. (2016, August 22). *More concerns about teacher migration*. Retrieved from http://rjrnewsonline.com/local/more-concerns-about-teacher-migration

Rudder, R. (2011). Managing teacher recruitment and migration: A case study of the Barbados experience. In Next steps in managing teacher migration, papers of the sixth commonwealth research symposium on teacher mobility, recruitment and migration. *Commonwealth Secretariat*. https://doi.org/10.14217/9781848591318-en

Saunders, A. (2016, August 18). Maths teachers leaving for jobs overseas. *Jamaica Observer*. Retrieved from Jamaica Observer website: www.jamaicaobserver.com/news/Maths-teachers-leaving-for-jobs-overseas_71170

Saunders, A. (2019, March 27). Thwaites: Education system lost over 100 maths, science teachers since January. *Jamaica Observer*. Retrieved from Jamaica Observer website: www.jamaicaobserver.com/news/thwaites-education-system-lost-over-100-maths-science-teachers-since-january_160480

Sives, A., Morgan, J. W., Appleton, S., & Bremner, R. (2005). Teacher migration from Jamaica: Assessing the short-term impact. *Caribbean Journal of Education, 27*(1), 85–111.

Thomas-Hope, E. (2018). *Migration in Jamaica: A country profile*. The UN Migration Agency. Kingston, Jamaica: International Organization for Migration [IOM].

Retrieved from IOM website: https://caribbeanmigration.org/sites/default/files/repository/migration_in_jamaica_-_profile_2018.pdf

Thomas-Hope, E., Knight, P., & Noel, C. (2012). *Migration in Jamaica: A country profile 2010*. Kingston, Jamaica: International Organization for Migration (IOM).

Virtue, E. (2018, September 16). Gleaner editors forum: Geography, history and religious education teachers also in short supply. *The Gleaner*. Retrieved from Gleaner website: http://jamaica-gleaner.com/article/news/20180916/gleaner-editors-forum-geography-history-religious-education-teachers-also

Wilson, N. (2016, July 3). Fast fix for migrating teachers – Education minister looks to technology to fill classroom vacancies. *The Gleaner*. Retrieved from Gleaner website: http://jamaica-gleaner.com/article/news/20160703/fast-fix-migrating-teachers-education-minister-looks-technology-fill-classroom

World Bank Group. (2018). *Learning to realize education's promise*. World Development. Retrieved from World Bank website: www.worldbank.org/en/publication/wdr2018

16

SUGGESTIONS FROM NATIONAL-LEVEL ACTORS ON HOW TO HANDLE RETENTION AND ATTRITION OF TEACHERS

A case study from Sweden

Laila Niklasson

Introduction

This chapter presents and discusses examples of how a selected number of national actors (government, unions and associations) are dealing with the retention and attrition of teachers in Sweden. I have used the term actors to refer to national actors, but a national actor like the Swedish Association for Local Authorities and Regions also includes organisers (municipalities) of K-12 (kindergarten to Year 12). As education systems differ from country to country, there is a need to give some brief background. Teacher education at university is tuition free, but in order to cover living costs (housing, food, transport, etc.) and books, most students take loans during their education, which lasts from three to five-and-a-half years. Students also receive a small grant from the state if they complete a certain number of credits during a semester.

Teachers and school leaders follow a national curriculum for all school sectors, but it is the organisers of K-12 who are responsible for overseeing the work undertaken in schools. Organisers are either public or private. Public organisers in Sweden encompass all 290 municipalities in the country. Private organisers can be non-governmental organisations, parent cooperatives, staff cooperatives or companies. Every principal must comply with the demands of the national curriculum, directives from the National Education Agency, various laws and regulations (such as the Education Act and Work Environment Act), and directives (an example is outdoor education as the profile for a preschool or additional routine policies) from the organisers. Teachers are recruited and paid by the organisers, not the state. Thus, the state and the organisers (private or public) are jointly responsible for ensuring that the education system functions well. This shared responsibility creates some tension between these two actors (state and the organisers), while the teachers' union and the association of school leaders attempt to balance national and local/organisational demands and needs to secure the best options for their members.

The responsibility for the education system is divided between the state, parliament and government at the national level; local authorities as counties; and most of the municipalities. The local authorities are associated with a national organisation called the Swedish Association for Local Authorities and Regions (SALAR). The parliament and government can influence the number of student teachers and fund in-service training at universities, but it is the local actors as municipality members (not counties) of SALAR and private organisers of K-12 education that actually employ the teachers and are responsible for quality in education.

The Swedish Government is fully aware of the current situation, in which a large cohort of teachers face retirement at the same time that there is a large increase of preschool children and pupils in all school sectors (The Swedish Government, 2019a). The Swedish National Agency for Education's website declared in 2018 that all children have the right to be taught by certified teachers. At the same time, they admit that almost a third of teachers are uncertified, and the number of uncertified teachers and preschool teachers is expected to increase to about 80,000 by 2031 (The Swedish National Agency for Education, 2019).

It is notable that schools in disadvantaged areas have a higher proportion of uncertified teachers. The national actors can influence the number of student teachers and fund in-service training at universities; SALAR is aware of the situation and supports municipalities' efforts to become attractive employers and thereby to improve their recruitment and retention of teachers. At the same time, SALAR is open to alternatives, such as assistant teachers and alternative ways to become a teacher, because it is unrealistic to think that student teacher recruitment will satisfy the current demand for teachers (Swedish Association for Local Authorities and Regions, 2019).

In summary, many actors are involved and different solutions are proposed to the problem of retention and attrition of teachers. This type of multilevel and multi-actor situation can be seen in studies from other countries (Kelchtermans, 2017; Towers & Maguire, 2017; Vagi & Pivovarova, 2017), which leads to the aim of this chapter: to study how different actors in Sweden describe the challenge of retention and attrition of teachers and suggest solutions.

The chapter continues with some examples of earlier studies, followed by discussion of the data collection and the research findings. The chapter ends with a discussion of the problems associated with teacher retention and possible solutions.

Broadening the question of retention and attrition

The first example of studies into teacher retention and attrition concerns why teachers are staying, and the subsequent two offer alternative ways of interpreting retention and attrition.

A Swedish study by Fransson and Frelin (2016) found that it was a sense of commitment in relation to teaching, and in particular their relationships with pupils, which made teachers stay in teaching for a long time (at least 15 years). Teachers who stayed felt confident about their competence. They also actively disregarded or ignored negative media coverage, as they perceived it to be untrue. When extra demands were required from education reform, they had the capacity to reframe the demands as supportive of pupils' learning; teachers changed their perception of the demands and interpreted them as core tasks. Supportive school-context factors were trust and recognition from colleagues, principals, former students and parents. Fransson and Frelin (2016) conclude that these factors need to be acknowledged as reasons for staying in teaching.

Alternative ways of analysing attrition are also suggested by Smith and Ulvik (2017). When they studied why some successful teachers in Norway left the teaching profession, they found that attrition could be discussed in terms of both resilience and agency. Teachers participating in the study were successful, managed their job and liked it; that is, they were resilient. However, after a while teaching no longer met their expectations. Instead of adapting further or developing professionally, they decided to leave teaching. Their reasons for leaving were both extrinsic, such as not having as much holiday as expected, and intrinsic, such as not having opportunities to develop; they could not act as agents for their professional ideas. Instead, they expressed their agency by leaving teaching. Smith and Ulvik suggest that leaving teaching should be interpreted as a sign not of a lack of resilience, but of competence to act.

Carlsson, Lindqvist and Nordänger (2019) have yet another analysis. They argue that defining attrition as leaving classroom teaching is too narrow. Instead, they argue that some who leave actually stay in educational settings, and some only take a break. If attrition is measured in too narrow a way, then teacher education could be devalued, despite the fact that a degree in education offers skills for working in an educational context or other professions. In a study from Sweden they found that from a school perspective, about 25 per cent of people in their sample (of 87 participants) left teaching, which means that 75 per cent actually stayed. If transferring to education administration and temporary parental leave are not counted as attrition, the proportion of those who stay is over 80 percent. In addition, from a societal perspective, if those who worked in an educational sector using their pedagogical competence could be added, the retention rate increases to over 85 per cent.

In comments from respondents, the authors found examples from leavers saying that the teacher training and experience had contributed to their own, individual development. They felt secure with a vocational education, and some were now engaged in non-governmental organisations that supported children. In conclusion, Carlsson et al. (2019) argue that it is better to broaden the definition of retention and analyse how the teaching profession contributes on societal, school and individual levels, and to accept some attrition due to lack of commitment or failure to manage the classroom situation.

Method

The aim of the study undertaken by the author, and used to underpin this chapter, was to explore how different actors described the challenge of handling retention and attrition of teachers, and to examine their suggested solutions to the challenge. The case study used a model from Kelchtermans (2017), who suggests what ways to study, and why a phenomenon is problematised. The study delves into these issues by studying, first, how retention and attrition are described by different actors (government, unions and associations), and, second, whether these issues are described as problems needing solutions or challenges needing a response (Kelchtermans, 2017).

After choosing questions, a purposive sampling was carried out (Bryman, 2008). It was decided to use terms such as 'competence provision' and 'teacher provision' via the internet to search for actors involved. From the search results, a judgement was made to study texts from the national government, a national association for local government, a national union for teachers and an association for school principals.

The selected documents were: two articles about future teacher provision from the Swedish Government (2019a, 2019b); two articles and two reports from the Swedish Association for Local Authorities and Regions (2018a, 2018b, 2018c, 2019); one article and two public-consultation comments (concerning teacher retention and professional development) from a labour union for teachers, The National Union of Teachers in Sweden (2018a, 2018b, 2019); and finally, three documents (concerning teachers' professional development) from an association for school leaders, the Swedish Association of School Principals and Directors of Education (2016, 2017, 2018). Each document was read several times looking for the two categories, problem and solution (Bryman, 2008). This yields both an actor perspective and a problem/solution perspective.

Findings

A summary is given of the documents from each actor, ending with the problems and solutions suggested by the actors.

The Swedish Government (2019a, 2019b) argues in two articles that measures need to be taken to change negative developments in Swedish schools (such as low results in international tests like the Programme for International Student Assessment [PISA]), and that the solution is to have certified and competent teachers. In general, the Swedish Government argues that there is a shortage of teachers, although few details on school form, subjects or regions, are supplied, and has decided on different measures that are aimed at encouraging teacher recruitment and retention. Teacher recruitment has now improved, partly because the government has increased the number of places in the teacher education programmes. The government has also suggested alternative ways of becoming a teacher; immigrants with previous experience or a degree in teaching should be offered supplementary education in a 'fast-track' route into teaching, and raising salaries could be aimed at making teaching more attractive. However, salary increases are only for those who can show special skills, for example, as pedagogical leaders in certain subjects (The Swedish Government, 2019a). These suggestions are implemented in higher education (with additional places paid by government) and by organisers of K-12. (See Table 16.1.)

The Swedish Association for Local Authorities and Regions (SALAR) (2018a, 2018b, 2018c, 2019) demonstrates that there has been an increase in the number of children in all school sectors, and that this is not matched by the current number of teachers. One reason is that large groups of teachers are retiring; another is that teachers are leaving teaching. However, they acknowledge that teachers are not more inclined to leave their profession than members of other professions. In general, three types of strategies have to be developed: strategies to increase the number of teachers; strategies to keep teachers; and strategies for organisational development and working methods.

For the first strategy to increase the number of teachers, creating additional places in the teacher programme is not enough, as it takes three to five years to complete teacher education; also required is the faster completion of the programme. Immigrants with teaching degrees should receive support, such as being offered a fast-track route into teaching. Existing teachers without a qualification to teach should be offered the chance to become qualified, sometimes with a salary. There is also a need to offer professional development to qualified in-service teachers. In addition, employment for retired teachers is suggested. SALAR supports various fast-track routes into teaching, for example, organisers hiring young people interested in teaching for short periods to let them try their hand as assistants.

For strategies to retain teachers in the profession, it is important to send a signal that teachers with experience are an important resource. Examples include one organiser giving teachers a bonus one year before retirement, another paying a bonus to teachers who stay for the first three years, and other organisers who top up the salary if teachers work some years after retirement age. The organisers of K-12 should be perceived as attractive employers, for example, by offering a health-enhancing workplace. SALAR supports the initiative where

TABLE 16.1 The Swedish Government's assessment of teacher provision

Problem	Solution
Too few people become teachers	• Increase the number of places in teacher education programmes. • Fast-track: Immigrants with previous experience or degrees in teaching should be offered supplementary education.
Too many teachers leave the profession	• Raise salaries for teachers who can demonstrate special skills.

students work part time in schools and study part time, with a salary. Other professionals could support teachers' work by becoming mentors or administrators, or by taking on some of the work that involves contact with families (2018a, 2018b).

As SALAR is recruiting for the public sector (2018c), they also have to consider the sector at large. They should represent public-sector work in a positive light, increase the diversity of recruitment (gender, immigrants) and offer more opportunities for salary increases; good results should lead to rewards. They suggest that the retirement age should be raised by two years. They also suggest increased digitalisation by, for example, developing distance learning in schools (2018b). (See Table 16.2.)

The National Union of Teachers in Sweden (2018a, 2018b, 2019) comment on the development of a professional programme for teachers and principals, which the union supports (The National Union of Teachers in Sweden, 2018b). Another suggestion concerned the introduction of professional development for the teaching workforce, not only teachers, that would entitle participants to payment at the same level as unemployment compensation. The union does not support this suggestion, objecting that teachers would lose full-time pension contributions during this time. The union makes the point that any professional development should only be for teachers and principals (National Union of Teachers in Sweden, 2018b).

In an article from January 2019 (The National Union of Teachers in Sweden, 2019), the union argues that the shortage of teachers continues and that in the next four years there will be a shortage of 80,000 teachers. Good working conditions and salaries will appeal to young people, encouraging them to choose the teacher programme, and will motivate in-service teachers to stay in their profession, further developing their competence. (See Table 16.3.)

TABLE 16.2 SALAR's assessment of teacher provision

Problem	Solution
Too few people become teachers	• Increase the supply of teachers through faster completion of teacher education programmes and better retention on these programmes. • Increase fast-track routes into teaching programmes. • Create a positive image of teaching. • Improve image of organisers as attractive employers.
Too many teachers leave the profession	• Demonstrate that many teachers are staying. • Encourage experienced teachers to stay after the usual retirement age. • Increase time in employment by two years. • Increase opportunities to increase salary. • Reorganise teaching with more distance learning. • Prioritise teaching over other activities. • Encourage assistants to take over teachers' non-teaching activities.

TABLE 16.3 The National Union of Teachers in Sweden's assessment of teacher provision

Problem	Solution
Too few people become teachers	• Good working conditions and good salaries. • Professional development programme for teachers and principals.
Too many teachers leave the profession	• Higher salaries, better working conditions. • Professional development programmes for teachers.

In 2016, the chairman of The Swedish Association of School Principals and Directors of Education argued that the latest reform of increased hours of instruction in mathematics was worsening the situation, due to the lack of certified teachers in mathematics. Because of the recent large influx of immigrant children, some classes have increased in size by 25 per cent and there is a shortage of both teachers and classrooms. In addition, there are municipalities with 30 per cent turnover among teachers. This turnover is partly due to increased salaries, where organisers compete with each other (The Swedish Association of School Principals and Directors of Education, 2016).

In 2017, The Swedish Association of School Principals and Directors of Education was positive about a revised curriculum for preschool children. However, the association emphasised that it is difficult to recruit enough preschool teachers in many parts of the country, and there is a severe lack of professional staff in this sector. The Association wants the government to take responsibility for managing a better balance between the preschool teacher programme and the demands of the labour market (The Swedish Association of School Principals and Directors of Education, 2017).

In 2018, the Association commented on a public consultation concerning professional development of teachers and principals (The Swedish Association of School Principals and Directors of Education, 2018). The suggestion of combining them into one single programme was dismissed. The Association argues that teaching and serving as a principal are two different professions, and should have two separate professional programmes, offered only to certified teachers. The programme should be organised according to career steps where induction (first job) is the first step for teachers. A suggestion that organisers of K–12 should get extra funding for allowing unqualified teachers simultaneously to work in a school and study in a teacher programme is supported. (See Table 16.4.)

Discussion: defining a problem and its solution

The study has shown how retention and attrition are described by different actors (government, unions and associations), and whether these issues are described as problems needing solutions or challenges needing a response (Kelchtermans, 2017). The study of the selected documents shows that three problems can be

TABLE 16.4 The Swedish Association of School Principals and Directors of Education's assessment of teacher provision

Problem	Solution
Too few people become teachers	• Increase the number of places in teacher education programmes. • Fast-track: Staff already working in preschools or schools, but without qualifications, should be able to participate in teacher programmes while working.
Teacher turnover is too high	• Minimise competition between organisers of K-12. • Introduce professional development programmes for teachers and principals.

traced: too few people become teachers, turnover among teachers is too high and too many teachers are leaving teaching.

Too few people become teachers

Among the selected national actors, there is agreement about where the basic problem lies. There is a shortage of certified teachers, especially in certain school sectors, such as preschool, and in certain subject areas, such as mathematics and science. A suggested solution is that the government should fund additional university places in the teacher programme to increase the number of teachers. As this programme takes several years to complete, another solution is to implement a fast-track route for aspiring teachers. Two solutions have been suggested: one for people working part time in school, who should be able to study part time, and one for immigrants who have previous education in teaching.

At a national level, realised on a local level, certified teachers need to be brought into every classroom, and this needs to be done very quickly. At the same time, the teacher programme has to maintain a certain level of quality in terms of knowledge, skills and attitude. If a fast-track route for teaching is available, should this be the route for all student teachers? Fast-track programmes can be difficult to implement because student teachers take loans for several years, and a fast-track route either shortens the period of the loan or the programme is subsidised. This means that there will be workplaces where some teachers have large loans to pay back and others have small or no loans. This also affects pension funding, because those who have taken a longer teacher education programme miss those years of pension contributions from an employer, which will especially affect student teachers who begin their education later in life.

High teacher turnover

The teachers' union supports higher salaries, but this suggestion is problematised by the school leaders' association, which already faces problems with organisers out-bidding each other to recruit teachers. In addition, some organisers do not have the means to raise salaries more than a few per cent each time there are salary negotiations with the unions. One explanation of why the school leaders' association is especially engaged with the issue may be that school leaders are responsible for hiring teachers, and are therefore directly affected at unit level. Turnover is presented here as teachers changing schools and still working as teachers. If the concept of turnover is broadened to also refer to teachers applying for administrative positions in schools, then the professionals are still in the education system (Carlsson et al., 2019). This makes it possible to depict turnover in a more positive light.

Too many teachers leave the profession

From the government's perspective, too many teachers are leaving teaching. On the other hand, SALAR wants to emphasise that teachers are not leaving their profession more than other professional groups. Even so, SALAR is just as inclined to highlight the lack of teachers.

Different actors have mentioned working conditions. The teachers' union indicates that it is national demands, particularly the goal-and-results system, which lead to test-driven teaching that causes attrition (Gallant & Riley, 2017). Among in-service teachers there is agreement about the problematic work situation and weak possibilities for professional development.

A solution proposed by the government is to give a pay raise to a group of teachers who can show special skills. This solution does not accord with research findings that show teachers mainly stay because of rewarding relationships (Fransson & Frelin, 2016); whether students choose the teacher programme and whether in-service teachers stay in the profession is not mainly a question of salary. In addition, selecting a group of teachers to receive higher salaries can be problematic, as it may create negative competition among teachers.

Finally, for some individuals, leaving teaching may be a necessary decision in order to preserve their health, and it should not only be perceived as an organisational problem (Yinon & Orland-Barak, 2017). If teachers perceive that combining their professional and personal life is difficult, action in the form of leaving teaching could be a positive choice (Gallant & Riley, 2017; Towers & Maguire, 2017).

The conclusion from the study is that it is difficult to balance the need to have staff (almost any adult) in the classroom with the need to have certified teachers for reasons of quality and out of respect for the professionals. Solutions with selective increases in salary, fast-tracks and assistants can be perceived as contrasting with the emphasis that teachers place on supportive relationships with students, colleagues and school leaders as reasons for retention.

References

Bryman, A. (2008). *Samhällsvetenskapliga metoder* [*Social research methods*]. Stockholm: Liber.

Carlsson, R., Lindqvist, P., & Nordänger, U. K. (2019). Is teacher attrition a poor estimate of the value of teacher education? A Swedish case. *European Journal of Teacher Education*, 42(2), 243–257.

Fransson, G., & Frelin, A. (2016). Highly committed teachers: What makes them tick? A study of sustained commitment. *Teachers and Teaching: Theory and Practice, 22*(8), 896–912.

Gallant, A., & Riley, P. (2017). Early career teacher attrition in Australia: Inconvenient truths about new public management. *Teachers and Teaching: Theory and Practice, 23*(8), 896–913.

Kelchtermans, G. (2017). "Should I stay or should I go?": Unpacking teacher attrition/ retention as an educational issue. *Teachers and Teaching: Theory and Practice, 23*(8), 961–977.

National Union of Teachers in Sweden. (2018a). Yttrande över delbetänkande av *Utredningen för ett hållbart arbetsliv över tid – Tid för utveckling* [*Comment on interim report from the investigation for a sustainable working life over time – Time for development*]. (SOU 2018:24). Stockholm.

National Union of Teachers in Sweden. (2018b). *Remissvar Med utvecklingsskicklighet i centrum – ett ramverk för lärares och rektorers professionella utveckling* [*Comment, With development skill in focus – a framework for teachers' and principals' professional development*]. (SOU 2018:17). Stockholm.

National Union of Teachers in Sweden. (2019, January 28). Krafttag krävs för att mota lärarkrisen [Strong measures are needed to deal with the teacher crisis]. *Upsala Nya Tidning.*

Smith, K., & Ulvik, M. (2017). Leaving teaching: Lack of resilience or sign of agency? *Teachers and Teaching: Theory and Practice, 23*(8), 928–945.

Swedish Association for Local Authorities and Regions. (2018a). *Elevboom och lärarbrist kräver flera åtgärder* [*Pupil boom and lack of teachers demand further actions*]. Retrieved from Sveriges Kommuner och Regioner website: https://skl.se/tjanster/press/nyheter/ nyhetsarkiv/elevboomochlararbristkraverfleraatgarder.14868.html

Swedish Association for Local Authorities and Regions. (2018b). *Skolans rekryteringsutmaningar. Lokala strategier och exempel* [*Recruitment challenges for school. Local strategies and examples*]. Stockholm.

Swedish Association for Local Authorities and Regions. (2018c). *Sveriges viktigste jobb finns i välfärden* [*Sweden's most important jobs are in the public sector*]. Rekryteringsrapport 2018 [Recruitment report 2018]. Stockholm.

Swedish Association for Local Authorities and Regions. (2019). *Personal och kompetensförsörjning skola* [*Staff and competence provision, school*]. Retrieved from Sveriges Kommuner och Regioner website. https://skl.se/arbetsgivarekollektivavtal/personalochkompetensforsorjning/ skola.11387.html

Swedish Association of School Principals and Directors of Education. (2016, August 18). Vi kräver en långsiktig lösning [We demand a long-term solution]. *Skolledarna, 6*(16). Retrieved from skolledarna website: www.skolledarna.se/Skolledaren/Ledaren/2016/ Vi-kraver-en-langsiktig-losning/

Swedish Association of School Principals and Directors of Education. (2017). *Förslag till reviderad läroplan för förskolan – remissvar* [*Suggestion for revised curriculum for preschool – referral*] (Dnr 2017:783). Stockholm.

Swedish Association of School Principals and Directors of Education. (2018). *Remissvar Med utvecklingsskicklighet i centrum – ett ramverk för lärares och rektorers professionella utveckling* [*Public consultation comment, with development skill in focus – A framework for teachers' and principals' professional development*]. (SOU 2018:17). Stockholm.

Swedish Government. (2019a). *Regeringens satsningar inom lärarområdet* [*Government investment within the teacher area*]. Retrieved from Regeringskansliet website: www.regeringen.se/ artiklar/2016/11/regeringens-satsningar-inom-lararomradet/

Swedish Government. (2019b, June 8). *Regeringens politik / högskola och forskning. Framtidens lärarförsörjning* [*Government politics / higher education and research. Future teacher provision*]. Retrieved Regeringskansliet website: www.regeringen.se/regeringens-politik/hogskola-och-forskning/framtidens-lararforsorjning/

Swedish National Agency for Education. (2019). *Lärarförsörjningen* [*Teacher provision*]. Retrieved from skolverket website: www.skolverket.se/om-oss/organisation-och-verksamhet/skolverkets-prioriterade-omraden/lararforsorjningen

Towers, E., & Maguire, M. (2017). Leaving or staying in teaching: A "vignette" of an experienced urban teacher "leaver" of a London primary school. *Teachers and Teaching: Theory and Practice, 23*(8), 946–960.

Vagi, R., & Pivovarova, M. (2017). "Theorizing teacher mobility": A critical review of literature. *Teachers and Teaching: Theory and Practice, 23*(7), 781–793.

Yinon, H., & Orland-Barak, L. (2017). Career stories of Israeli teachers who left teaching: A salutogenic view of teacher attrition. *Teachers and Teaching: Theory and Practice, 23*(8), 914–927.

17

THE CHALLENGES OF STAFFING SCHOOLS IN A COSMOPOLITAN NATION

Rethinking the recruitment and retention of teachers in Australia through a spatial lens

Philip Roberts and Natalie Downes

Introduction

The popular narrative in Australia is that 30–50 per cent of teachers leave the profession in the first five years (Weldon, 2018) and that there is a looming teacher shortage (Sullivan, Johnson, & Simons, 2019). However, there is essentially no solid evidence base for these claims (Weldon, 2018), with most claims based upon the more comprehensive USA and UK data (AITSL, 2017). For instance, existing data do not account for staff movement across sectors that has been shown to be around 20 per cent of the workforce (Weldon, 2018). Similarly, with females making up 74 per cent of the workforce (Willett, Segal, & Walford, 2014), movement in and out of the workforce, and into part-time employment, are not well accounted for. To address this, the national teacher registration body, with its state and territory affiliates, is working on a national teacher workforce data project that will produce quality workforce data. Better understandings of the true situation regarding teacher demand is important as student numbers are increasing along with Australia's growing population (ABS, 2018), and there is a generally accepted ageing of the workforce.

Most research that has been conducted in Australia has tended to be qualitative studies on why teachers leave (Weldon, 2018). Here, a general consensus has been the impact of major policy changes over the last decade that are often associated with audit cultures and performativity (Sullivan et al., 2019). These are seen as increasing oversight and accountability of teachers and the loss of professional autonomy, somewhat ironically, in the name of enhanced professionalism. The constant 'blaming' of teachers by politicians and the media for an apparent decline in the quality of education and associated outcomes has been linked to a decline in demand for teaching degrees, which has arguably been exacerbated by an increase in entry standards to the profession (Heneberry, 2020).

The Australian education system

In order to appreciate the complexities associated with attracting and retaining teachers in Australia, it is necessary to provide a brief overview of the Australian education system. Australia is a federal system of seven states and two territories, each of which has its own education system. The federal, national government has no constitutional authority over schools. However, the federal government has the greatest revenue-raising capacity and consequently exerts a degree of power over the states and territories through coercion related to funding. This includes general annual funding distributed to states to provide services, such as education, special grants, its funding of universities including pre-service teacher training and a national teacher registration body and curriculum authority.

Furthermore, the Australian system is comprised of government schools and two types of non-government schools – Catholic system schools and independent schools. The states and territory governments are only responsible for running government schools, though all schools must comply with state and territory registration requirements. Adding to the complexity is that the federal government directly funds the non-government school sector, with states responsible for the government schools. Consequently, school funding politics is an ongoing issue of debate in Australia. Over the last 30 years, the share of the Catholic and independent 'non-government' sector has been increasing. In 2018, nationally 65.7 per cent of students were enrolled in government schools, 19.7 per cent in Catholic schools and 14.6 per cent in independent schools (ABS, 2018). On a socio-economic status (SES) scale, independent schools are typically made up of the most advantaged students, government schools the least advantaged and Catholic schools occupying the middle.

Geographically, Australia occupies a vast space, being the only nation and continent. It has a highly urbanised population with over 85 per cent of the population living in urban areas, within 50 kilometres of the coast. Indeed, the greater Sydney and Melbourne areas comprise nearly half the population of Australia (ABS, 2016). Australia uses a geographical classification, the Australian Statistical Geography Standard (ABS, 2011), to describe areas from major cities through to remote areas, based on distance, population density and access to services. In policy, and related staffing research, the non-city areas are often referred to as rural, regional and remote. For our purposes here we use 'rural' as a collective term for all these unless noted otherwise.

The social system underpinning the Australian education system becomes important as low SES schools are hard to staff (Sullivan et al., 2019; Weldon, 2015) along with rural schools – themselves often classified as low SES by virtue of location. One contributing factor appears to be the different resource of sectors, with independent schools, for instance, having the lowest student-teacher ratio of all sectors, making them more desirable employers. However, it would appear that the socio-cultural contexts of low SES, and rural, communities have some relationship to staffing difficulties.

In ongoing research using social cartography drawing upon the Australian Bureau of Statistics (ABS) census data for 2016, we are examining the relationships between low SES communities, teachers and hard-to-staff urban schools. Given that most Australian teachers are middle class and of Anglo ethnic heritage (Han & Singh, 2007) it becomes important to consider who the teachers are. The latest research (Willett, Segal, & Walford, 2014) shows that 82 per cent of the Australian teaching workforce were born in Australia, with 89 per cent born in a Commonwealth country (including those born in Australia), with the United Kingdom, New Zealand, South Africa and India the most common overseas countries of birth. We find that those who classify their heritage as Australian or North West European comprise about 71 per cent of the population but 82 per cent of the teaching workforce, with significant under-representation in all Asian heritage backgrounds and North African and Middle Eastern heritage. Notably, only 1.3 per cent of the workforce identify as Aboriginal and Torres Strait Islander, compared to 3.5 per cent of the population. This is a particular issue for students in non-metropolitan communities where a school can have a population of 60–100 per cent Aboriginal or Torres Strait Islander students.

Urban hard-to-staff schools tend to be in low SES communities and communities with high percentages of the population having a non-Anglo heritage; these are often defined by a particular ethnic heritage. Similarly, more remote hard-to-staff schools tend to be located in majority Aboriginal and Torres Strait Islander communities. In urban areas, we also find in our research that teachers do not live in these low SES, and highly ethnic, communities. Instead, we find that teachers are more likely to live in more advantaged, less densely populated suburbs with a high majority Anglo ethnic heritage, and that many commute up to an hour for work. Given the population densities, and numbers of schools, in these urban areas, the only plausible conclusion is that teachers are commuting en masse into these communities. This raises questions about 'why' teachers are not living in the communities they work in, and the broader socio-cultural forces at play. To be fair, this also means that those working with more advantaged communities are not living with those students; however, schools in these locations are not hard to staff. Indeed, teachers born outside of Australia are more likely to work in higher SES schools (Willett, Segal, & Walford, 2014).

Towards a spatial perspective

In the remainder of this chapter we will briefly refer to hard-to-staff urban schools before looking in more detail at hard-to-staff rural schools. In this separation, and more generally, we raise the spectre of the production of the spatial dimension. This can be seen through reference to the socio-cultural dimension of urban contexts and more particularly in relation to rural contexts. In doing so, we draw upon the spatial turn in social theory and educational research (Gulson & Symes, 2007) to suggest that most existing approaches to the attraction and retention of staff in hard-to-staff schools have been informed by redistributive justice notions, which are organised around the distribution of teachers in order to redistribute human resources or provide economic compensation for working in 'less desirable' social contexts.

Extending this idea, the accountability and performative notions noted are linked to the 'neoliberal social imaginary' (Rizvi & Lingard, 2010) which, valuing economic advancement and mobility in a modern globalised world, are inherently cosmopolitan (McLeod, 2012; Popkewitz, 2008). The resultant system of ideas and reasoning tends to marginalise the rural (Corbett, 2010) by positioning it as embracing old, unproductive, inefficient and inward-looking ways (Brett, 2011), and we suggest is in operation in marginalising low SES urban communities who are also not part of this global mobility elite (McLeod, 2012). Furthermore, this 'normalising' of the global urban experience develops a metrocentric (Roberts & Green, 2013) system of reasoning in education that produces metro-normative standards of achievement that value a globally linked imagined urban space over all others. For instance, rural and low SES communities are where hard-to-staff schools are more often located, and those which tend to be associated with lower achievement from literacy and numeracy to senior secondary are associated with lower student and school SES (Chesters, 2019). Coupled with the argument that being blamed for poor achievement is a reason teachers leave (Sullivan et al., 2019), it would seem that there is potentially an important relationship to explore here in terms of what the system, and those working in it, value.

Interestingly, there are no state or federal programmes or incentives aimed at urban hard-to-staff areas. While the spatial organisation of cities appears to be related to school staffing, it also seems to work against any special programmes, as the ability to live in the city and commute is assumed to be adequate. Such an assumption reinforces the implicit city-rural binary. The only special approaches that relate to hard-to-staff urban schools do so incidentally and include scholarships for pre-service teachers in specific subject areas where there are shortages (e.g., mathematics, physics and chemistry) and male teachers. A recent analysis by McGrath and Van Bergen (2017) of trends over 50 years showed a growing decline of male teachers in primary and secondary schools, especially in government schools, although not in Catholic schools, and noted that there are no existing programmes to address this trend. While hard-to-staff urban schools experience high turnover, they are generally not affected by systemic staff shortages. Many issues here are analogous to the international experience (Sullivan et al., 2019) and often relate to spatial organisation of cities and their related social segregation.

The situation in rural schools

The situation is a more complex in rural areas, as location is associated with some characteristics of low SES communities that create local economic circumstances that exacerbate distance and isolation for teachers. The staffing of rural schools in Australia has been an intractable problem since the advent of compulsory primary education (Downes & Roberts, 2018) and remains a major dilemma and the subject of recent federal inquiry (Halsey, 2018). Nationally, 29.3 per cent of Australian students are in rural, regional or remote contexts; however, schools in these contexts make up 47 per cent of all schools (Halsey, 2017). Furthermore, government schools make up 84 per cent of all rural and regional schools and nearly all in outer-regional or remote areas, making education in these communities primarily a state or territory government responsibility.

Nationally, and within each state or territory, the provision of quality education in rural, regional and remote areas is a major ongoing concern. On average, rural students have lower rates of literacy, numeracy, school completion, school qualifications and university entrance and completion than metropolitan students (Halsey, 2018). The major focus to address this has been on the attraction and retention of quality teachers, as without staff, all other reforms are essentially meaningless. However, even with an ongoing focus, the provision and retention of staff remains an intractable problem.

In a recent review into the research on staffing rural schools (Downes & Roberts, 2018), we identified the major themes and foci in the literature. The first major theme was the opportunities and challenges of staffing rural schools. This research tended to identify the challenges, such as distance, isolation, smaller class sizes and accessing subjects in the senior years, but would then reframe these as positives associated with connecting to place, individual student attention in smaller classes and school-community partnerships. This work was largely seen as setting the context for the other themes that referred more to specific approaches and research projects.

The major focus over the last two decades has been pre-service teacher preparation, which has included advocacy for specialist pre-service training and professional experience placements, supported by numerous small local research studies (Beutel, Adie, & Hudson, 2011; Jenkins & Cornish, 2015; Sharplin, 2010; Trinidad, Sharplin, Ledger, & Broadley, 2014; White & Kline, 2012). These university-based projects have tended to focus upon the importance of understanding 'place' and approaches to support pre-service teachers in rural schools, to advocate for specific pre-service education to prepare teachers for rural schools. However, besides this persistent research focus, there is no broad adoption of specific pre-service or professional experience approaches by universities or in departmental policy. Finally, an emerging focus in the research, and associated practice, has been school leadership. This leadership focus centres on the notion of 'rural difference' and the need for different and specific preparation of rural school leaders (Roberts & Downes, 2019).

Retaining teachers in rural areas

It is evident upon reflecting on this research that most work has tended to be aimed at encouraging teachers to consider working in rural areas. Very little seems to be focused on 'retention' – save perhaps mentoring and professional development needs of early career teachers. Most concerning, however, was the realisation that over the last 20 or so years very little 'new' thinking has occurred. In general, the research seems a variation on persistent themes or pre-service preparation and rural difference and, sadly, has not had a major impact on education policy in Australia (Halsey, 2018). Hence, our suggestion here to start considering issues of attracting and retaining teachers from a socio-spatial perspective.

For instance, while staffing shortages remain a major issue, most vacancies are ultimately filled in rural areas. It is just that they are quickly followed by another vacancy due to high staff turnover (Halsey, 2018). Thus, we agree with Sullivan et al.'s (2019) suggestion that a focus on teacher attrition is overdue, as ultimately retention (should be) responsive to policy intervention. Indeed, as they note, high staff turnover is acknowledged to be very disruptive to schools and student learning (Sullivan et al., 2019), so there is an imperative on the side of the state and territory governments to attend to this. However, while a compelling position, retention remains an issue in rural areas regardless of multiple approaches to encourage retention (Halsey, 2018). This, we suggest, is because existing approaches do not attend to the spatial dimension of a teacher's experience, or on the impact of standardised assessments of teacher quality and student achievement on their professional identity and career progression. Instead, we have ambiguous references to attrition as a function of location without broader explanation or analysis (Weldon, 2018; McKenzie, Rowley, Weldon, & Murphy, 2011).

To illustrate this point, we refer now to a recent review we have undertaken of state and territory government incentives to attract teachers to, and retain them in, rural schools across Australia. At this point we remind you, the reader, that state and territory governments are essentially the only provider of schools in rural areas in Australia. We have grouped these approaches under three categories: financial, professional conditions, professional development. The first group of incentives targeting pre-service teachers includes financial incentives and takes the form of bonds that cover university fees in return for taking up a rural position for a minimum number of years upon graduation, and compensation while on professional experience, including a stipend and housing costs. The ability to gain a permanent position faster through preferential treatment, and the opportunity to gain experiences helping with career progression are promoted as positive professional conditions. Access to mentoring and learning through placement are promoted as professional development opportunities. These last two also relate to the idea of promoting the profession, and rural teaching, as a positive career that makes a real impact in the world. However, these are all essentially aimed at attracting prospective teachers into the profession.

In-service teacher incentives are much more significant, and broader in scope, than those aimed at pre-service teachers. The main focus is again financial, predicated upon the notion of compensation for perceived disadvantages of the location, such as isolation, access to goods and services and increased costs in locations including services and rental accommodation. Teachers are supported by a relocation subsidy from the government department that oversees schools, but to encourage them to stay, longer cash incentives, rental subsidies, travel subsidies and additional leave are also offered and increase with time. This increase of benefit with time is aimed at retention and minimising the perverse impact of the main benefit in professional conditions – transfer benefits, the guaranteed move to another location of the teachers' preference (i.e. the city) after a minimum period of service – that ultimately encourage teachers to leave (White, 2019).

Ironically, one of the main approaches over many years to attracting teachers to rural schools has been ensuring they can leave, and be guaranteed a job in a location they find more desirable (Roberts, 2004). Other than these approaches outlined, some states and territories offer limited additional leave, with staff in the smallest state and the smallest territory having access to study-related sabbatical leave after they have remained for a minimum number of years beyond those needed for cash incentives. There are also provisions to access additional professional development support and related leave, though in reality this merely makes allowance for the extra travel time often required to access professional development.

Conclusion: rethinking retention in rural schools

Overall, incentives are near universally framed from a deficit perspective of the rural and seek to elicit individual rewards as motivation. They frame rural communities as far away, remote from services and culture that are valued, and a cost impediment in accessing housing, services and basics foods. They are undesirable and, by association, those that live there are undesirables. Notably this is framed from the perspective of the desirability of the city, and all it affords in a cosmopolitan nation. Consequently, we have an intractable problem limited by a collective failure of imagination and without regard for rural places.

In such a negative construction, it is no wonder that professional conditions in rural schools are not seen to be on a par with city schools, especially when the hallmarks of the profession are themselves framed in the experience of the majority of teachers (Roberts & Green, 2013). Here we return to Sullivan et al.'s (2019) argument that the prevailing performative culture of education undermines professionalism and encourages teachers to leave.

We see in the approaches to staffing rural schools, and the absence of focus on hard-to-staff city schools, no attempt to engage with the professional conditions within these schools as constructed in their place. In seeking models of professionalism that are universal, and context-free, policy has by design separated schools from their communities, and teachers from their students. For instance, one missing piece in the staffing puzzle is recruiting from local communities, both rural and urban. However, to address perceptions of poor quality due to falling international test rankings, most state and territory governments have introduced a variety of new entry requirements to enter teacher training, such as minimum grades in English and math in their final year of high school or minimum grades in their end of school certificate. At a university level, minimum grades throughout the degree, and mandatory literacy and numeracy tests before graduation, have been introduced. These essentially block rural students entering education degrees as the schools they attend often have lower achievement levels in secondary education. Furthermore, many rural students don't meet university entry requirements or find the cost of relocation to university, usually in the city or larger town, prohibitive. Ironically, one state has introduced a ban on teachers being trained through online courses, further disadvantaging rural students from becoming teachers. Instead, an imagined nation is valorized, and those who subscribe to this notion, rewarded with entry to the profession. For this reason, we have endeavoured throughout this chapter to situate our narrative of hard-to-staff schools in a socio-spatial dimension. By so doing, we bring attention to the metro-normative framing of rural schooling, and invite you, the reader, to imagine how we might reconstitute the teaching profession in these contexts, in the interests of the least advantaged. Given the perennial failure of redistributive, economically motived incentives, it is time to throw out the old ways and try something radically different.

References

Australian Bureau of Statistics [ABS]. (2011). *Australian Statistical Geography Standard (ASGS): Volume 1 – Main Structure and Greater Capital City Statistical Areas, July 2011.* (1270.0.55.001). Retrieved from www.abs.gov.au/AUSSTATS/abs@.nsf/DetailsPage/1270.0.55.001July%202011

Australian Bureau of Statistics [ABS]. (2016). Education and work (May 2015). *TableBuilder.* Findings based on use of ABS TableBuilder data.

Australian Bureau of Statistics [ABS]. (2018). *4221.0 – Schools, Australia, 2018.* Retrieved from www.abs.gov.au/AUSSTATS/abs@.nsf/DetailsPage/4221.02018?Open Document

Australian Institute for Teaching and School leadership [AITSL]. (2017). *Spotlight: What do we know about early career Teacher attrition rates in Australia?* Retrieved from www.aitsl.edu.au/tools-resources/resource/spotlight-what-do-we-know-about-early-career-teacher-attrition-rates-in-australia

Beutel, D., Adie, L., & Hudson, S. (2011). Promoting rural and remote teacher education in Australia through the Over the Hill project. *International Journal of Learning, 18*(2), 377–388.

Brett, J. (2011). Fair s: Country and city in Australia. *Quarterly Essay, No. 42.* Melbourne: Black Inc.

Chesters, J. (2019). Alleviating or exacerbating disadvantage: Does school attended mediate the association between family background and educational attainment? *Journal of Education Policy, 34*(3), 331–350.

Corbett, M. (2010). Standardized individuality: Cosmopolitanism and educational decision-making in an Atlantic Canadian rural community. *Compare, 40*(2), 223–237.

Downes, N., & Roberts, P. (2018). Revisiting the schoolhouse: A literature review on staffing rural, remote and isolated schools in Australia 2004–2016. *Australian and International Journal of Rural Education, 28*(1), 31–54.

Gulson, K. N., & Symes, C. (Eds). (2007). *Spatial theories of education: Policy and geography matters.* London: Routledge.

Halsey, J. (2017). *Independent review into regional, rural and remote education – Discussion paper.* Canberra: Commonwealth of Australia. Retrieved from Australian government website: https://docs.education.gov.au/node/44526

Halsey, J. (2018). *Independent Review into Regional, Rural and Remote Education – Final Report.* Canberra: Commonwealth of Australia. Retrieved from Australian government website: https://docs.education.gov.au/node/50281

Han, J., & Singh, M. (2007). Getting world English speaking student teachers to the top of the class: Making hope for ethno-cultural diversity in teacher education robust. *Asia-Pacific Journal of Teacher Education, 35*, 291–309.

Heneberry, B. (2020, January 16). Schools face 'critical' teacher shortage in 2020. *The Educator Australia.* Retrieved from the Educator website: www.theeducato ronline.com/k12/news/schools-face-critical-teacher-shortage-in-2020/269422#. XiFNm9Pv2SY.twitter

Jenkins, K., & Cornish, L. (2015). Preparing pre-service teachers for rural appointments. *Australian and International Journal of Rural Education, 25*(2), 14–27.

McGrath, K., & Van Bergen, P. (2017). Are male teachers headed for extinction? The 50-year decline of male teachers in Australia. *Economics of Education Review, 60*(October), 159–167.

McKenzie, P., Rowley, G., Weldon, P., & Murphy, M. (2011). *Staff in Australia's schools 2010: Main report on the survey.* Australian Government Department of Education, Employment and Workplace Relations (DEEWR): Canberra, Australia. Retrieved from VOCEDplus website: www.voced.edu.au/content/ngv%3A50342

McLeod, J. (2012). Educating for 'world-mindedness': Cosmopolitanism, localism and schooling the adolescent citizen in interwar Australia. *Journal of Educational Administration and History, 44*(4), 339–359.

Popkewitz, T. S. (2008). *Cosmopolitanism and the age of school reform: Science, education, and making society by making the child.* New York: Routledge.

Rizvi, F., & Lingard, B. (2010). *Globalizing education policy* New York: Routledge.

Roberts, P. (2004). *Staffing an empty schoolhouse: Attracting and retaining teachers in rural, remote and isolated communities.* Sydney, NSW: New South Wales Teachers Federation.

Roberts, P., & Downes, N. (2019). The rural difference trope: Leader perceptions on rural, regional and remote schooling difference. *Leading & Managing, 25*(2), 51–65.

Roberts, P., & Green, B. (2013). Researching rural place: On social justice and rural education, *Qualitative Inquiry, 19*(10), 765–774.

Sharplin, E. (2010). A taste of country: A pre-service teacher rural field trip. *Education in Rural Australia, 20*(1), 17–27.

Sullivan, A., Johnson, B., & Simon, M. (2019). Introduction. In A. Sullivan, B. Johnson, & M. Simon (Eds.), *Attracting and keeping the best teachers* (pp. 1–11). Singapore: Springer.

Trinidad, S., Sharplin, E., Ledger, S., & Broadley, T. (2014). Connecting for innovation: Four universities collaboratively preparing pre-service teachers to teach in rural and remote Western Australia. *Journal of Research in Rural Education, 29*(2), 1–13.

Weldon, P. (2015). *The teacher workforce in Australia: Supply, demand and data issues.* Policy Insights No. 2. Camberwell: ACER.

Weldon, P. (2018). Early career teacher attrition in Australia: Evidence, definition, classification and measurement. *Australian Journal of Education, 62*(1), 61–78.

White, S. (2019). Recruiting, retaining and supporting early career teachers for rural schools. In A. Sullivan, B. Johnson, & M. Simon (Eds.), *Attracting and keeping the best teachers* (pp. 43–159). Singapore: Springer.

White, S., & Kline, J. (2012). *Renewing rural and regional teacher education curriculum, final report 2012*. Australian Learning and Teaching Council. Retrieved from www.rrrtec.net.au/PDFs/PP9-1320%20Deakin%20White%20Final%20Report%20 2012%5B1%5D.pdf

Willett, M., Segal, D., & Walford, W. (2014). *National teaching workforce dataset data analysis report*. Canberra: Department of Education. Commonwealth of Australia.

AFTERWORD

Tanya Ovenden-Hope and Rowena Passy

The international context of an efficient, appropriate and sustained supply of high-quality teachers is one of great concern. The authors in this book demonstrate that there is an international discord between the actions of 'agencies' that control the training and development of teachers and the recommendations of experts on teacher education in relation to teacher recruitment and retention. This dissonance challenges sensibility, in that we should be working together to ensure that we have enough quality teachers to educate the increasing world population.

The United Nations Sustainable Development Goal 4: Quality Education (UN, 2015) demands a collaborative approach to teacher supply in their vision for education, which should:

> Ensure inclusive and equitable quality education and promote lifelong learning opportunities for all.
>
> *(UN, 2015, p. 14)*

And

> By 2030, substantially increase the supply of qualified teachers, including through international cooperation for teacher training in developing countries, especially least developed countries and small island developing States.
>
> *(UN, 2015, p. 17)*

It seems hard to imagine that the least developed countries will receive the substantial international support required for increasing their number of qualified teachers if, as suggested in this book, the developed nations are struggling to achieve their own teacher number needs. The urgency in securing a collaborative, sustainable solution that proactively addresses workforce supply and shortages in schools is one that should be met with an immediate government response.

The term 'quality' has been used many times within this book to describe the type of teacher to be ideally recruited or retained in the professional. There are occasions that the authors acknowledge that this ideal has been superseded by the need to simply have an adult in the classroom. This is despite high quality teaching being demonstrated to be a main determinant in a child's positive learning experience and attainment (Sutton Trust, 2011; Higgins, Cordingley, Greany, & Coe, 2015). In Chapter 14 we hear from Donitsa-Schmidt and Zuzovsky that in Israel teacher shortages are being met by an increasing number of unqualified teachers with serious implications for a quality education:

> The Jewish sector's teacher shortage has led to school principals employing large numbers of unqualified teachers, thus jeopardizing the Hebrew-speaking schools' educational quality.

The same story is told in Sweden by Niklasson in Chapter 16, where uncertified teachers are recruited to fill teacher shortages with serious consequences for quality of education and for perceptions of professionalism:

> it is difficult to balance between the need to have staff (almost any adult) in the classroom and the need to have certified teachers for reasons of quality and out of respect for the professionals.

Authors in this book have shown that the appointment of unqualified teachers is increasing in schools in many countries, including England. Ovenden-Hope and Luke explain in Chapter 9 that educational policy reform in England through the Academies Bill (HM Government, 2010) allowed new powers to be given to schools in 2012 'to regulate their own teaching supply, including the appointment of unqualified teachers into teaching roles, and were able to call them teachers, effectively deregulating teaching'. This last point is important as it demonstrates the erosion of professionalism for teaching, regardless of whether an unintended consequence, by government policy. Allowing teaching to become a job that can be done by a competent adult without a teaching qualification or a degree undermines the status and value of teaching as the highly skilled profession it is and should be.

The overview of the typical international government and agency response to teacher shortages seen in different chapters in this book is to offer financial incentives to recruit teachers. However, as See, Gorard, Morris and El-Soufi's systematic review of research findings in this area demonstrated in Chapter 11, these bursaries and grants given to those training to teach, or recently qualified (predominantly in the most hard to recruit to subjects, or schools), may attract teachers initially to teaching, but do not lead to long-term retention.

> There is little evidence that any approaches other than financial incentives work for recruitment, and no good evidence yet of anything else that works for retention, in high need areas.

Roberts and Downes are critical of this approach in Chapter 17, stating that 'given the perennial failure of redistributive, economically motived, incentives it is time to throw out the old ways and try something radically different'. This is a particularly pertinent observation, as See and colleagues (Chapter 11) highlight unintended negative consequences of financial incentives in that 'it is not clear that such external motivation is desirable, or attracts the best teachers'. We should consider the real cost to the profession, and to our children, of government and agencies' short-term supply fixes that attract recruits who do not view teaching as a long-term career and do not develop the skills that enable high-quality teaching. This approach to teacher recruitment and retention does little to show any value in teaching or enhance the quality or standing of teaching as a profession.

We argue that teaching in all countries (and sectors) requires long-term, structured investment beyond a political party term in order to create a sustainable system of high-quality teachers. This lack of strategic planning and support at a structural level is an international concern in need of full and fast consideration. Short-term 'fixes' for teacher recruitment and retention do not work. It seems ridiculous that some developed countries, such as England, have a more long-term, systematic and evidence-based approach to developing transport systems (Department for Transport, 2019) than they do education. To achieve the ambition of the United Nations Goal 4, something has to change in how governments view and treat education, and there needs to be a recognition of the importance of long-term investment for long-term stability in the teaching in our schools.

In Chapter 1, Howson articulates clearly the active role required of government in securing teacher workforce supply:

> A modern economy needs an educated workforce. It should not be beyond the powers of politicians to ensure such a workforce is available to teach every child that the state is responsible for educating by designing a system that provides sufficient well-trained teachers, with the highest quality preparation, and where they are needed by schools. Government should also create an appropriate career development programme that helps teachers develop their skills and expertise, as well as helps them create a career within the state school system.

While Noble–Rogers acknowledges in Chapter 2 that some factors affecting having enough teachers in the classroom are outside of the government's control in England, such as an increase in pupil numbers and competition from other graduate professions, he also argues that in England 'the measures adopted by the government prior to 2019 were ad hoc, piecemeal and did not sufficiently address the roots of the supply crisis'.

Sadly, the evidence provided by the authors in this book is one of governments internationally reacting to the teacher shortages and poor supply rather than pro-actively engaging in a long-term solution that includes a 're-professionalising' of teaching. Teaching appears to have become synonymous with poor work-ing conditions, accountability and reduced autonomy. Cordingley and Crisp demonstrate in Chapter 10 that there is a real possibility of enhancing teacher recruitment and retention if the development of teachers' professional identi-ties is supported 'through a dynamic combination of CPDL [continuing profes-sional development and learning] and teacher leadership'. This in essence means embracing teachers' professionalism and 'celebrating' this with long-term, struc-tured investment in professional development and learning. This approach, insti-gated in initial teacher training that establishes 'professional norms of openness to learning . . . attentive to instructional practices, continual improvement, col-laboration, collegiality' (Chapter 12), will enable teachers to feel accountable to their students and to each other as lifelong learners within a profession.

CPDL is considered in this book as an essential element for teacher recruit-ment and retention, whether it is provided through subject associations, as described in Chapter 6, or to continue the development of pedagogy and prac-tice, as in Chapter 4. Professional development is located in both personal and public professional teacher identity. The simplest definition of 'professional' is all that is needed to understand why we have an international crisis in teacher recruitment and retention:

> Professional is having a 'type of job that is respected because it involves a high level of education and training'.
>
> *(Cambridge Dictionary, 2020, para. 4)*

The variability and/or limited access for teachers to CPDL, such as in educa-tionally isolated schools (Chapter 8) and rural, hard-to-staff schools in Australia (Chapter 17) begins to challenge adherence to a 'high level of education and training' and the provision of high-quality teaching. Dig deeper and you dis-cover that some 'teachers' are not qualified at all. We know that teachers will do their best for their pupils with whatever resource they have. However, as was argued in Chapter 5, without self-efficacy teachers lose confidence in their ability to do their job effectively and this can make them leave. Structured, long-term, high-quality, high-level training and development is essential for a job to be seen and experienced as professional. This is not currently the case for teaching.

A change in government attitude towards teaching could potentially lead to an essential societal shift towards the role as a career. In China, teachers who followed a particular programme are 'guaranteed basic working and living conditions' (Chapter 13). Hordatt Gentles argues in Chapter 15 that the Jamaican government needs to enhance the role and treat teachers as professionals, an argument replicated for many of the countries in this book:

> It is critical that the government invests in improving the job and work context of teaching in Jamaica. Helping teachers to feel valued, autonomous and respected must be a priority. This can be accomplished through policies that facilitate more professional autonomy and empower teachers to engage in professional collaboration about issues affecting student learning.

In order for teaching to become an attractive professional career of choice, it must be experienced as an attractive professional career by those in it. The current teacher recruitment and retention crisis has made governments consider, at the very least, how to replace those leaving teaching. In England, the shoots of hope are emerging from new government reform that recognises the absolute need to make things better for teaching as a profession. The recruitment and retention strategy (DfE, 2019) aims to 'support a career offer that remains attractive to teachers as their careers and lives develop' (DfE, 2019, p. 24). As Georgina Newton argues in Chapter 3, a teacher 'feeling valued can protect against both push and pull factors out of teaching'. If governments value teachers, understand that high-quality teaching is essential to both developed and developing countries as 'a fundamental building block to national success' (Cordingley and Crisp, Chapter 10) and invest in long-term strategic planning for a highly skilled workforce, then we may see our schools fully populated by qualified teachers that 'ensures an inclusive and equitable quality education' (UN, 2015, p. 14) for all.

References

Cambridge Dictionary. (2020). *Cambridge Dictionary online*. Retrieved from https://dictionary.cambridge.org/dictionary/english/professional

Department for Education [DfE]. (2019). *Teacher recruitment and retention strategy*. London: DfE. Retrieved from gov.uk website: https://assets.publishing.service.gov.uk/government/uploads/system/uploads/attachment_data/file/786856/DFE_Teacher_Retention_Strategy_Report.pdf

Department for Transport. (2019, June). *Department for Transport single departmental plan*. London: Department of Transport. Retrieved from gov.uk website: www.gov.uk/government/publications/department-for-transport-single-departmental-plan/department-for-transport-single-departmental-plan-2

Higgins, S., Cordingley, P., Greany, T., & Coe, R. (2015). *Developing great teaching: Lessons from the international reviews into effective professional development* [summary]. London: Teacher Development Trust. Retrieved from Teacher Development Trust website: http://tdtrust.org/about/dgt

HM Government. (2010). *Academies Act*. London: HM Government. Retrieved from legislation.gov website: http://www.legislation.gov.uk/ukpga/2010/32/pdfs/ukpga_20100032_en.pdf

Sutton Trust. (2011). *Improving the impact of teachers on pupil achievement in the UK – Interim findings.* London: Sutton Trust.

United Nations [UN]. (2015). *Transforming our world: The 2030 agenda for sustainable development.* Resolution adopted by the General Assembly on 25 September 2015. A/RES/70/1. Retrieved from United Nations website: www.un.org/ga/search/view_doc.asp?symbol=A/RES/70/1&Lang=E

INDEX

Note: Page numbers in *italics* indicate figures, and those in **bold** indicate tables.